ken yeang

the
skyscraper
bioclimatically considered

a design primer

AD. ACADEMY EDITIONS

This book is dedicated to my mother, Louise.

ACKNOWLEDGEMENTS

In writing this book, I acknowledge the help of the many who have given their time
and ideas freely: Professor Lyn Beedle, the Director of the Council on Tall Buildings
and Urban Habitat; its executive council and its staff; the many engineers who have
offered their ideas and notes for the text; my former doctorate dissertation
supervisor and friend, Professor John Frazer; Professor Ivor Richards for his advice;
Dennis Sharp who provided many critical comments; Dr Kisho Kurokawa as mentor
and guide; Professor Alan Balfour as critic to many of the architectural designs;
Dr Takekuni Ikeda for his encouragement; Professor Peter Cook who has reviewed
my work ever since my AA days; Professor Leon van Schaik for his support of the
ideas; Professor Bryan Lawson for his critical conversations; Tom Barker, Tony
Fitzpatrick and many others at Ove Arup & Partners; Mui Heng Chor of Jurutera
Perunding LC Sdn Bhd; Norman Disney & Young; Akira Suzuki; Derek Trowell;
Melanie Richardson; Guy Battle and Chris McCarthy for their enthusiasm;
Elaine for the design of the book; Tim Evans for his work on the text; the many
others who have contributed comments; and finally, my partner, Tengku Dato Robert
Hamzah and the staff of TR Hamzah & Yeang Sdn Bhd.
(Ken Yeang)

First published in Great Britain in 1996 by
ACADEMY EDITIONS

An imprint of
ACADEMY GROUP LTD
42 Leinster Gardens, London W2 3AN
Member of the VCH Publishing Group

ISBN 1 85490 431 0

Distributed to the trade in the USA by
NATIONAL BOOK NETWORK, INC
4720 Boston Way, Lanham Maryland 20706

Printed and bound in Malaysia

contents

Nagoya
Barchrometer
Nagoya, Japan,
Latitude 35.10°N

ken yeang

foreword

Our intention here is not to provide a step-by-step design manual for skyscraper design that 'leads from the sketch to completed building'. This is, of course, impractical. The design of a skyscraper is such a huge and complex undertaking that it is simply not possible to map out the entire design process and assemble the set of design considerations in one single volume.

Our treatise here is essentially a *design primer*. As a primer, it is simply a set of helpful reminders for the designer, outlining the range of considerations in skyscraper design. It summarily reminds the designer of, or brings his attention to, those aspects that are essential, particularly from a *bioclimatic* point of view.

A design primer should suggest tried and tested propositions as well as offer new solutions to the designer, especially when encountering varying programmatic, site and climatic conditions. Our guidelines serve to steer the designer rapidly through the quagmire of information on skyscraper design towards an efficient process of arriving at a workable solution. (In other words, its purpose is to facilitate design decisions.)

However, it is also hoped that this primer might direct skyscraper designs towards a low-energy future, and that the ideas therein might engender new innovative approaches and new inventions by others to further advance the design and technology of this building type.

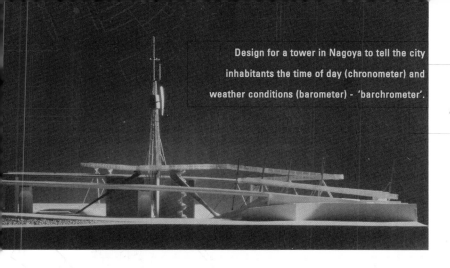

Nagoya

Barchrometer

Illustrated here are examples from the numerous experiments and design studies we have carried out. In most instances, these have been subjected to the usual trials and tribulations of professional architectural practice, as well as the multitude of constraints commonly imposed on any building project (such as those of site, client, approving authorities, costs, etc).

R&D (Research and Development) is regarded as comprising creative work undertaken on a systematic basis in order to increase the stock of knowledge which is then used to devise new applications. Following on from this, the design examples which relate to the text in this book may be regarded as derived essentially from an R&D-motivated approach, but it is an RD&D (Research, Design and Development) approach that is interpreted in a pleasurable way by design.

Unfortunately, many of the design propositions had to evolve through a discontinuous process of RD&D. This discontinuity is not necessarily detrimental but it can affect the completeness of the development of the proposition; by this we mean the RD&D work in a professional architectural firm is inevitably intermittent and, in most instances, evolved 'on the run'.

Our RD&D work is not carried out (as it would be in a full-time laboratory or research station) in a continuum. These propositions and their testings evolve only as they become part of the on-going work in a professional architectural practice. Here, some of the research was done in-house; the rest was done through consultants elsewhere.

The unfortunate consequence of this architectural practice-based RD&D is that propositions can progress (and then be tested) only where they are permitted by external constraints. In other words, the RD&D can progress only as and when the various commissions and projects in the architectural practice are designed, developed and (if successful) built. The constraints on an architectural project are numerous and generally outside the control of the designer.

Where pertinent, more emphasis is placed on certain aspects of skyscraper design that require greater elucidation for the new designer (eg. the design of the building's elevator configuration). Efforts have been made to ensure that a sufficient level of detail is provided to guide the designer in designing these specialised parts.

5

While many important aspects of skyscraper design are elaborated in greater detail elsewhere (such as in the many monographs of the Council on Tall Buildings and Urban Habitat (CTBUH)), it is likely that the practising architect will still lament the lack of a comprehensive and authoritative guide to designing this building type. Similarly, bioclimatic design strategies can be found to be more comprehensively covered elsewhere (eg. in Koenigsberger et al, 1974 and Olgay et al, 1963) although not in their application to skyscraper design.

The many monographs on tall buildings contain material that is either of insufficient detail or inversely, too detailed. Many of these can be so topically specific (especially when they are written as 'working papers') that they are of no practical use to the designer. Over-specificity negates their usefulness when guiding the inexperienced designer along the tortuous route of designing a tall building.

We owe the title of our book to Louis Sullivan's 1896 essay, 'The Tall Building, Artistically Considered'. Here, the skyscraper's design is discussed with regard to how it might be configured and designed in an alternative approach to that conventionally taken to make it responsive to the climate. This is the 'bioclimatic' approach: it is design for human comfort and low-energy consumption, based on the meteorological data of the locality.

6

ken yeang
TR HAMZAH & YEANG SDN BHD
(KUALA LUMPUR)
1996

Menara

Mesiniaga,

Kuala Lumpur,

Latitude 2°N

the skyscraper

'The skyscraper is a potent symbol of power and domination. The higher we build the more power we appear to command. Overcoming the most fundamental of all forces, gravity, this is nowhere more graphically demonstrated than in the space rocket, and even that is a skyscraper whilst still on the earth.'

PROFESSOR BRYAN LAWSON

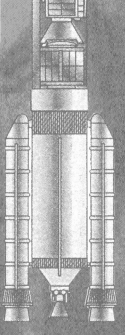

New Launcher Ariane 5, 51.37m (15 storeys)

The first known office building
was designed for the Medicis
in Florence, Italy, in 1560.
This Renaissance palace
was called the Uffizi
('office' in Italian) and was
used for administrative
functions. During the same
decade in Japan, Osaka Castle,
an administrative centre for the
feudal lord, was completed.

introduction

We must initially fully grasp what a daunting task it is for both the client and the architect to undertake the creation of a skyscraper. At the outset of an enterprise there are already a huge number of considerations that must be taken into account, almost all simultaneously. These include the site FARs (Floor Area Ratios), optimum footprint utilisation, building configuration and its permissible 'envelope', the design of marketable floor-plates, elevator planning and configuring, M&E (Mechanical and Electrical) systems integration, structural grids and floor-to-floor heights, foundation and substructure design, and many others.

The question at this point, then, is why should the designer burden himself further with additional considerations such as *bioclimatic* ones?

The answer depends essentially on whether the designer accepts the objectives of the **bioclimatic approach** – that is, to seek by design a *low-energy, passive building* and *better occupant comfort* – as being vital issues. If he does, we might contend that rather than complicating skyscraper design the bioclimatic approach will, in effect, simplify it.

In the bioclimatic design approach, the low-energy imperative is achieved through *passive means* (such as through shaping the built-configuration, placement of the building components, and selection of materials), rather than through the use of electro-mechanical devices and systems. While these electro-mechanical devices and systems might subsequently be added to the building's M&E and facade systems to further enhance its low-energy performance, these should be regarded as secondary to design by low-energy passive means.

Where a skyscraper's built form was wrongly configured at the outset, any subsequent electro-mechanical devices and systems would first need to correct some of the previous mistakes in

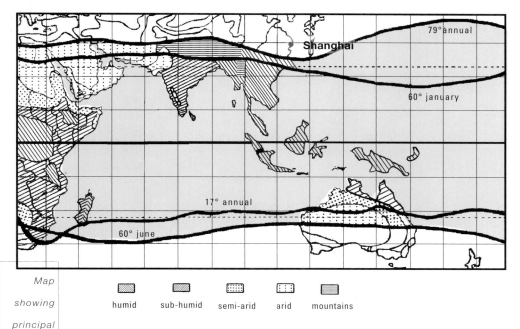

79° annual

Shanghai

60° january

17° annual

60° june

humid sub-humid semi-arid arid mountains

Map

showing

principal

climates

the built configuration (those parts of the building not designed along bioclimatic design principles). Having to undertake such corrective measures to rectify earlier design mistakes simply makes a mockery of undertaking low-energy design in the first instance.

The global economy today is clearly increasingly aware of *energy* as a scarce resource; the need to conserve energy and design for a sustainable future is becoming imperative for all designers.

9

Shanghai

Armoury

Tower,

Pudong,

Latitude 31.14°N

designed with Norindar
Hamzah & Yeang
International, Beijing
(Mr Song Guofu)

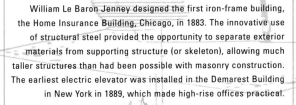
nineteenth-century
high-rise building

William Le Baron Jenney designed the first iron-frame building,
the Home Insurance Building, Chicago, in 1883. The innovative use
of structural steel provided the opportunity to separate exterior
materials from supporting structure (or skeleton), allowing much
taller structures than had been possible with masonry construction.
The earliest electric elevator was installed in the Demarest Building
in New York in 1889, which made high-rise offices practical.

In practice, we might describe architecture
as a craft, one which is variable and that may even appear whimsical
to the layman. Consequently, an energy imperative might provide a
theoretical respectability to the craft where the designing of energy-
efficient enclosures gives us the potential to transform architectural
design from a variable craft into a confident science. The theory of
skyscraper design might, in the future, be derived in part from the
ethic of energy conservation.

10

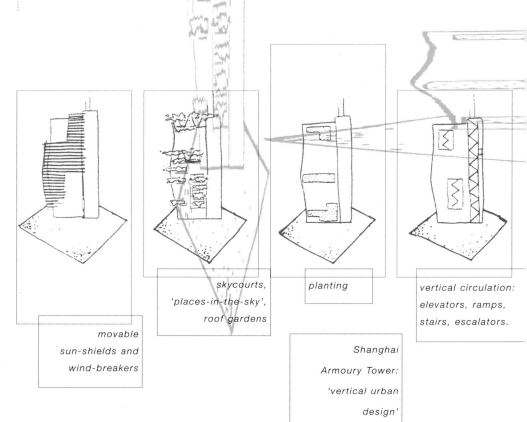

skycourts,
'places-in-the-sky',
roof gardens

planting

vertical circulation:
elevators, ramps,
stairs, escalators.

movable
sun-shields and
wind-breakers

Shanghai
Armoury Tower:
'vertical urban
design'

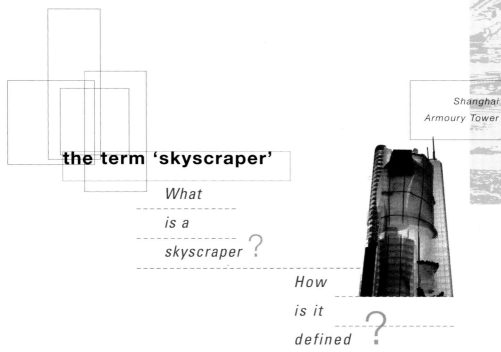

the term 'skyscraper'

What

is a

skyscraper ?

How

is it

defined ?

Shanghai Armoury Tower

Around 1890, the term 'skyscraper' was coined to describe 'the multi-storey office building type' which was being built predominantly in the central areas of Chicago and New York in the USA.

By 1884, 'skyscraper' was being used as an adjective to describe tall buildings; its first use as a noun occurred around 1889. As late as 1933, the Oxford English Dictionary still provided six different definitions of the word 'skyscraper', which included one for a high-standing horse and another for a very tall man! Finally, by the advent of World War I, the term had become sufficiently common place to refer primarily to the *tall building type*.

The term is preferable to others such as the 'tall building' or the 'high-rise' because it does not imply relativity. For example, how tall does a building have to be to be considered a 'tall building', and how high does it have to rise to be 'high-rise'?

The 'skyscraper' is also regarded by many as an American invention, along with the movie palace and the fast-food restaurant. Some probably regard it as one of America's greatest inventions because of its worldwide impact on our contemporary urban human habitat.

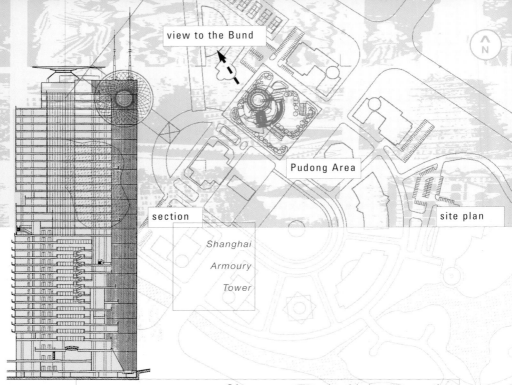

view to the Bund

Pudong Area

section

site plan

Shanghai
Armoury
Tower

Of course, we should be aware that mankind has been building tall structures for centuries (such as pagodas in China, temples in Wat Arun, Thailand, pyramids in Egypt, and the towers of San Gimignano in Italy). In many parts of the world, the creation of tall buildings has symbolised human endeavours.

Since the beginning of human organisation, the height of buildings has been limited to a person's ability to climb stairs. For centuries, buildings reached their commercially optimum height at about four to five storeys.

Skyscrapers, however, did not evolve from their four or five-storey predecessors which were simply 'walk-up' buildings: the skyscraper is considered to be a unique building typology.

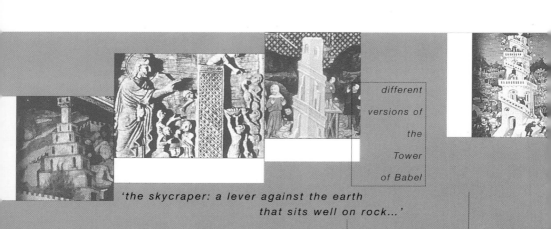

different

versions of

the

Tower

of Babel

'the skycraper: a lever against the earth
that sits well on rock...'

PROFESSOR LEON VAN SCHAIK

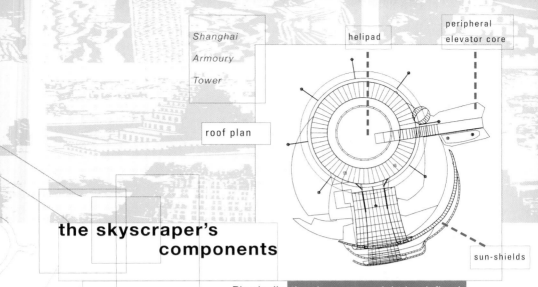

helipad

peripheral
elevator core

roof plan

sun-shields

the skyscraper's
components

Physically, the skyscraper might be defined
as a *multi-storey building, generally constructed using a structural
frame, provided with high-speed elevators, and combining extraor-
dinary height with ordinary room-spaces, such as would be found in
low buildings.*

The Council on Tall Buildings and Urban
Habitat (CTBUH) initially considered tall buildings as being of *ten storeys*
or over because that had been the cut-off height for fire-fighting from
ladders in New York City. Although today's fire-engine ladder can reach
higher than ten storeys, this broad criterion remains.

Another definition is in the ASHRAE (American
Society of Heating, Refrigeration and Air-conditioning Engineers) *Handbook of Fundamentals* (1989) which categorises a high-rise building as one
in which its height (H) is more than three times its cross-wind width (W).

Recently, the CTBUH (L Beedle) wrote: 'a
multi-storey building is not defined by its height or number of floors.
The important criterion is whether or not the design is influenced by
some aspect of 'tallness'...It is a building whose height creates different conditions in the design, construction, and operation from those
that exist in 'common' buildings of a certain region and period.'

13

*the spiralling
ramp as a land-
scape theme*

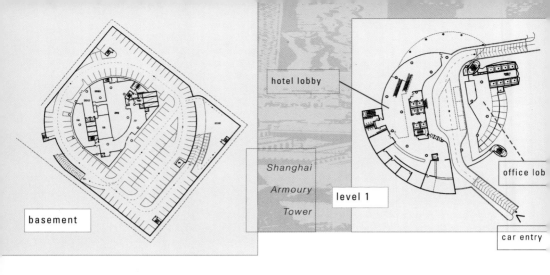

hotel lobby

Shanghai
Armoury
Tower

level 1

office lob

car entry

Technologically, the skyscraper is the culmi-
nation of a number of building inventions, such as the structural-frame
with wind-bracing, new methods of making piling and foundations,
high-speed elevators, air-conditioning systems, flush-toilets, large
pieces of glazing and window-framing, advanced telecommunications
and electronics, advanced indoor-lighting, ventilation, and cleaning
technologies.

Spatially, a skyscraper can be regarded
(especially by the commercially-minded developer) as being simply an
intensification of large areas of built space concentrated over compar-
atively small parcels of land area (or over small building footprints). The
skyscraper enables more usable floor-space to be placed over a small
plot of land by simply going higher. It allows more cash to be made
from the land, with more goods, more people and more rents derived
from one place.

Consequently, because of its evident com-
mercial objectives, the goal of the developer is obviously to achieve high
structural efficiency with minimum premium-for-height. Very often (and
unfortunately so) what happens is that the executive managers of the
developer determine the building's typical floor-plate and, having
devised the workspaces, leave the architects the role of simply designing
the building's outside envelope.

14

La Ville Radieuse
by Le Corbusier,
Paris,
Latitude 48.52°N

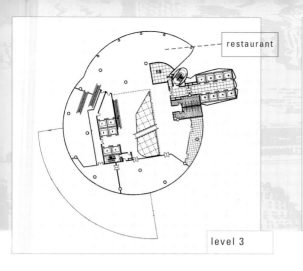

restaurant

level 3

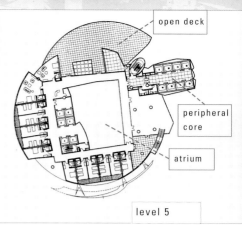

open deck

peripheral core

atrium

level 5

Because skyscrapers are such intensive developments, they are obviously major financial investments and commitments for their developers: hence, cost becomes a critical factor. However, regardless of whether the building is low-rise or high-rise, in all those instances where costs have been given precedence over the aesthetic, human or poetic aspects of architectural design, the built forms that inevitably result are more often than not bland, inarticulate boxes.

The crucial issues for the designer, then, are how to meet the developer's commercial objectives while at the same time giving meaning and scale to the built form as well as providing user-friendly spaces both within and without, and also fulfilling other environmentally-responsive considerations.

15

1931. The Empire State Building was completed in New York City. A speculative venture during the Great Depression, it was the largest office building in the world at that time.

'... as old technology reaches its limits the age of the super-skyscraper dawns, driven by emergent new forms and new technologies – the ultimate building becomes a city itself...'

PROFESSOR IVOR RICHARDS

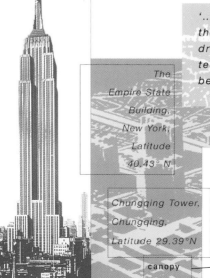

The Empire State Building, New York, Latitude 40.43° N

Chungqing Tower, Chungqing, Latitude 29.39°N

canopy

level 7

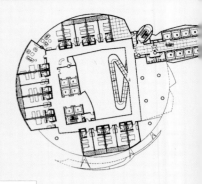

level 10

design criteria

Although the skyscraper has North American origins, this invention and massive piece of contemporary technology can be found in other areas, such as Europe and the Far East. Architects in these locations, faced with having to design intensive high developments in dense urban contexts (whether in Berlin or in Shanghai), obviously seek appropriate criteria to guide the design of this building type. Where are these to come from? Should the designers replicate the models found in North America but dress them up differently?

An obvious starting point is to look at the historical precedents of the locality, but this is not realistic in practice. In the skyscraper's contemporary role as multi-storey business premises or residences, there are no historical or regional precedents and it is unlikely that we will find models for contemporary skyscraper design in even the largest of traditional or colonial buildings (where these exist). This is because the sheer scale and bulk of the modern-day skyscraper by far exceeds those of the largest traditional precedents.

16

life in the
Concrete
Jungle,
'the North American origins
of the skyscraper'

Menara
Mesiniaga,
Kuala Lumpur,
Latitude 3.5°N

peripheral
core
position

variable facade treatment

sun-roof

gymnasium

open
escape stair

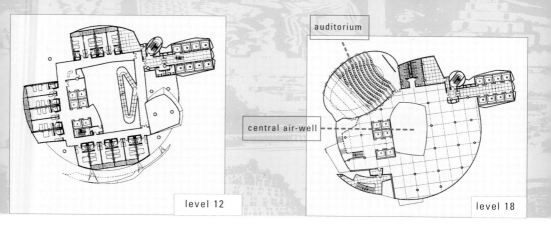

auditorium

central air-well

level 12

level 18

Clearly, if designers can find no historical precedents for the new skyscrapers that are fervently being built in Tokyo, China or Germany, for example, how are they to design the tall building in these places far removed from North America?

Louis Sullivan's 1896 essay, 'The Tall Building, Artistically Considered', proposed an approach to handling the aesthetics of the tall building, formulating the concept of the 'three part sky-column'. He based his theories on the functional and expressive qualities of the three parts of the skyscraper: the base, the shaft and the crest. However, while these can provide a useful aesthetic structure (as exemplified in the Flatiron Building, NYC), they provide very little else. This structuralist view is simply the formal sub-division of the skyscraper's built form into three categories to assist their shaping and styling. It does not offer other solutions as to how these segments are to be shaped.

What is needed is an endemic approach that will enable the designer to relate the skyscraper to different cultures and places.

'Skycrapers will provide society with the means to live and work in creative contact and avoid the destructive spilling-out of cities as an urban sprawl into the countryside...'

TONY FITZPATRICK
OVE ARUP & PARTNERS

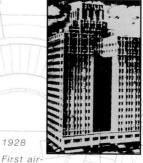

1928

First air-conditioned office

The first large office building to be fully air-conditioned was the 21-storey Milam building in San Antonio, Texas. The building had a central refrigerating source in the basement and a series of smaller units on every other floor. Cool air was distributed to each office through metal ducts and warm air was returned through the hallways.

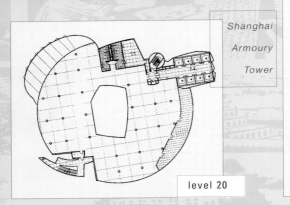

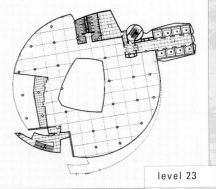

Shanghai Armoury Tower

level 20

level 23

the bioclimatic skyscraper

A question frequently asked is: why do the facades of some skyscrapers look the same on all sides, when the contextual environment (meteorologically, physically, geographically, etc) of each side of the building is not the same?

The design of bioclimatic skyscrapers, however, demands a *variable approach* to facade treatment and building performance since the location's sun-paths are different for each facade at different times of the day, year and latitude in the hemisphere (see the Shanghai Armoury Tower).

The climate-responsive approach seeks year-round comfort, using entirely passive energy means where possible to reduce energy consumption. The bioclimatic approach also has the potential of being an ecologically benign approach if other sustainable design factors such as the selection of materials and ambient energy sources are also taken into consideration.

The **bioclimatic skyscraper** might be regarded as a new genre of the tall building type. Simply stated, it is the application of the (already well-known) bioclimatic approach to building design to skyscraper design.

We can define the bioclimatic skyscraper as a tall building whose built form is configured by design, using passive low-energy techniques to relate to the site's climate and meteorological data, resulting in a tall building that is environmentally interactive, low-energy in embodiment and operations, and high quality in performance.

The fundamental premise is that the understanding and incorporation of the external and internal environmental aspects of the skyscraper will contribute to its architectural expression.

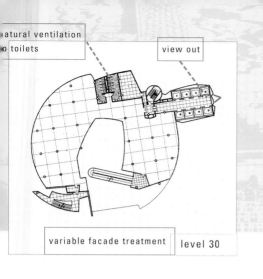

natural ventilation o toilets

view out

variable facade treatment | level 30

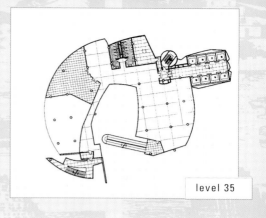

level 35

The outcome of the bioclimatic design approach should be a 'high quality' building. In the past, much 'bioclimatic-based architecture' was related to low-cost, low- and medium-rise architecture, especially in tropical climates and mostly in 'Third World' locations. This has inadvertently led the term 'high-rise' to have connotations of low-standards and poor quality. This should not be the case: the bioclimatic approach is applicable to *all* climatic zones and can be applied to high quality buildings as well.

We might contend that as a consequence of this design approach, the emergent skyscrapers might be regarded as a different genre to those based on existent design approaches, which are ubiquitous in all the major cities of the world.

19

Shanghai

Armoury Tower

peripheral core position

sky courts

variable facade in all directions depending on climatic responses and site context.

Of course, the pressing question is: what is the relevance of the bioclimatic skyscraper and why is it beneficial? To answer this, we can list the features and benefits of the bioclimatic skyscraper as follows:

FEATURES	BENEFITS
PASSIVE LOW-ENERGY FEATURES	Contribute to a sustainable future
LOW-ENERGY PERFORMANCE	Achieved through the building configuration (instead of an 'additive' approach through the addition of electro-mechanical devices)
SOLAR AND WIND-RELATED ORIENTATION	Either through singular or combined climatic-responsive solutions
NATURALLY SUNLIT SPACES WITH VIEWS OUT FROM LIFT LOBBIES, STAIRCASES, TOILETS	Results in a more human building and provides better awareness of place
NATURAL VENTILATION TO LIFT-CORES, TOILETS, STAIRCASES	Creates a healthier built environment and is lower in energy to operate
OTHER NATURAL VENTILATION AND WIND-ENERGY OPPORTUNITIES	Lower in energy to operate
SKYCOURTS AS PRIVATE COMMUNAL SPACES	Greater user satisfaction
SKYCOURTS AS WIND-CONTROLLED ZONES	Natural ventilation and landscaping opportunities
SKYCOURTS AS SUN-RECEIVING SPACES	Greater user satisfaction and low-energy benefits
INTERSTITIAL SPACES	Bioclimatic applications as well as flexible allowance for future expansion by the building users and reduction of facade wind vortices
CLEAR-GLAZING	Better light quality reaches the internal areas for greater user satisfaction
SOLAR-CONTROL THROUGH PASSIVE DEVICES	Reduce energy consumption
VERTICAL LANDSCAPING, PLANTING AND GARDENS-IN-THE-SKY	Enable a more human environment with healthier micro-climate near the perimeter of the facades
LIFT-CORES AS SOLAR AND WIND BUFFERS	Reduce energy consumption
ENVIRONMENTALLY-INTERACTIVE EXTERNAL-WALL	Greater responsiveness to variable seasonal changes
GREATER USER COMFORT AND AMENITIES THROUGH BIOCLIMATIC RESPONSES	Greater user satisfaction
LIFT/STAIR LOBBIES AS COMMUNAL ROOMS AND REFUGE ZONES	Greater user safety and satisfaction
GREATER INTER-FLOOR CONNECTIVITY THROUGH NATURALLY-VENTILATED RAMPS, STAIRS, ETC.	Greater accessibility and the recreation of access conditions resembling the ground-plane
HIGH-QUALITY BUILDING AS A CONSEQUENCE OF BIOCLIMATIC APPROACH	For greater user comfort

Of course, we must be aware that besides climatic criteria, there are many other criteria for design, such as economics, culture, building programme, site contours, views, etc. However, a locality's climate is probably its most durably endemic characteristic (besides the site's bedrock).

As the location's most endemic factor, *climate* provides the designer with a legitimate starting point for architectural expression in the endeavour to design in relation to place, because climate is one of the dominant determinants of the local inhabitant's lifestyle and the landscape's ecology.

At the level of design and town planning, the approach provides us with an ecologically-responsive high-rise built environment which affords intensive land use in the existing city, and leads towards a sustainable future.

The benefits to the community of the bioclimatic design approach are high-rise architecture and urban design (see Chapter 9) that environmentally and physically perform differently (and probably appear different) to the conventional high-rise architecture that was built from the 1950s to the 1990s.

On the premise that both intensive developments and tall buildings are inevitable in our cities, the bioclimatic skyscraper will contribute to reduced energy consumption in the built urban environment and will be more ecologically beneficial than the conventional skyscraper since it achieves this *passively*. At the same time, the bioclimatic skyscraper provides a more aesthetically fulfilling, human and safer high-rise built environment for its occupants.

Generally stated, our bioclimatic design approach might be regarded as a subset of the ecological design approach.[1]

It is also contended that it will generally simplify rather than complicate the design of the skyscraper. By employing the basic bioclimatic energy-conserving principle of providing natural ventilation and sunlight to the elevator and stair-core areas, the need for mechanical pressurisation-ducts to elevator lobbies and stair-shafts is eliminated, thereby simplifying the design and lowering the capital costs at the same time (see Chapter 2).

Note

1 K Yeang, *Designing with Nature*, McGraw-Hill, NYC, 1995.

the bioclimatic approach

Bioclimatology is the study of the relationship between climate and life, particularly the effects of climate on the health and activity of living things.

The approach offers the designer an endemic solution by focusing on the relationship between the architectural form and its environmental performance in relation to the climate of the place. The resulting built form then illustrates how an understanding of the environmental aspects of design that already influence the culture and life of that locality can contribute to architectural expression. At the same time the approach helps minimise dependence on non-renewable energy sources.

Until the 1960s the bioclimatic design principles (the 'principles of designing with climate') were relatively advanced for low- and medium-rise buildings. During the 1940s and 50s in schools of architecture in Canada and the USA, architectural response to climate had been an integral part of professional education – determining the size of an overhang to a window had a widely-held importance then, similar to the correct sizing of a beam. But by the 1960s, in most schools, this standard of climatic response became unfortunately displaced by other priorities. Cheap oil prices enabled designers to negate the environmental factors of a place which led to the proliferation of the internalised-environment and architecture with high levels of energy consumption.

SHANGHAI ARMOURY TOWER

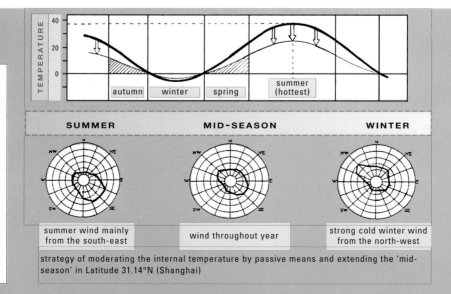

strategy of moderating the internal temperature by passive means and extending the 'mid-season' in Latitude 31.14°N (Shanghai)

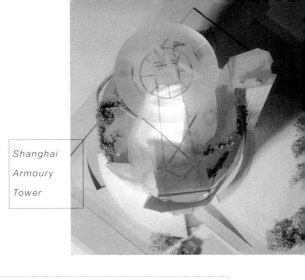

From the 1960s to today, there has been inadequate development of bioclimatic concepts with regard to the high-rise building. The justification for greater attention to this are evident. Apart from other building typologies, the skyscraper is a novel (ie. non-traditional) building type possessing new technological systems. It should inevitably demand its own set of design and planning premises.

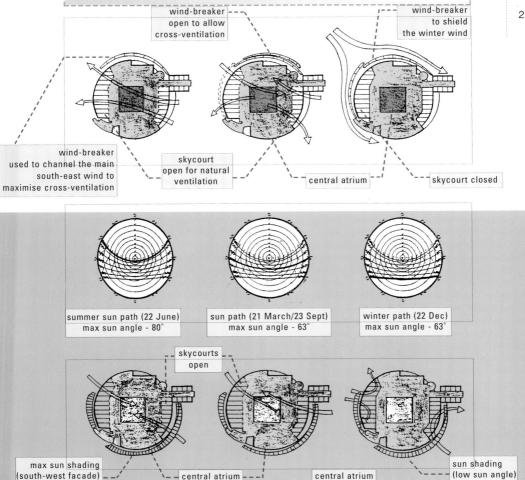

SUMMER	MID-SEASON	WINTER

wind-breaker open to allow cross-ventilation

wind-breaker to shield the winter wind

wind-breaker used to channel the main south-east wind to maximise cross-ventilation

skycourt open for natural ventilation

central atrium

skycourt closed

summer sun path (22 June) max sun angle - 80°

sun path (21 March/23 Sept) max sun angle - 63°

winter path (22 Dec) max sun angle - 63°

skycourts open

max sun shading (south-west facade)

central atrium

central atrium

sun shading (low sun angle)

the bioclimatic
rationale

A question often asked is what is the rationale for designing according to meteorological data? This is particularly important since designing a tall building to take advantage of its location's climate leads inevitably to a departure (whether to a greater or lesser extent) from purely economic criteria (ie. the building will cost more than the norm). For instance, the provision of sun-shading to the facades will increase the thickness of the skyscraper's external wall. The use of external lift cores in the bioclimatic skyscraper might, in some instances, use space less efficiently than the central core layout, or might obstruct the view, albeit marginally. Return-on-Investment (ROI) analysts might well ask what justifications we have for this departure, besides, of course, reasons of architectural expression.

The most obvious justification for the bioclimatic design approach to the skyscraper is the lowering of life-cycle *financial and energy costs* which arises from lowering the energy consumption in the operations of the building. These savings can be as much as 30% to 60% of the overall life-cycle energy costs of the building since, during its entire life cycle, the bulk of its costs lie clearly in its operational phase (see Chapter 8). Thus significant savings in operational costs justify the climatically-responsive design features despite a moderately higher initial capital construction cost.

Another factor is the beneficial effect on the occupants of the skyscraper. The climatically-responsive skyscraper enhances its users' well-being providing a more human

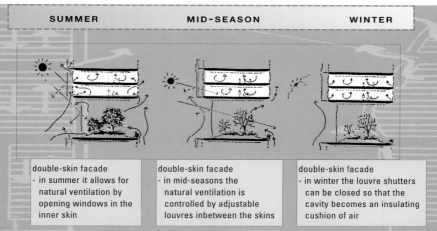

SHANGHAI ARMOURY TOWER

SUMMER	MID-SEASON	WINTER

double-skin facade
- in summer it allows for natural ventilation by opening windows in the inner skin

double-skin facade
- in mid-seasons the natural ventilation is controlled by adjustable louvres inbetween the skins

double-skin facade
- in winter the louvre shutters can be closed so that the cavity becomes an insulating cushion of air

high-rise environment. Better natural ventilation to the internal spaces results in a healthier internal environment thereby increasing overall business productivity.

The climatically-responsive design approach also provides the building's occupants with the opportunity to experience both the external environment of the locality and the changing diurnal and seasonal variations (as against a constant dull internalised condition). This avoids them spending their working hours (a significant part of their day) in an inhuman artificial environment that remains essentially the same throughout the year.

A further justification is the *ecological* one. Designing with climate results in the reduction of the overall energy consumption of the building through the use of passive devices (as against the use of energy-driven electro-mechanical devices). This results in operational cost savings which translate to minimise the use of electrical energy resources (meaning savings in the use of non-renewable fossil fuels). The lowering of energy consumption further reduces the overall emission of carbon dioxide and waste-heat which lowers the overall air-pollution and heat-island effect. Every KWh of energy conserved in the building constitutes the reduction of the negative environmental impacts on the biosphere arising from the extraction, production, distribution and utilisation of that KWh unit of energy, hence contributing to a more sustainable future.

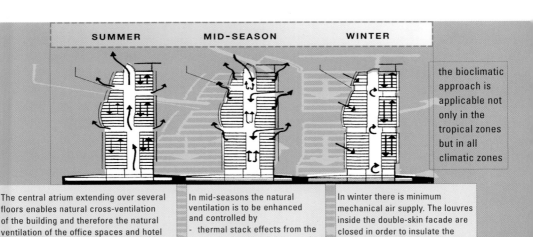

SUMMER — MID-SEASON — WINTER

the bioclimatic approach is applicable not only in the tropical zones but in all climatic zones

The central atrium extending over several floors enables natural cross-ventilation of the building and therefore the natural ventilation of the office spaces and hotel corridors next to the atria

In mid-seasons the natural ventilation is to be enhanced and controlled by
- thermal stack effects from the thermal flue (atrium)
- wind suction

In winter there is minimum mechanical air supply. The louvres inside the double-skin facade are closed in order to insulate the building with an air cavity

There is also the regionalist design justification (discussed earlier). When viewed in the overall perspective of human history and built settlements, the climate of a place is the single most constant factor in our landscape, other than geological structure. Whilst the socio-economic and political conditions of any location may change almost unrecognisably over a period of, say, one hundred years (as may its culture, politics and aesthetic sensibilities), its climate remains more or less constant in its cyclical course (excluding, of course, minor changes and environmental variations in temperature, sunshine, rainfall, etc).

The history of human settlements shows us that with accumulated human experiences and imagination, the architecture of the human shelter evolved diversely in response to the differing challenges of various locations and climates. Evidently, the ancients recognised regional design adaptation as an essential principle of architecture. The climatically-responsive building might be regarded, then, as endemically having a greater design 'fit' with its design programme.

LE CORBUSIER HIT THE HEADLINES IMMEDIATELY ON HIS ARRIVAL IN NEW YORK WHEN HE DECLARED THAT THE SKYSCRAPERS WERE TOO SMALL AND TOO CLOSE TOGETHER.

HE CALLED HIS SKYSCRAPER THE 'CARTESIAN SKYSCRAPER'. IN PLAN IT WAS LIKE A HEN'S FOOT.

TO THE PRIVATE SECTOR (REAL ESTATE DEVELOPERS AND BIG BUSINESS CLIENTS), LE CORBUSIER'S 'CARTESIAN SKYSCRAPER' IDEA MUST HAVE SEEMED HOPELESSLY UNTENABLE AS IT THREW AWAY SO MUCH POTENTIALLY PROFITABLE LAND FOR 'USELESS' PARKS.

'The Cartesian skyscraper as a salvation for the American city'
Le Corbusier (late 1930s)
New York, Latitude 40.43°N

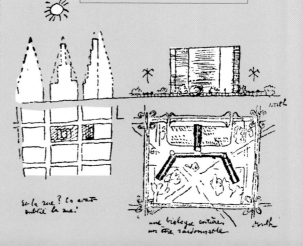

land use
and other initial
considerations

A proposed skyscraper's net and gross space use and the site's development plot ratios are usually among the considerations of the developer when looking at a plot of land for intensive development. Each plot of land (especially in the business areas of a city) generally has 'permissible allowances' for its development determined by the local planning authorities (ie. its plot ratio).

In optimising the usually small land area, the skyscraper's economics obviously seek the maximum internal area on each floor (net rentable areas or NRA), and the maximum gross building area (the gross floor area or GFA) for its site (ie. maximum plot ratios and minimum 'net-to-gross' ratios).

In order to achieve these economic objectives, the following design criteria are inevitably critical:

- MINIMUM EXTERNAL WALL THICKNESS
- MINIMUM VERTICAL SUPPORT SIZE
- MINIMUM HORIZONTAL-SUPPORT THICKNESS
- MINIMUM VERTICAL CIRCULATION (IN THE SERVICE CORE)
- MINIMUM FLOOR-TO-FLOOR HEIGHT

The cost-saving justifications for these criteria are obvious. For instance, having minimum external wall thickness reduces vertical structural member sizes (ie. column widths). An efficient service core layout increases the net rentable floor area per typical floor.

Minimum horizontal-support thickness and floor-to-floor heights lower structural costs and the area of external cladding and hence construction costs generally.

However, there are some who argue that if minimum cost and maximum financial optimisation are the only objectives for design, the resultant architecture will be self-evident 'built-diagrams' as 'bunkers'.

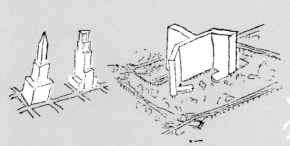

re - formation cellulaire de la ville

However, besides costs, there are, of course, other important issues which need to be considered when designing skyscrapers. As already discussed, these include enhancing the environment of its occupants (thereby improving their well-being and hence productivity), and conserving energy (thus translating initial capital costs arising from energy conservation design measures into long-term financial benefits).

Then there are marketing issues where the appearance of the building might enhance the corporate image of the company.

THE INITIAL PRE-DESIGN CONSIDERATIONS IN SKYSCRAPER DESIGN INCLUDE THE FOLLOWING:

- The designer usually starts by finding out the extent of permissible built-up space for the plot of land. He initially analyses the site using its plot ratio (or FAR, the Floor-Area-Ratio) to ascertain the permitted built-up area for that plot area. This is simply the 'site area' multiplied by the 'permitted plot ratio' for the site (eg. if the site area is 'x' and the permitted plot ratio is 1:12, then the permissible gross floor area, or GFA, is '12x').

- From these analyses, the designer then makes other numerical assumptions based on 'assumed building efficiencies' to derive the net rentable/saleable area (in relation to the total gross built-up areas for the plot). For example, he might assume that the overall net-to-gross ratio percentage is at an efficiency of 75% (although a higher efficiency is usually attainable), in which case the net rentable/saleable area (or NRA) for the proposed building is '75% of 12x'.

'the over-styled skyscraper' or 'skyscraper design as packaging'

the bioclimatic ant hill in the monsoon zone (complete with overhangs and sunshading)

the ant hill in the hot arid zone as a climatically-responsive skyscraper

28

- The extent of car-parking provisions and where these are to be located. Whether these are located above ground or below ground in basements or elsewhere (eg. in car park-structures) may be a factor in the analysis affecting costs, building height and usable ground floor area (eg. if basements are provided, ramps to the basement will reduce the ground floor net-area). A useful guide to determining car-park area is 35 sq m per car park (inclusive of bay area and driveways).

- Other factors include delineating the permissible building envelopes (which may include height restrictions) and permissible building footprints or plinth-ratios (usually described as a percentage of the site area).

- From these figures, initial financial analyses are calculated by the designer (or the developer) to establish a construction and development budget that makes the project viable, taking into account other costs such as legislative development charges, saleable/rentable rates, financing costs, construction costs, fees, etc.

- In the above financial analyses, the end-user and real estate marketing requirements for the building may affect the building areas and configuration, including the likely tenancy requirements (or owner's requirements if the building is owner-occupied), and the need for the provision of additional marketing features in the design.

- Budgetary constraints and ROI (Returns on Investment) studies are done at this stage. These will influence the form of construction and the level of provision of the building's M&E system as well as the level of building finishes (ie. the quality of building).

29

For the developer, the skyscraper is a 'money-making machine': the more the built-up space, the more the rental.

Skyscraper as packaging

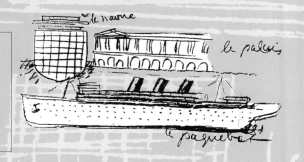

- General site planning is also evaluated. However, as most skyscrapers are on compact urban sites, crucial design considerations include the extent of road widening, the extent of building set-back lines from boundary lines, the extent of building volume in relation to provision of fire-engine access (eg. access to facades), the extent of permissible basement lines, location of vehicular ingress, egress and 'drop-off' points, and other town planning related requirements.

- Alternative building configurations for the plot may be evaluated at this stage depending on the permissible building envelope and height restrictions (if existent), the preferred floor-plate sizes (a market-related decision and dependent also on whether the built-up space is for 'institutional', 'professional' or 'corporate' tenants or for indeterminate tenants).

- Floor-plate planning and configuration, service-core location, floor-to-floor height considerations in relation to floor clear-spans, fire escape distances and dead ends, tenancy options (eg. single-tenant, double-tenant, multiple-tenant or a combination), extent of wash room provisions, access distance to window and sunlight, acceptable floor-depths from sunlit-windows, corner-office situations and preferences, and other interior architectural requirements are also evaluated and determined.

- Elevator planning and configuration are generally analysed early on to determine likely core size and configuration (see Chapter 2), the level of building floor-plate efficiency (having deducted the service-core area), the need for the provision of sky lobbies (if the elevator configuration is multi-zoned), the provision of firemen's elevator(s) and a freight/service elevator, the need for lobby separations (if it is a multiple-use building), the provision of protected fire lobbies, etc.

- M&E system integration and options also need to be initially considered as these depend on expected user and marketing requirements. Different systems will have varying mechanical plant room requirements and distribution systems which will affect building efficiencies and floor-to-floor heights.

- Initial decisions may be made early on the structural *grids* in relation to beam spans, ceiling grids, car-parking integration, window mullion spacings, likely partitioned room sizes and tenancy situations, column-free floor preferences, etc.

- Subsoil and water table conditions will also influence piling design, sub-structural design, structural design, floor-plate design, the location of cores and structural columns, basement provision, etc. In some localities soil improvements may be necessary (eg. sub-structural grouting). Soil tests are preferably undertaken prior to commencing design.

- Mandatory and market-preferred car-parking requirements and provisions may affect structural grids (eg. transfer beams, if not coinciding) and the building's configuration.

- The total period of building (from start to finish of the project) may involve the consideration of a 'fast-track' method of construction and alternative building systems (eg. precast versus in-situ, reinforced concrete frame construction vs steel-frame construction, etc), 'jump-start' construction, 'top-down' construction, 'fly-form' shuttering, all of which may affect design and costs, etc.

- In addition, the designer also has to consider the built form's aesthetics and design concepts, when integrating the above by design.

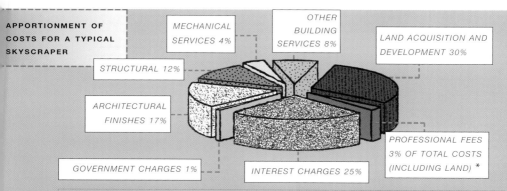

APPORTIONMENT OF COSTS FOR A TYPICAL SKYSCRAPER

MECHANICAL SERVICES 4%

OTHER BUILDING SERVICES 8%

LAND ACQUISITION AND DEVELOPMENT 30%

STRUCTURAL 12%

ARCHITECTURAL FINISHES 17%

GOVERNMENT CHARGES 1%

INTEREST CHARGES 25%

PROFESSIONAL FEES 3% OF TOTAL COSTS (INCLUDING LAND) *

Source: Hira, A, Paks, M, 'Design and Construction of Cores for Tall Buildings – achieving TQM through Multi-Disciplinary approach'; presented at Conference, Sluvice, Poland, 13-15 Oct 1994

* NB: Professional fees are expressed here as a percentage of the total costs including land, but are usually given as a percentage of construction costs (here @ 7.5%).

These considerations are usually studied in detail by the designer at the start of a skyscraper's 'concept design' stage. Although at this stage the design often remains no more than a diagram of the intended project and a simple statement of its intentions, the involvement of the designer is essential (ie. rather than leave all these analyses to the building economist or the owner). This is because the evaluation and resolution of many of these analyses (although tentative at this stage) will influence design development at later stages.

These conceptual design considerations provide the designer and/or owner with the basic figures and bases to negotiate plot ratios, height limitations, configurations, etc with the relevant local planning or approving authorities or with financial institutions (for development and financing purposes) or with potential 'anchor' tenants.

A skyscraper is certainly a massive financial undertaking involving major commitment and risk-taking, in most instances. This is even more the case when the project has no confirmed key tenant, or 'anchor tenant', and when the developer embarks on an entirely speculative venture. In many such cases, the skyscraper's commercial priorities tend to override architectural aspects leading inevitably to 'jerry-built' architecture – boxes devoid of any qualities. In such instances, the remaining opportunities for the architect might be the development of unique 'marketing features' (building features that could enhance sales and rentals). This is certainly not a desirable situation to be in.

vertical
circulation

- structural stiffening
- solar buffer
- wind buffer
- emergency refuge zone
- communal places
- vertical urban linkages
- events spaces

'How many relationships begin in a lift car or on an escalator? ...pressed within the doors of a crowded lift... with tightly-packed strangers. ...As the lift opened I was kissed on the lips. True love? It was a cousin of mine'

PROFESSOR
LEON VAN SCHAIK

vertical circulation

Movement within the skyscraper consti-
tutes the skyscraper's vertical circulation systems. These are the
means by which the skyscraper's users access the floors.

The skyscraper's vertical circulation com-
ponents are the staircases, escalators, elevators, dumb-waiters and
all the means of vertical access and service to the building. These are
usually located in 'cores' and these vertical 'service cores' and 'risers'
play a key part in the design and shaping of the typical floor-plate.

As with any architectural project, the build-
ing's circulation systems are an important part of its design parti. The
effectiveness of the circulation system is ultimately the test of whether
the skyscraper works as a building. If a skyscraper's circulation systems
do not work, then the building does not work. In the case of the skyscraper, its vertical circulation system has to be one of the foremost
design considerations.

Elevators are an essential part of the circu-
lation system for a skyscraper, much as the circulation of blood to the
heart is for the human body. It cannot be stressed enough to the
designer that the successful functioning of a skyscraper depends
almost entirely upon the successful functioning of its elevator system
as its main circulation system.

configuration

In the initial stages of design, the designer
ascertains the extent of buildable net rentable areas (NRA) and gross
floor areas (GFA) in the proposed skyscraper and these figures are used
as the bases for elevator configuration design. These areas are usually
apportioned over the entire height of the building and it is at this stage
that the typical and atypical floor-plates are generally configured.

It is at this very preliminary stage of design,
when the designer is still shaping the floor-plates and the skyscraper's
built form and finalising the building height, that he prepares a diagram
of the proposed elevator configuration, showing the number of banks of
elevators, the expected number of stops, the transfer floor(s), the likely
segregation of the regular passenger elevators from those serving the
car-park floors, etc. This diagram is drawn with a tabulation of the
approximate apportionment of built area over the entire building
(see table and diagram opposite).

Example of area tabulation and elevator configuration diagrams:

FLOOR	LEVEL	NET (NRA)	SERVICE	GROSS (GFA)	CAR-PARK	CAR-PARK	EFFICIENCY
BASEMENT	B3-B1	0	1,229	-	150	59,365	-
GROUND	1	2,274	2,231	4,105	-	-	55%
BANKING	2	9,799	2,231	12,034	-	-	81%
BANKING	3	9,799	2,231	12,034	-	-	81%
CAR PARKING (15 levels)	4-18	0	6,148	-	548	249,525	-
LIFT FLOOR	19	7,769	2,231	10,000	-	-	78%
OFFICE (15 levels)	20-34	AVE 12,799	2,231	AVE 15,030	-	-	85%
LIFT FLOOR	35	7,769	2,231	10,000	-	-	78%
OFFICE (15 levels)	36-50	AVE 12,799	1,585	AVE 15,030	-	-	89%
PENTHOUSE	51	9,270	1,585	10,858	-	-	85%
PENTHOUSE	52	3,218	1,585	4,803	-	-	67%
TOTAL	51	438,544	76,210	514,754	695	308,890	85%
GROSS				823,644			

TENTATIVE AREA TABULATION PREPARED BY THE DESIGNER OF THE PROPOSED BUILDING

EXAMPLE OF FORMAT FOR
ELEVATOR ANALYSIS OF
A **52**-STOREY BUILDING
WITH **3** BASEMENT
LEVELS OF CAR-PARKING

No. of
elevators:

3 car-park
zone lifts

6 banking
and lower
offices
zone lifts

6 upper
offices
zone lifts

• = lift opening

Initial schematic diagram
prepared by the designer
to show the number of
lift shafts and proposed
lift door openings.

(See above table for
areas of each of the
floors in the elevator
configuration diagram)

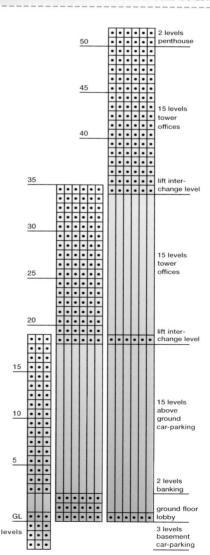

2 levels
penthouse

15 levels
tower
offices

lift inter-
change level

15 levels
tower
offices

lift inter-
change level

15 levels
above
ground
car-parking

2 levels
banking

ground floor
lobby

3 levels
basement
car-parking

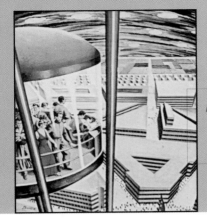

From these the elevator suppliers (or the elevator engineer), using their formulae, analyse the building based on an estimated population density per floor (a 'rule-of-thumb' is 1 person per 15 sqm).

They then prepare summary charts (containing such information as alternative Average Waiting Times (AWT), handling capacities, type of lift cars, elevator speeds, etc, with alternative elevator configurations). From these analyses, the designer evaluates and develops the skyscraper's floor-plates and built form until they meet both his aesthetic and technical criteria (see 'Requirements for Elevator Selection Service' table, pages 48-49). (Note: the end column in the table on pages 196-197 provides a preliminary guide for determining the numbers of elevators required to serve a building.)

Generally, the elevator configurations are decided upon by the designer who takes into consideration a number of other factors such as: typical floor-plate sizes, typical floor-plate efficiency, staircase positions, tenancy options, views outward, M&E risers and routes, structural system options, etc.

Once the designer is satisfied that his entire set of criteria has been met, the number of elevators is decided upon, and their configuration provides the general basis for firming up the floor-plate design.

the contemporary
safety elevator

An elevator or lift is defined as a car that moves in a vertical shaft to carry passengers or freight among the levels of a multi-storey building.

Although there are between 72,000 and 94,000 pieces in the average elevator, the basic components are:

- machine and brake
  (for hoist and the car)

- elevator-car

- controller

- selector

- counterweight

- travelling cables

- ropes
  traction cables

- governor

- guide rails
  (for car and
  counterweight)

- buffer (or springs)

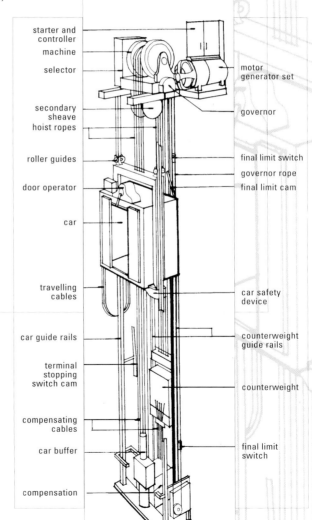

starter and controller
machine
selector

secondary sheave
hoist ropes

roller guides

door operator

car

travelling cables

car guide rails

terminal stopping switch cam

compensating cables

car buffer

compensation

motor generator set

governor

final limit switch
governor rope
final limit cam

car safety device

counterweight guide rails

counterweight

final limit switch

floor-plate design

Future Interactive Panel at elevator lobby

In planning the configurations and layout of the skyscraper's elevators, the main staircase is usually grouped with the elevators so that should the latter be unserviceable, the staircase becomes an alternative means of escape and is readily accessible. As these usually run all the way up the building, the M&E riser ducts are also located in the same vicinity.

Structurally, the elevator core walls are often used as shear walls in the skyscraper, especially integrated with concrete frame construction for the superstructure and are often referred to as the 'service-core'. However, recent trends indicate a move towards non-structural core walls (eg. gypsum fire-rated walls) to reduce overall building weight and to make use of other parts of the structure for stiffening (eg. facade bracing).

Early consideration by the designer of these vertical circulation components is important because they determine the shape, layout plan and efficiency of the typical floor-plate. Attention must be paid to the floor-plate design at the preliminary design stage since it is generally repeated many times over the height of the skyscraper (if some level of economy is desired). Clearly, the consideration of the number of floors which it is necessary to access through the service-core is important. Other aspects that affect the floor-plate's design include the direction of the best views out, which levels provide the best views, the permissible ground floor plinth area (the area generating the highest income), the car-parking grids in relation to the floor-plate structural configuration, etc.

ADVANCED ELEVATOR-CAR DESIGN #1 (FOR SCHINDLER MANAGEMENT LTD)

THE 'TOURER'

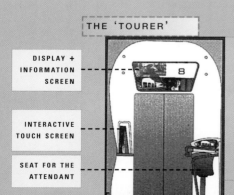

DISPLAY + INFORMATION SCREEN

INTERACTIVE TOUCH SCREEN

SEAT FOR THE ATTENDANT

This is a proposal for an advanced elevator-car design called the 'Tourer' which brings back to the contemporary elevator-car the traditional lift car attendant, especially vital in super-tall skyscrapers when travel times exceed 160 seconds.

In the elevator-car of today, where travel distances are longer than before, the elevator-car attendant serves as a 'tour guide'.

> *'Vertical circulation...has for too long been the poor relation of horizontal circulation. He who makes the two equal will conquer the 21st century.'* MARTIN PAWLEY

Of crucial economic interest to the developer is the net-to-gross area's 'efficiency' (expressed as a percentage) of the typical floor-plate (ie. NRA ÷ GFA x 100%). The more efficient the typical floor-plate, the more net area the developer gets and the more income will be derived from the building.

Generally, a floor-plate efficiency should not be less than 75%, unless the site is too small or too irregular to permit a higher level of floor-use efficiency. Floor-plate designs using clever devices (eg. scissor-stairs, pressurised lift-shafts, dispersal of toilets, etc) can increase efficiency up to 80-85% per typical floor. The implementation of efficiency measures also requires a good understanding of the local fire-codes determining the need for fire-protected lobbies and escape-stair positions.

39

service-core positions
in the
bioclimatic skyscraper

In the bioclimatic skyscraper, the location of the service-core is important both in relation to the quality of the internal spaces of the building and to the site's sun-path which varies depending on the latitude in which the building is located (eg. whether in the cold, temperate or tropical zones, etc). The position of the service-core is a key consideration in the planning of the bioclimatic skyscraper's floor-plate and in determining its configuration.

THE ELEVATOR ATTENDANT'S NEW ROLES ARE TO:
- monitor the elevator controls' override systems
- manage the elevator-car and its passengers in case of emergencies
- interact with the building's Intelligent Systems and the building's Command Centres through an AV screen at his station
- communicate with the building's reception (at ground level), the reception of all floors, and with the building's facilities (eg. restaurants, car-park floor, etc)
- interact with passengers as tour guide and attendant to make travel comfortable and cheerful

ELEVATOR ATTENDANT STATION

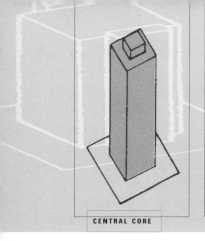
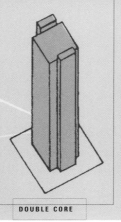
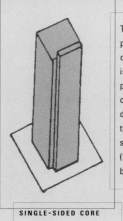

The size of the floor-plate in the 'side-core' configuration is restricted by the permissible distance of the furthermost dead end corner to the fire-protected stair lobby (limited by the local building codes).

Besides their obvious structural ramifications, service-cores determine which parts of the building's peripheral walls will have further external window-walls. These can also affect the building's thermal performance and the direction of the views outside.

Essentially there are three possible configurations of core position:

- CENTRAL CORE
- DOUBLE CORE
- SINGLE-SIDED CORE

40

Generally, the service-cores in the bioclimatic skyscraper should be located at the *periphery* of the floor-plate to allow natural sunlight and ventilation to the elevator lobby, stair and toilet areas.

The benefits of a peripheral core position are:

- NO FIRE-FIGHTING PRESSURISATION DUCT IS NEEDED (IE. LOWER FIRST COSTS AND OPERATING COSTS)
- IMMEDIATE VIEW OUT FROM ELEVATOR LOBBY WITH GREATER 'AWARENESS OF PLACE'
- PROVISION OF NATURAL VENTILATION TO THE CORE SPACES
- PROVISION OF NATURAL SUNLIGHT TO THE CORE SPACES
- A SAFER BUILDING IN THE EVENT OF TOTAL POWER FAILURE
- THE CORES CAN SERVE AS SOLAR-BUFFERS TO THE BUILDING

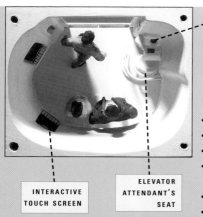

ELEVATOR ATTENDANT'S CONTROL PANEL

THE 'TOURER'

ABOVE THE CAR DOOR IS A LARGE-SCREEN FLAT VIDEO MONITOR WHICH CAN SHOW SINGLE OR MULTIPLE VIEWS OF:

- the next floor
- information on the floor
- information on the climate outside (eg. raining, snowing, etc)
- information on building activities for the day (for the information of passengers)
- urgent messages for passengers, etc
- any other information relevant to passengers

INTERACTIVE TOUCH SCREEN

ELEVATOR ATTENDANT'S SEAT

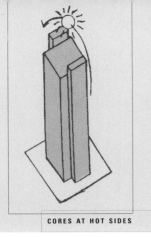

CORES AT HOT SIDES

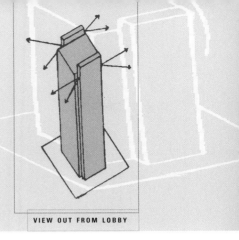

VIEW OUT FROM LOBBY

The double-core configuration offers many benefits: the two cores can be located on the 'hot' sides, acting as thermal 'buffer-zones' to the internal spaces. For instance, in hot-humid climates the solar path is generally east-west along the Equator. Studies have shown that where the service-cores are located on the 'hot' sides of the building (ie. east and west sides) significant savings can be achieved in the air-conditioning load as a consequence of this configuration (ie. with window-openings running north-south and cores on the east and west sides). This placement of the cores would meet the first two objectives above, preventing heat gain in those user-spaces which require greater cooling than the core areas, and providing a buffer (as a form of 'spatial' thermal insulation) to the hot sides of the building that would in turn maximise cooling loss away from the user-spaces.

In temperate and cold climates, the core-position could be organised to protect from the cold winter winds (eg. on the north-east and north-west).

41

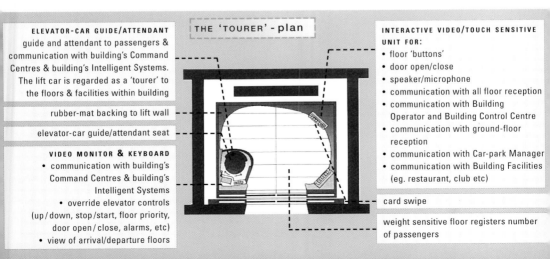

ELEVATOR-CAR GUIDE/ATTENDANT
guide and attendant to passengers & communication with building's Command Centres & building's Intelligent Systems. The lift car is regarded as a 'tourer' to the floors & facilities within building

rubber-mat backing to lift wall

elevator-car guide/attendant seat

VIDEO MONITOR & KEYBOARD
• communication with building's Command Centres & building's Intelligent Systems
• override elevator controls (up/down, stop/start, floor priority, door open/close, alarms, etc)
• view of arrival/departure floors

THE 'TOURER' - plan

INTERACTIVE VIDEO/TOUCH SENSITIVE UNIT FOR:
• floor 'buttons'
• door open/close
• speaker/microphone
• communication with all floor reception
• communication with Building Operator and Building Control Centre
• communication with ground-floor reception
• communication with Car-park Manager
• communication with Building Facilities (eg. restaurant, club etc)

card swipe

weight sensitive floor registers number of passengers

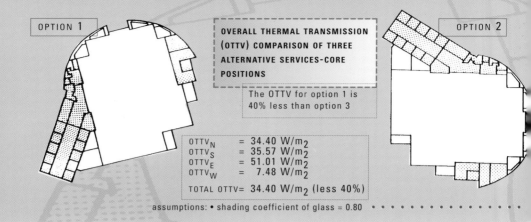

OVERALL THERMAL TRANSMISSION (OTTV) COMPARISON OF THREE ALTERNATIVE SERVICES-CORE POSITIONS

The OTTV for option 1 is 40% less than option 3

$$OTTV_N = 34.40 \text{ W/m}_2$$
$$OTTV_S = 35.57 \text{ W/m}_2$$
$$OTTV_E = 51.01 \text{ W/m}_2$$
$$OTTV_W = 7.48 \text{ W/m}_2$$

TOTAL OTTV = 34.40 W/m$_2$ (less 40%)

assumptions: • shading coefficient of glass = 0.80 • • • • • • • • • • • • •

natural ventilation and sunlight to service-cores

Natural ventilation can be justified for two primary reasons: firstly, for comfort, such as in the reduction of humid conditions (as in the tropics), and secondly, for energy-conservation by reducing the need for mechanical ventilation (see Chapter 5).

Free air movement should be encouraged around human body surfaces and throughout the building, so that the evaporation process increases and some degree of comfort can be achieved. The exchange of indoor air with fresh outdoor air can provide cooling and the moving air can also act as a heat-carrying medium.

In the case of the bioclimatic skyscraper, outdoor breezes could be fully utilised not only to ventilate elevator lobbies and staircases and terraces but also (when required) to pass through the whole building for structural cooling. The higher wind speeds at the upper levels of the building could be fully utilised as a cooling element in the tropics or in temperate zones during summer. To some extent, convective cooling through stack-effect could be used to take advantage of the building's height during the period of low wind.

THE 'TOURER' - section

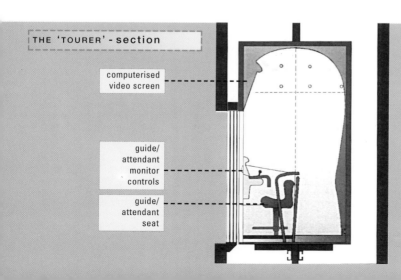

computerised video screen

guide/ attendant monitor controls

guide/ attendant seat

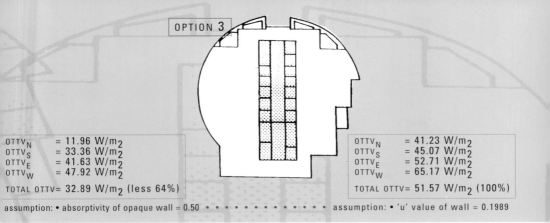

$OTTV_N$ = 11.96 W/m$_2$
$OTTV_S$ = 33.36 W/m$_2$
$OTTV_E$ = 41.63 W/m$_2$
$OTTV_W$ = 47.92 W/m$_2$

TOTAL OTTV = 32.89 W/m$_2$ (less 64%)

assumption: • absorptivity of opaque wall = 0.50

$OTTV_N$ = 41.23 W/m$_2$
$OTTV_S$ = 45.07 W/m$_2$
$OTTV_E$ = 52.71 W/m$_2$
$OTTV_W$ = 65.17 W/m$_2$

TOTAL OTTV = 51.57 W/m$_2$ (100%)

assumption: • 'u' value of wall = 0.1989

The designer should ensure that the service-cores (those parts of the tall building which contain the elevator shafts, elevator lobbies, main and escape stairways, riser-ducts, toilets and other service rooms) should have, wherever possible, natural ventilation, besides of course, sunlight and a good view out. This principle dictates a *peripheral* rather than a central-core position. Placed externally, further energy savings can be achieved through reduced requirements for mechanical ventilation, artificial lighting and the need for mechanical pressurisation-ducts for fire-protection (as mentioned above).

By providing a pleasant view from these areas, the users of the building can look out and experience the natural environment almost immediately as they exit from the elevator car onto the landing with the opportunity to experience natural sunlight and ventilation. This is considerably more desirable than the central-core situation where the building users leave the elevator car only to enter an artificially-lit, windowless, upper-floor lobby or passageway.

43

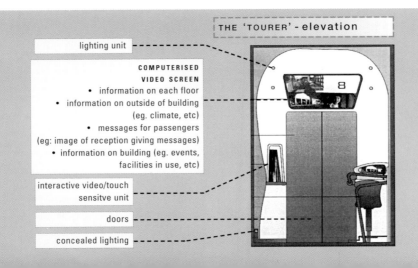

THE 'TOURER' - elevation

lighting unit

COMPUTERISED
VIDEO SCREEN
• information on each floor
• information on outside of building
(eg. climate, etc)
• messages for passengers
(eg: image of reception giving messages)
• information on building (eg. events,
facilities in use, etc)

interactive video/touch
sensitve unit

doors

concealed lighting

We might further contend that peripheral cores create a safer building. For instance, in the NYC World Trade Center bombing incident, the building users tripped over each other in the darkness while trying to locate the escape staircases and had immense difficulty escaping in the dark. This might have been averted had the staircases been on the periphery of the building, hence receiving natural sunlight and ventilation.

sky lobbies

For buildings significantly above 25 storeys, it is recommendable to adopt an elevator 'zoning concept'. Here, each zone (or 'segment') is served by a group of lifts with separate entrances and is limited by transfer floors or *sky-lobbies*.

At the NYC World Trade Center, this technique is used to minimise the space required for elevators. The 110-storey tower is divided into three segments. The lower segment, the first 41 floors of the tower, has four banks of six elevators each; similarly the middle and upper layers each have their own banks of six elevators. At the 44th and 78th floors there is a 'sky lobby' connected to the main floor by eleven high-speed shuttle elevators.

ADVANCED ELEVATOR-CAR DESIGN #2 (FOR SCHINDLER MANAGEMENT LTD)

THE 'COACH'

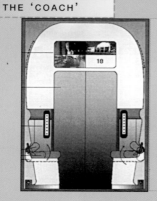

The 'Coach' design is similar to the coach-car of the city's subway. During peak periods of use, vertical supports slide out from the sides of the cabin and strap-handles also slide down from the ceiling for passengers to hold on to as the car moves up or down or stops and starts. While with contemporary designs and controls for elevators, these devices might be regarded as superfluous, they contribute to a greater passenger sense of security, increased comfort and well-being, especially when travelling up or down a large number of floors in a packed car.

In other zoned buildings, escalators are used to increase the transfer between the lobbies, if on separate floors.

In the elevator programming, the high-rise elevators of the lower section, which are arranged to serve the sky lobby, should not be arranged to serve the latter during peak traffic periods. If they do, building users will find it more convenient to ride to the sky floor and take the lower section elevators down to their floor, creating a two-way traffic on the elevators during peak period.

Without the sky lobby arrangement, the sky-scraper designer will find that necessary shafts for conventional local and express elevators serving all floors will consume almost the total areas of the lower floors. With the sky lobby arrangement, the space above the lower bank of lifts can be 'reclaimed' for office use thereby increasing the efficiency in the net areas in the upper levels of the building.

the contemporary elevator

Modern elevators are electrically propelled, either by cables, sheave and counterweight; by a winding-drum mecha-nism; or by an electro-hydraulic combination. Multiple cables (three or more) increase both the traction surface with the sheave and the safety-factor; cable failure is rare.

Along the sides of the cabin are seats that move out/in at three positions.
In position 1, the seats serve as 'butt-seats' during reasonably busy periods. During low periods of use the seats protrude totally outward into position 2 to become full seats for passengers' comfort.
In position 3, the seats are totally recessed into the cabin wall during peak use.

'If the skyscraper were nothing more than equal spaces sliced up
vertically (as universal spaces), it would be totally boring.'

AKIRA SUZUKI

The drive-motor usually operates with alternating current (AC) for slower speeds and direct current (DC) for higher speeds. With the DC motor, the speed is varied by varying the field strength of a DC generator, and direct connection of the armature of the generator with the armature of the drive-motor. For high-speed operations, a gearless arrangement is used, usually with cable wrapped twice around the sheave.

The traction elevator may have an unlimited rise; however, rises exceeding 30.48m require compensating ropes.

Current R&D is in high-speed linear motor elevators that service the whole building, and go up and over and down and around, rather like an intercity rail.

46

safety devices

Elevators lifted by hoisting ropes are required to have platform 'safeties', devices designed to clamp onto the steel guide rails upon activation, quickly braking the elevator to a halt. The safety device, usually mounted below the car platform, is actuated by a speed governor through the rope. The rope pulls the safety to the 'on' position in the event of governor over-speeding and continued downward motion of the car. The device first cuts off the elevator power; if over-speed continues, it applies the safety-brake.

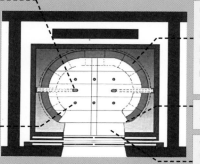

THE 'COACH' - plan

VERTICAL SECURITY POLE
pole that slides into three positions
depending on the number of passengers
within, especially when travelling many
floors:
position 1 - recessed - max peak period
position 2 - half extension - peak period
position 3 - full extension - non-peak period

EXTENDABLE HANG BAR
the hang bar is able to assume three
different heights dependent on the number
of passengers in the lift car:
position 1 - high level - max peak period
position 2 - mid level - peak period
position 3 - low level - non-peak period

PIVOT SEAT
seat that can be adjusted
in three positions
position 1 - butt seat - peak period
position 2 - full seat - non-peak period
position 3 - recessed seat - maximum
peak period

elevator push buttons
for manual control

weight-sensitive floor to register
number of passengers

automatic
control system

Most modern elevators are automatic, using various control systems to operate elevators in groups or individually. The earliest automatic control system, single-automatic-push-button, gave a rider exclusive use of the car for a trip (eg. in small apartment buildings and freight elevators).

Most skyscrapers use a group-automatic operation that controls two or more cars as a group, keeping them spaced within a specified operating interval. Group-automatic operation is used if traffic is heavy and two or more elevators are operating. Recent advances use fuzzy logic and neural networks to improve despatching and waiting times.

elevator doors

Separate outer- and inner-car doors are essential parts of the modern elevator system. The two usually employ the same type of operation (eg. centre-opening, two-leaf, single-slide). Doors are opened and closed by an electric motor on the car. Door speed in closing is regulated to avoid injury to persons caught in the closure. A sensor electrically reverses the door if it responds to an object in closing. Photoelectric controls and electronic proximity devices are also employed to control door reversal. Hoistway doors are designed so that they are always closed before the elevator can operate.

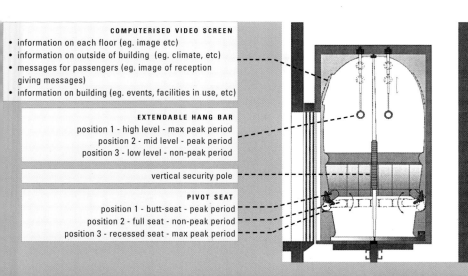

COMPUTERISED VIDEO SCREEN
- information on each floor (eg. image etc)
- information on outside of building (eg. climate, etc)
- messages for passengers (eg. image of reception giving messages)
- information on building (eg. events, facilities in use, etc)

EXTENDABLE HANG BAR
position 1 - high level - max peak period
position 2 - mid level - peak period
position 3 - low level - non-peak period

vertical security pole

PIVOT SEAT
position 1 - butt-seat - peak period
position 2 - full seat - non-peak period
position 3 - recessed seat - max peak period

THE ELEVATOR SYSTEM MUST BE DESIGNED TO PROVIDE SERVICE WITHIN THE FOLLOWING CRITERIA:	EXCELLENT SERVICE	GOOD SERVICE	FAIR SERVICE
COMMERCIAL BUILDING			
Up-peak interval :	28 secs	30 secs	35 secs
5-minute up-peak handling capacity :	14-15%	13-13.5%	11-12%
HOTEL BUILDING			
Two-way lobby traffic:	35-40 secs	45-50 secs	55-60 secs
5-minute up-peak handling capacity:	14%	13%	12%

Note: the designer evaluates his elevator configurations based on these critiria

elevator design and configuration

Elevator layout and configuration depends very much on the building design itself and on the criteria used. Building users will generally tolerate many inconveniences, most of which can be changed. However, it is crucial to ensure that the elevator design and configuration is correct from day one as the service-core in a skyscraper is usually fixed and elevator systems are almost impossible to change after construction.

Elevator design for the skyscraper is the process of selecting for a given building the optimum:

- NUMBER OF ELEVATORS
- TYPE OF ELEVATORS
- ELEVATOR CAPACITIES
- ARRANGEMENT OF ELEVATORS

The rules, restrictions and criteria vary according to building type (office, hospital, hotel, residential units, learning institutions, etc), occupancy and geographic location.

The optimum system, therefore, not only satisfies the appropriate performance criteria, but also minimises costs and building core space and contributes to a viable and successful project.

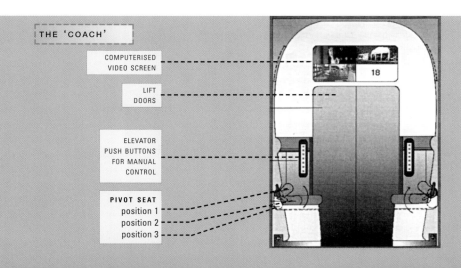

THE 'COACH'

COMPUTERISED VIDEO SCREEN

18

LIFT DOORS

ELEVATOR PUSH BUTTONS FOR MANUAL CONTROL

PIVOT SEAT
position 1
position 2
position 3

	EXCELLENT SERVICE	GOOD SERVICE	FAIR SERVICE
APARTMENT BUILDING			
Two-way lobby traffic:	50-55 secs	60-65 secs	70-75 secs
5 minute handling capacity :	7%	6%	5%
CAR-PARK BUILDING			
Two-way lobby traffic:	35 secs	40 secs	50 secs
5 minute handling capacity :	13.5-14%	12.5-13%	11-12%

The two common performance criteria for design are:

- THE AVERAGE WAITING INTERVAL (EXPRESSED IN SECONDS)
- THE 5-MINUTE HANDLING CAPACITY (EXPRESSED AS A PERCENTAGE)

In order to obtain the figures for the above performance criteria for a particular design, elevator traffic analyses have to be carried out by computer analysis of the building population (derived from net areas multiplied by number of persons per sqm), number of floors, average floor height (ie. travel distance), and elevator speed and capacity. However, there are no hard and fast standard criteria and these may vary (see table above).

49

SUGGESTED ELEVATOR CAPACITY

	COMMERCIAL	HOTEL	APARTMENT	CAR-PARK
884kg (13 persons)	-	-	yes	yes
952kg (14 persons)	yes	-	yes	yes
1088kg (16 persons)	yes	yes	yes	yes
1360kg (20 persons)	yes	yes	yes	-
1564kg (23 persons)	yes	yes	-	-
1768kg (26 persons)	yes	-	-	-

Source: M, Shirow,
Ghost in the Shell, Dark Horse Comics,
Milwaukie, USA, 1995

It is likely that the elevators of the future will be wall-mounted room-size 'wall climbers' which will either be an integral part of the new skyscrapers or 'clipped-on' to the existing skyscraper facades (after renovation and upgrading).
Being exposed on the outside of the building, these have natural ventilation opportunities (non-inclement climate permitting).

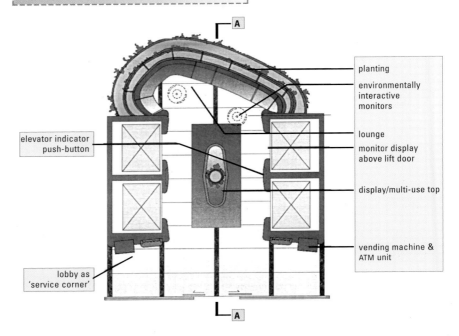

- planting
- environmentally interactive monitors
- lounge
- monitor display above lift door
- display/multi-use top
- vending machine & ATM unit
- elevator indicator push-button
- lobby as 'service corner'

50

SECTION A-A

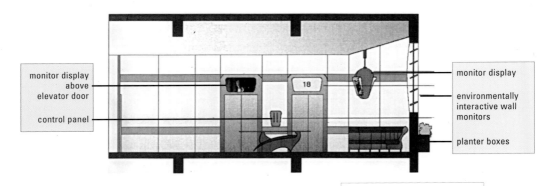

- monitor display above elevator door
- control panel
- monitor display
- environmentally interactive wall monitors
- planter boxes

Shanghai Armoury Tower

hotel elevator-lobby

*'If you have a daily fight just to get into your room,
the skyscraper just doesn't work.'* MELANIE RICHARDSON
DEREK TROWELL

THE OFFICE ELEVATOR-LOBBY AS 'SERVICE CENTRE'

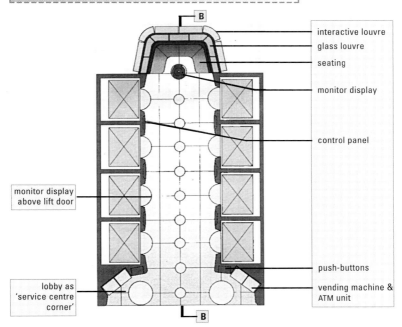

- B

interactive louvre
glass louvre
seating
monitor display

control panel

monitor display
above lift door

push-buttons
vending machine &
ATM unit

lobby as
'service centre
corner'

- B

SECTION B-B

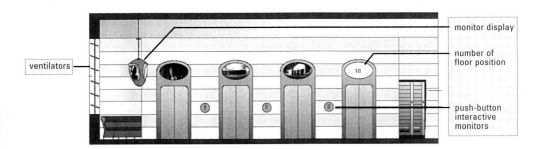

monitor display

number of
floor position

ventilators

18

push-button
interactive
monitors

Shanghai Armoury Tower

office elevator-lobby

INTEGRATION OF THE ELEVATOR CONTROLS WITH THE SKYSCRAPER'S INTELLIGENT BUILDING SYSTEMS

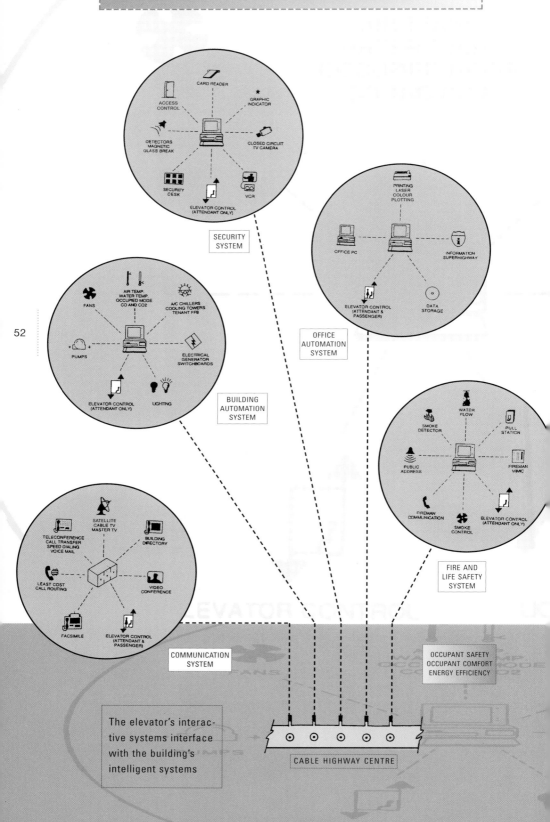

52

The elevator's interactive systems interface with the building's intelligent systems

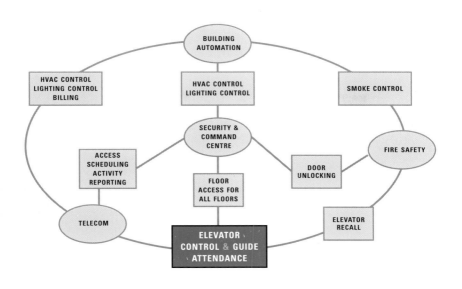

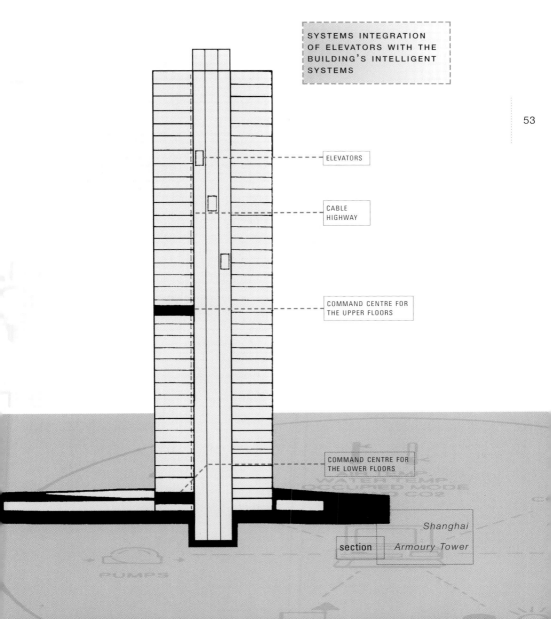

SYSTEMS INTEGRATION
OF ELEVATORS WITH THE
BUILDING'S INTELLIGENT
SYSTEMS

53

ELEVATORS

CABLE
HIGHWAY

COMMAND CENTRE FOR
THE UPPER FLOORS

COMMAND CENTRE FOR
THE LOWER FLOORS

Shanghai

section *Armoury Tower*

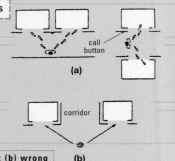

A TWO-CAR GROUPINGS

For a two-car group, side-by-side arrangement is best, passengers face both cars and react immediately to a direction lantern or arriving car.

Separation of the elevators should be avoided, excessive separation tends to destroy the advantages of a group operation. (see diagram b)

call button

(a)

corridor

two-car arrangements: (a) preferred; (b) wrong   (b)

traffic flows

A study of traffic flows in an office building reveals several peak periods throughout a normal day. These peaks usually include 'morning up-peak', 'two-way lunch peak', and 'afternoon down-peak'. The most onerous of these, and the traditional period over which acceptable lift performance is judged, is the 'morning up-peak', or more particularly, the worst five minutes during the 'morning up-peak'.

population density

Above-ground population is normally established by applying a density factor to the nett rentable area (NRA) calculated for each floor of the building. It is quite common for NRA not to have been established prior to undertaking lift performance calculations. Indeed NRA cannot be established accurately until the service-core has been fixed.

In the early stages of designing the elevator configuration, the designer can assume an efficiency factor to gross floor area (GFA) which should already be established. An efficiency factor of 80-85% is a safe assumption (ie. NFA ÷ GFA x 80-85%).

Population densities will also vary depending on building type, height and occupancy, as well as geographic location (eg. city fringe vs CBD). Densities in terms of 'sq m of NRA per person' for a diversified commercial office building should be assumed as:

SINGLE SEGMENT BUILDING	11	N/A	N/A	N/A
TWO-SEGMENT BUILDING	11	N/A	12	N/A
THREE-SEGMENT BUILDING	11	12	13	N/A
FOUR-SEGMENT BUILDING	11	12	13	14

NRA PER PERSON (IN SQ M)

54

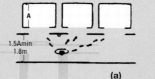

1.5Amin
1.8m

(a)

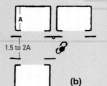

1.5 to 2A

(b)

three-car arrangements: (a) preferred; (b) acceptable

Population densities should never be based solely on historical data produced by estate agents or building managers from existing buildings. The figures opposite produce a certain level of service irrespective of actual occupancy. The greatest danger in applying lower density rates is that should actual building usage or occupancy change, resulting in higher population, the level of elevator performance will deteriorate and may be unacceptable. However, these figures are becoming lower as a result of telecommuting and 'hot-desking' (see Chapter 3).

A good check on the acceptability of an elevator system is to compare its theoretical performance with similar existing buildings, applying consistent base data. Another important check is to consider the effect on elevator system performance with one elevator out of service: at least a 'fair to good' level of service should be aimed for under such conditions.

As indicated earlier, elevator performance criteria vary according to building type, geographic location with respect to CBD's and major transport facilities, nature of occupancy, and type of traffic flow. The common performance criteria for a diversely tenanted commercial office building are based on a five minute morning up-peak condition and measure:

A QUANTITY

The five minute handling capacity (%) being the number of passengers handled in a five-minute period, expressed as a percentage of total above-ground building population.

B QUALITY

The perceived level of service, expressed in terms of the interval of departure of elevators from the ground floor = 'average waiting interval' (AWI) (seconds). Note: AWI is not to be confused with 'lobby waiting time' (LWT). However, the two are related and typically LWT = 60% x AWI.

FOUR-CAR GROUPINGS

Four elevators in a group are common in large, busier buildings. Experience has shown that a two-opposite-two arrangement is the most efficient.

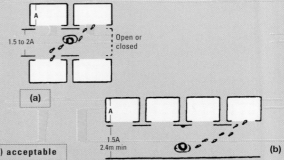

1.5 to 2A

Open or closed

(a)

1.5A
2.4m min

(b)

four-car arrangements: (a) preferred; (b) acceptable

C TRAVEL TIME

Travel time is the maximum time taken for the last passenger to reach his destination after leaving the ground floor.

For example, the travel times in relation to the performance criteria for a diversely tenanted commercial office building are as follows (see also page 49):

LEVEL OF SERVICE	EXCELLENT	GOOD	FAIR
AWI (SECONDS)	28	30	35
5 MINUTE HANDLING CAPACITY			
(% OF POPULATION)	14-15	13-13.5	11-12
TRAVEL TIME (SECONDS)	100	120	<150

traffic analysis

There are many variables in calculating elevator system performance including: number of elevators, type of drive, arrangement of elevators, speed and acceleration rates, door types and clear opening widths, elevator-car size, shape and capacity. All these factors can have an effect on the calculated results. The optimum solution, therefore, relies on a combination of the knowledge and experience of the designer, some trial and error, and mathematical calculation.

Before suitable computer programmes were available for these calculations, elevator configuration performances were calculated long-hand, using a complex formula. A well written computer programme allows rapid processing of base data, providing a means of obtaining fast, accurate traffic analysis for a number of options. Factors affecting the performance of lifts include:

SIX-CAR GROUPINGS

Groups of six elevators are often found in large office buildings, public buildings and large hospitals. They provide the combination of quantity and quality that an elevator service requires in these busy buildings. Arrangement of the six cars as three-opposite-three is the preferred architectural core scheme.

The dimension of the lobby must be no less than 3m. If the lobby is to be used as a passage as well, its width should be no less than 3.6m.

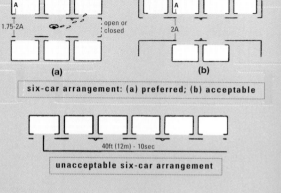

1.75-2A   open or closed   2A

(a)   (b)

six-car arrangement: (a) preferred; (b) acceptable

40ft (12m) - 10sec

unacceptable six-car arrangement

general planning

On the planning of elevator layouts for tall buildings, the two basic rules are:

- ALL ELEVATORS IN A GROUP OF ELEVATORS SHOULD SERVE IDENTICAL LANDINGS
- ELEVATORS SHOULD SATISFY THE MAJORITY OF USERS AND NOT THE MINORITY

multiple rises

Generally stated, any office building of twenty or more floors cannot be effectively served by a single rise of lifts. Often, buildings of fifteen to twenty floors also struggle to meet performance criteria, particularly in terms of maximum travel time - the 'Milk Run' effect (ie. a person residing on the top level, usually paying the highest rent, could be receiving an unacceptable level of service). In these cases, it is prudent to consider multiple-segmented lift systems (ie. sky-lobbies).

Each segment or zone is treated as a 'separate building' in terms of performance calculations.

Every effort should be made to achieve a 'balanced' system, (ie: consistent levels of performance throughout all segments). This often means the higher the segment, the fewer the number of local floors that can be accommodated per segment (eg. a twenty-floor building may be split into twelve low-segment floors and eight high-segment floors.)

Whenever multiple rises are used, a floor-to-floor 'transfer' should be provided. This will allow travel between zones without returning to the ground floor.

When using multiple rises, the designer should endeavour to restrict local floors within each zone to no more than fifteen floors per segment.

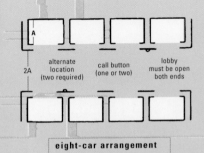

E   EIGHT-CAR GROUPING

The largest practical group of
elevators in a building, eight
cars, four-opposite-four

eight-car arrangement

multiple entry levels

Every effort should be made to avoid multiple entry levels.
Such a condition has a dramatic effect on lift performance.

If unavoidable (eg. in a building with two street frontages at
significantly different levels), additional elevator capacity will be
required to achieve acceptable performance.

car-parking floors

Car-parking floors have a marked effect on elevator system
performance, more so if such floors are above ground level than if below.

If the car-park floors are integral with the building or if there
are intermediate floors for car-parking, it is recommended that there
be separate car-park elevators.

When one or two car-parking floors are designed for a building, all main elevators should be designed to serve all such levels.
Alternatively, and necessarily if more than two car-parking floors are
present, a separate shuttle elevator or elevators can be provided to
transfer car-park users to and from the ground floor.

The designer might endeavour to avoid car-parking floors
above the ground floor, as this results in a situation similar to multiple
entry levels.

The designer should also avoid restricting service to car-
parking floors to a selected elevator or elevators within a group.

special purpose floors

For mixed-use buildings (eg. offices with apartments, with
hotels, etc) it is recommended that there are separate groups of elevators for different building uses, with separate elevator lobbies. This will
reduce the congestion at the main entrance levels by splitting the waiting
population. It also enables the different performance criteria for varied
building uses to be achieved.

goods elevators

Dedicated goods elevators are recom-
mended in all office skyscrapers. Such elevators should serve all levels
of the building from loading dock to roof plant room level.

In very large skyscrapers, the number of
goods elevators might be determined on the basis of one elevator per
25,000-30,000 sq m of NRA.

unconventional
approaches to
elevators

When typical floors exceed 2,000 sq m NRA
and/or when the number of floors above-ground is forty or more, consideration should be given to incorporating a sky-lobby system.
Should a sky-lobby system be feasible, it may also be appropriate to
utilise double-deck elevator-cars with such a system.

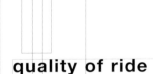

quality of ride

The quality of ride experienced within an elevator car has in recent times become a high priority for building owners and occupants. Hence special consideration must be given to design features which will contribute to providing a good quality of ride. Design features to be considered for high-rise installations include the following:

- **elevator shaft area**

To reduce the possibility of the elevator-car suffering from the effects of wind buffeting, elevator shaft area should be at least 20% greater than that of the car platform area.

- **guide rails**

The car guide rail sections with fixing points at a maximum spacing of 2.4 m are required to provide a rigid running surface for the car guides.

- **guide-rail alignment**

Guide-rail fixings must allow for vertical movement in order to avoid rail distortion due to settlement of the building.

Adjustable-type rail fixing-brackets are recommended as a means of fine-tuning the alignment of guide rails.

- **car guides**

Roller type car guides fitted with a tyre compound suited to local conditions and approximately 30 cm in diameter will be necessary to achieve a satisfactory quality of ride.

Spacing between upper and lower guide rollers on the car frame should be at the maximum practicable distance.

EXAMPLES OF BUILDING CODE INFLUENCE ON EXIT STAIRS' LOCATION

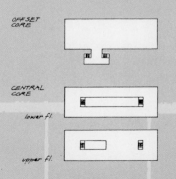

OFFSET CORE

OFFSET CORE creates large travel distance to exits and, therefore, should not be used in large buildings. It also violates the common-sense definition of remote exits. *

CENTRAL CORE

lower fl.

upper fl.

CENTRAL CORE remote ends are used for stair location. This results in good code compliance but creates some problems when the elevator core drops off in upper floors, as one stair will tend to float.

- **pendulum car**

  The pendulum car arrangement provides a means of reducing the negative effects produced by poor guide-rail alignment. Whilst the pendulum car should be considered for new high-rise projects, this arrangement may also be appropriate for refurbishment projects which suffer poor ride quality.

service-core layout
and
space requirements

The layout or arrangement of the skyscraper's vertical transportation system may generally be assumed to be subject to architectural requirements. Careful consideration should be given to balancing any special architectural features with the need to provide an efficient service-core layout which will ease loading and unloading at landings and also minimise restrictions to pedestrian traffic at the main entrance lobby.

General design requirements for elevator core layout and requirements are as follows:

- **elevator car sizes and shapes**

  Elevator car capacity (kg) is established according to clear inside platform area. Passenger loading is then calculated allowing 68kg per person.

  A 'comfortable' car capacity for the skyscraper is 1,088 kg (16 people) to 1,768 kg (26 people).

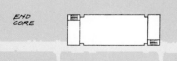

END
CORE

END CORES have no dead-end corridors created by stair locations and are perhaps the safest solution. An additional advantage is that elevator lobbies can have a window. The main drawback is the loss of exterior office space. This is also good for the bioclimatic skyscraper as the service-cores are at the floor-plate's periphery. ∗

∗ indicates the preferred configuration for the bioclimatic skyscraper

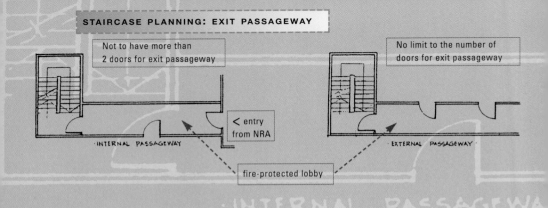

Not to have more than
2 doors for exit passageway

No limit to the number of
doors for exit passageway

< entry
from NRA

·INTERNAL PASSAGEWAY·

·EXTERNAL PASSAGEWAY·

fire-protected lobby

·INTERNAL PASSAGEWA

Car shapes influence the elevator's 'actual' carrying capacity and also its efficiency in loading and unloading. Wide, shallow cars generally accommodate most passengers and have a much higher loading and unloading efficiency when compared with narrow, deep cars. With the exception of emergency/stretcher elevators and dedicated goods elevators, cars for office buildings should have an aspect ratio (width to depth) of between 1:2 and 1:3. For example, 1,360 kg for a 20 person capacity lift, internal dimensions should be in the range 1.94 m wide x 1.6 m deep to 2 m wide x 1.56 m deep.

• elevator door types and sizes

The type best suited to passenger elevators in office buildings is the two panel centre bi-parting type due to its fast and efficient operation.

Door sizes (clear opening width) should be consistent with car size and shape, and more importantly, designed to achieve the best efficiency for a particular building.

Elevator-car loading and unloading efficiencies rely heavily on door width and speed of operation.

In theory, only 1.1-m-wide doors (or larger) allow two abreast transfer. In practice, such transfer is only likely with 1.2-m-wide doors.

The most common door sizes used for office skyscrapers have widths of 1.1 m or 1.2 m.

Door widths relate directly to internal well widths (ie: the wider the doors, the wider the elevator well required to accommodate them).

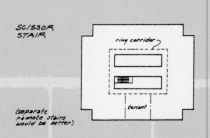

SCISSOR
STAIR

ring corridor

tenant

(separate
remote stairs
would be better)

SCISSOR STAIRS make sense only when floor areas need not be subdivided, or when in a very small building. The problem is threefold in a large building with multiple tenants: first, the exits are not remote by any common-sense definition; second, the maximum travel distance to the stair becomes excessive; third, the maximum dead-end corridor length becomes excessive. The creation of a ring corridor around the core solves the dead-end problem, but creates a real estate agent's nightmare in terms of lost rentable space.

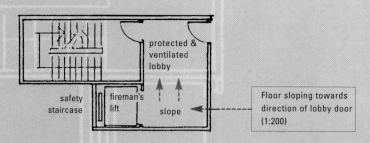

protected &
ventilated
lobby

safety
staircase

fireman's
lift

slope

Floor sloping towards
direction of lobby door
(1:200)

Door sizes need to be considered in conjunction with car sizes and shapes to ensure both the optimum elevator system and the minimum core space are achieved.

- **elevator shafts**

Elevator shafts are sized according to car shapes and sizes, and door sizes, with due consideration to the space requirements for guide-rails and brackets, counterweight systems, running clearances and space for other ancillary equipment. As previously discussed, sufficient air space should always be provided around cars and counterweights to minimise buffeting and air-borne noise during operation.

A bank of two, three or four elevators in line should share a common fire-protected shaft without a dividing structure, hence avoiding a single enclosed elevator shaft. Where single enclosed elevator wells become necessary for structural reasons, the designer must ensure air relief slots (ideally, full-height vertical slots) to allow adequate air relief.

- **elevator core and lobby planning**

'Outward facing' elevators (ie. facing the NFA) prove to be the most efficient, as on typical floors the lobby is included as part of the NRA (NB. some building codes require fire-rated elevator doors and pressurised elevator shafts). Such an arrangement also allows a good access/wider lobby at ground floor level, to handle traffic peaks more efficiently.

'Inward facing' elevators can also have lobbies included as part of the core but are less efficient in terms of NRA vs GFA. For inward facing elevators, the designer must ensure both ends of the lobby are kept open.

63

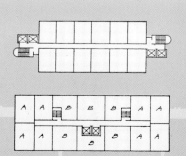

No dead-end corridor *

Dead-end corridor conforms to most major codes (40 not maximum). Occupants in apartment 'A' are blocked from both stairs if there is a fire in the corridor between their door and the first stair. Occupants in apartment 'B' have a choice of direction in case of a fire.

* indicates preferred configuration for the bioclimatic skyscraper

encirclement wall

window opening
1.4 m²

window can be opened
when required

special open space
according to height
of building

protected staircase space

stairway

ventilation space

fire-
protected
lobby

enclosed wall

fireman's
lift

ventilation space

The width of the lobby should generally be twice the depth of the elevator cars it is serving. For a single line of elevators, a minimum lobby width of 2.5 m is recommended.

Lobbies should not be used as a common or public passageway at the ground floor.

In multi-segment buildings, care should be taken that separately identifiable lobbies are provided for each group of elevators, particularly at the ground floor where clear signage is essential.

64

Generally, the arrangement of elevators and lobbies within a building core is quite flexible with many workable solutions, some more efficient than others.

staircases, exits
and life-safety

For the skyscraper, elevators are not considered 'legal exits' in a fire emergency because they may fail to operate and can actually become lethal devices by delivering people to the wrong floor or worse, trapping them. Moreover, elevator shaft doors cannot close tightly and the elevator shafts (unless fire-pressurised and/or with high fire-rated doors) connecting the floor containing the fire to the rest of the building often contain smoke. Usually during a fire, the fireman at the fire control command room immediately

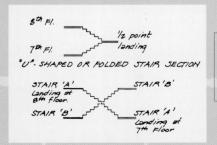

The designer has certain obligations regarding his design regardless of whether the prevailing code sets a maximum dead-end corridor, permits no dead end, or allows any length of corridor.

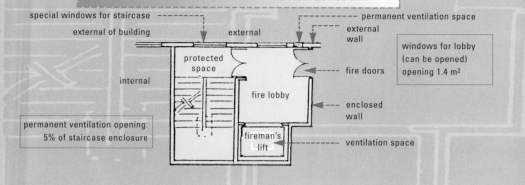

special windows for staircase

external of building

internal

external

protected space

fire lobby

fireman's lift

permanent ventilation opening: 5% of staircase enclosure

permanent ventilation space

external wall

windows for lobby (can be opened) opening 1.4 m²

fire doors

enclosed wall

ventilation space

brings all elevators down to the ground floor and uses the designated fireman's elevator (and/or any other) for fire-fighting use.

It follows that both the number and location of staircases and exits are critical parts of the skyscraper's life-safety system.

escape staircases
and protected lobbies

One of the decisive form-givers in any major building is the location of its required means of egress. This is separate from the location of decorative or ceremonial staircases.

Although the local building codes go into great detail describing exit requirements and the way in which exiting enclosures must be constructed, the key points below have a major impact on building design:

1 Use of the building (eg. office, apartment, store or hospital, etc).

2 Total number of people in the building as a determinant of the required number of separate exits.

3 Limitations on the maximum travel distance permitted to reach an exit enclosure.

4 Provision for a choice of paths to an exit, and a choice of exits in case one exit is blocked.

5 Provision that exits must lead the occupants to a safe area.

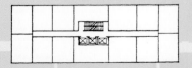

A 'scissor-stair' does not fold on itself at a landing halfway between floors. Rather, it is a straight run from floor to floor. Two such straight-run stairs can be placed in one shaft to considerably reduce costs.

Note: Items 1, 2 and 5 are taken directly from the building codes. Items 3 and 4 require proper proportioning and shaping of spaces by the skyscraper designer in order to comply with a specific maximum dead-end corridor length. This proportioning can have a dramatic effect on the overall shape of the building: for example, most building codes will not permit any dead-end corridors in a hospital; therefore the stairs must be located at the ends of the building.

SOME FIRE AUTHORITIES ADOPT THE FOLLOWING PREMISES FOR ESCAPE:

- HUMANS CAN BE IN A SMOKY SITUATION FOR ABOUT 3 MINUTES BEYOND WHICH THERE WILL BE FAINTING OR ASPHYXIATION.

- DURING FIRE WITH THICK SMOKE, HUMANS CAN GENERALLY MOVE ABOUT 12 METRES PER MINUTE.

- FOR CERTAIN AREAS INVOLVING 'DEAD ENDS', OCCUPANTS MUST BE EVACUATED WITHIN 1 MINUTE AND THE TRAVEL DISTANCE FOR 'DEAD ENDS' MUST BE NOT MORE THAN 12 METRES.

Generally, and depending on the distance of the furthest point to the staircase, there should be at least two staircases for the skyscraper because if one of the staircases is on fire, there will still be the other for the occupants to escape by. These staircases must be fire-protected:

- PROTECTED STAIRCASES MUST HAVE A STAIRCASE LOBBY AND SMOKE LOBBY. THE PURPOSE OF HAVING THE SMOKE LOBBY IS TO ACT AS AN INITIAL PROTECTION BEFORE THE HEAT AND SMOKE PENETRATES THE STAIRCASE ENCLOSURE.

- THE SMOKE SHOULD NOT ENTER THE STAIRCASE LOBBY BECAUSE IT CAN SPREAD TO THE WHOLE BUILDING AND THE FIREMEN WILL BE UNABLE TO ENTER THE BUILDING.

- THE STAIRCASE LOBBY AND SMOKE LOBBY ARE PLACED WHERE THE FIREMEN WILL PUT ON THEIR BREATHING APPARATUS AND PREPARE TO ENTER THE STAIRCASE INVOLVED.

- THE STAIRCASE AND FIRE-PROTECTED AREAS MUST HAVE THE RELEVANT FIRE-RATED DOORS (EG. 1/2 HOUR, 1 HOUR, 2 HOUR, 4 HOUR). THESE DOORS ARE TO PREVENT SMOKE AND HEAT FROM PENETRATING THE STAIRCASE ENCLOSURE IN ORDER TO CREATE A CLEAR PASSAGE FOR ESCAPE AND ALSO TO ENABLE FIREMEN TO CONDUCT INTERNAL FIRE-FIGHTING EFFECTIVELY.

the
interior life
in the sky

- re-creation of ground conditions (in the sky)
- accessibility to sunlight & openable windows
- various tenancy options
- various tenancy types
- transitional spaces
- a new form of interior life

'...an interior life where every kind of need for leisure and recreation, work and home, commerce and business are satisfied in a vertical complex of magnificent spaces with outer rings and inner atria and unbelievable views...'

PROFESSOR
IVOR RICHARDS

the floor-plate

Physically, the skyscraper is a series of 'floor-plates of built space' stacked one on top of another in a tower. Of primary concern to the designer are the design decisions that affect the quality of life on these floors, especially when these floors are so high above ground level. These decisions include aesthetic as well as engineering and economic considerations.

Can these spaces be humanised in view of their vertical remoteness from the ground plane? What can make them attractive and fulfilling to occupy, rather than allowing their distance from the ground plane to be detrimental and a negative factor?

In any event, much consideration must be given to the floor-plate design in relation to its effect on the sky-scraper's occupants, since it is often repeated (varying in shape as required and/or where variances are deemed efficiently acceptable). This principle applies, regardless of whether the skyscraper is an office, a hotel or an apartment building.

ramps linking
the skycourts

Hitechniaga Tower,

Kuala Lumpur,

Latitude 2°N

linked sky-
courts &
urban design
in the sky

COMPARISON OF SPACE PER WORKER

sq m
25
22.2
20
15   14.8   14.2
10   8.6
5
JAPAN   US   GERMANY   SINGAPORE

configuring
the floor-plate

Our first consideration is the size of the floor-plate itself (ie. its NRA and GFA). This is essentially a marketing decision depending on the city and country in which the skyscraper is located. If the building is a hotel, it may depend on the number of rooms per floor which is related to the housekeeping systems for that country. There may also be building regulations which specify the maximum distance any worker can be from a window (eg. 6 m in Germany), in which case the resultant floor-plates become either very small or shallow in depth.

In the bioclimatic skyscraper, consideration must also be given to: the option of natural ventilation for the floor-plate (eg. through the availability of openable windows); the penetration of sunlight into the floor-plate; and the quality of the internal life of the user of the floor-plate which should resemble as closely as possible the existent conditions at the ground plane (eg. the proximity of greenery and landscaping which are both components of a healthy environment).

The floor-plate configuration in relation to the service-core position must further allow for different tenancy options (eg. single-tenant, double-tenant, multiple-tenant), each option having different partitioning, fire-escape, protected fire-lobby or corridor and floor efficiency (ie. NRA percentage) implications.

Furthermore, the design of the skyscraper's floor layout, besides responding to the commercial considerations of the building, should also take account of human habits and local cultural patterns of living and working, privacy and community, all of which develop in relation to the locality's climate.

The design of the internal spaces should have some degree of humaneness (provision of skycourts, etc), some degree of visual interest (views out or to internal atrium spaces), and some degree of physical scale (aesthetically appropriate floor-to-ceiling height that is higher that the norm of 2.5 m).

69

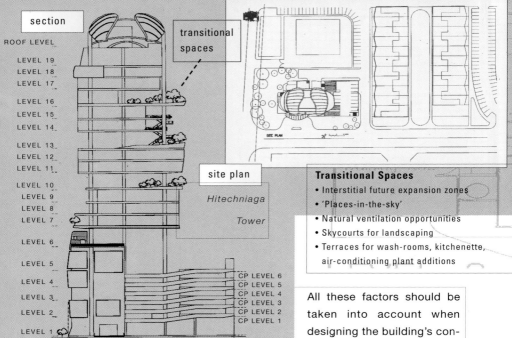

section

ROOF LEVEL
LEVEL 19
LEVEL 18
LEVEL 17
LEVEL 16
LEVEL 15
LEVEL 14
LEVEL 13
LEVEL 12
LEVEL 11
LEVEL 10
LEVEL 9
LEVEL 8
LEVEL 7
LEVEL 6
LEVEL 5
LEVEL 4
LEVEL 3
LEVEL 2
LEVEL 1

transitional spaces

site plan

Hitechniaga

Tower

CP LEVEL 6
CP LEVEL 5
CP LEVEL 4
CP LEVEL 3
CP LEVEL 2
CP LEVEL 1

Transitional Spaces
- Interstitial future expansion zones
- 'Places-in-the-sky'
- Natural ventilation opportunities
- Skycourts for landscaping
- Terraces for wash-rooms, kitchenette, air-conditioning plant additions

All these factors should be taken into account when designing the building's con-figuration, determining its floor-depth, positioning its entrances and exits, providing for human move-ment through and between spaces, and setting the building's orientation and external views. Generally stated, the building's floor-plate should provide a human environment, interest and scale, sunlight to reach internal areas, suf-ficient ventilation and so forth.

some considerations for designing the floor-plate

- Users tend to have a preferred core-to-perimeter dimension of 8 m to 10 m where a majority of space should be within about 10 m of the glass-line.

- The maximum dimension from core to glass has remained relatively sta-tic over the last twenty years as it is recognised that the highest return for office developments is achieved within a high percentage of the space located within an 8 m zone (two office modules) of the perimeter glazing. In certain countries, the local building codes restrict the depth that a desk can be away from the window to two-and-a-half times the height of the window. Lever House (NYC) established the distance of approximately 8 m from the window to the furthest desk as a minimum and made the building depth 16 m. The trend today is for office widths of glass-to-glass wall of 1.35-1.8 m, allowing for natural ventilation.

- Maximum flexibility in space planning can be achieved where 80% of the floor area is located generally within this 8 m zone.

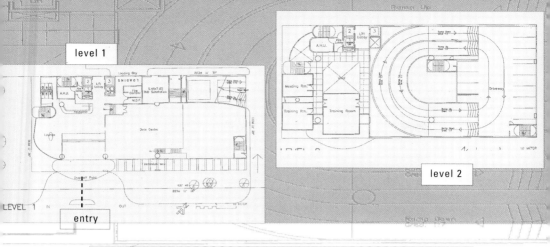

level 1

level 2

LEVEL 1

entry

- The average space per person for tall buildings ('population density') had varied from 1 person/10 sq m twenty years ago, to 1 person/13 sq m today (see page 54). With telecommuting and hotelling, in situations where less than 50% of staff have desk ownership, the average space per person can go down to 10 sq m with over 25% of the space for meeting spaces.

- The NRA per floor varies from country to country, generally depending on whether the building is owner-occupier or speculative. If it is the latter, the size is dependent on market conditions, lot size and built form. The optimum in South-East Asia is about 800 sq m to 1,000 sq m whereas in Europe the floor-plate areas are about 500 to 2,500 sq m, elsewhere they might be around 1,200 sq m to 2,000 sq m.

- A more compact floor-plate plan reduces cross-floor travel distances, benefitting inter-office communications.

- Net-to-gross ratio (NRA vs GFA) should not be less than 75%, although 80% to 85% is considered appropriate.

- Corner offices (executive 'power zones') and the articulation of the facade can be used to provide more corner-office conditions through a higher perimeter-glass-to-floor-area ratio.

- When the service-core becomes disproportionately large, travel distances, both to elements within the core and to points on the floor, can reach the stage where they are no longer acceptable to the market. The trend is to provide a number of smaller floors where interconnection is enhanced.

- The primary office partitioning zone at the facade is around a 2 x 4 m module for two offices.

- The floor-plate configuration and position of core, escape stairs and toilets should efficiently allow for various tenancy options (single, double and multiple) and different tenant types (eg. institutional tenants requiring large rooms such as for dealer's rooms, professional firms, tenants requiring small offices, and corporate tenants requiring many large 'director-size' rooms).

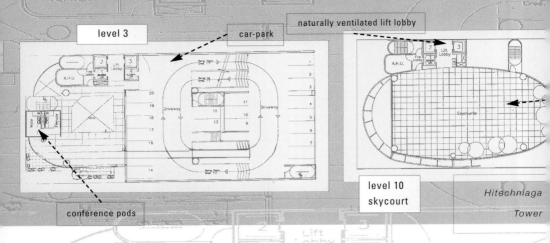

level 3

car-park

naturally ventilated lift lobby

level 10
skycourt

Hitechniaga
Tower

conference pods

- The structural grids, mullion grids, office partitioning grids and ceiling grids should coincide (eg. 600 mm x 600 mm modules).

- Structural column-spacings and grids are organised according to the occupant's spatial requirements. In instances where the office floor-plates are located over the car-park, a structural grid with columns spaced at 8.4 m-centres will enable three car-park bays to be placed between the structural grid at the car-park level.

- The preferred sill levels at about 73 cm and 78 cm from the floor.

- The requirements for electrical power appear to be increasing from 12 watts/sq m (ten years ago) to about 170 watts/sq m today.

- The service-cores should never divide the floor-plate into two. The occupants from one side of the floor-plate must be able to traverse to the other side without having to go across the public service-core lobby.

- Toilets can be designed to be accessible directly from the lettable space in the event of single tenancy.

- The main staircase must be near the elevators in the event of a power-failure.

- AHU (air handling unit) rooms must facilitate ducting into the office, hotel or apartment floor without having to go through fire-protected lobbies to reduce the need for fire-dampers in the ducts.

- AHU and duct access panels should open out to public areas for easy access for servicing.

- Stair cores should be kept to not more than two per floor-plate (ie. one main stair and one escape stair), even if floor-plates are large. NB: This excludes the ceremonial stair.

1936 Design for
open-plan

Frank Lloyd Wright designed the Johnson Wax Administration Building in 1936. Most of the clerical force worked in one large square room, seated at specially designed desks and chairs.

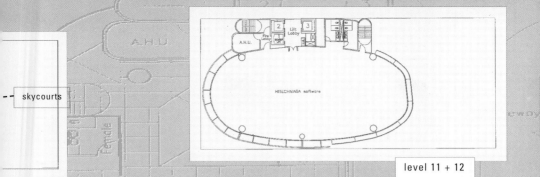

skycourts

internal life

If the bioclimatic skyscraper's architecture is to be justified as a new genre of building type, it must transcend being a clever reorganisation of external building forms and superficial changes to facades.

Essentially, the skyscraper's design must create a new and significant *form of internal life* for its inhabitants that has not existed before in other genres of the same type.

Looking at the changes in the internal life of the tall building today, we first find that the skyscrapers built in the nineteenth century had an interior life that showed their subdivision and management hierarchies and reflected the corporation's departmental systemisation. What tended to happen was that the entrepreneurial developer commissioned the architects to design the built form and outside envelope (or 'skin'), while the corporation's managers devised the internal life and work spaces.

In this process, natural light admission became the crucial factor in skyscraper design. The executive 'corner office' (with its 270° view) acquired its significance as an indicator of status and power, followed by the importance flexibility gained in the re-arrangement of internal partitioning, furniture and equipment which in turn affected the socio-political relations within the office. The politics of space planning then led to the regulation of permissible depths for a desk from a sunlit window (see pages 69 and 70).

73

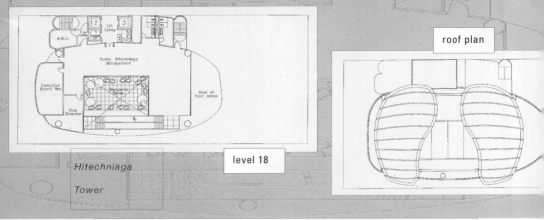

In the internal space planning of the floor-plates, an intricate pattern of enclosure, concealment and visual surveillance also emerged in these offices which helped reinforce boundaries between different kinds of staff, and between employees and the public. Managerial 'eyes of power' and controls operated across desks, past filing-cabinets, through perforated partitions and elevator grills.

Since the invention of the skyscraper in the nineteenth century, there have been many technological advances in skyscraper design, such as those enabling their construction to greater heights (eg. high-strength concrete and other structural innovations), and those which create more electronically responsive systems. However, inadequate attention seems to have been paid to innovation in the internal life for the users of skyscrapers, or their *life-in-the-air*.

a vertical
urban design

Conventional urban design carried out at the ground-plane is concerned with such aspects as place-making, vistas, creating public realms, civic zones, linkages, figure-ground, massing of built forms, etc. This type of thinking must now be extended upwards.

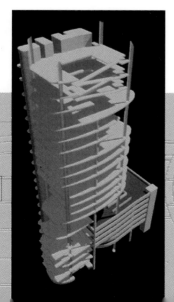

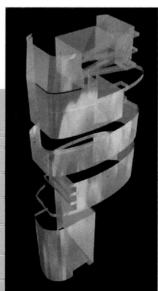

Hitechniaga

Tower

structure

glazing

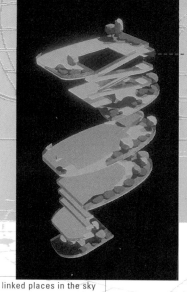

skycourts

linked places in the sky

solar shields

If we compare the built mass of a typical low-rise nineteenth-century urban design with that of a high-rise development in the twentieth century, the built-up mass in a few high-rises in any locality would exceed that of several blocks of the traditional city. The point is that urban design in the twenty-first century must be vertical rather than horizontal. The applications for this new approach to urban design and town planning deserve greater study.

All the conventional considerations in the ground-plane of any typical urban design project need to be applied to the vertical plane of the skyscraper, such as the provision of places in the sky, vista considerations at the upper levels (both horizontally as well as vertically upwards and downwards), linkages in the sky (eg. through secondary staircases, passageways, bridges, ramps between floors, etc), public realms, etc.

fresh-air environment

Contemporary skyscrapers are developing healthier internal environments with spaces that encourage greater incoming fresh air and room air changes. An indicator of this development is the reduction of 'itchy eyes', a common complaint which tends to reduce productivity. While this may be achieved through mechanical means, there is a greater justification for natural ventilation in the bioclimatic skyscraper.

In temperate zones the hot summer season may still need air-conditioning and the winter seasons require heating, but the mid-seasons might make greater use of natural ventilation by a design to extend the periods of mid-seasons to at least 70% of the year, resulting in significant reduction in energy consumption.

• The skyscraper is a specialised building type and because of its intensive mass and size it is important to get the design correct at the outset before construction. Unlike low-rise buildings, rectification of faulty design is more difficult or sometimes impossible during construction of the buildings.

• The efficiency of the skyscraper can be improved in the following ways:

a Location of the service-cores and escape staircase in a configuration that facilitates: single-, double- and multiple tenancy options.

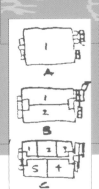

b Location of toilets for single-tenancy options, which can be entered directly from the tenant's space (NB: efficiency can be increased by as much as 5%).

For the new office environment, the ability and option to control fresh air and natural ventilation appear to be an overriding priority for over 60% of office occupants. Internal layouts should give maximum opportunity for openable windows to be accessible to all.

One solution in internal space-planning is to place all circulation at the perimeter of the floor-plate so that everyone has access to a window, to views and to daylight. The partitioned rooms and offices should be located within the inner parts of the floor with the work-stations located at the spatial zone in-between the partitioned spaces and the windows, so that the majority of the office's users (ie. 60%) have direct access to natural sunlight and openable windows.

In current offices about 39% of employees are likely to work in individual offices or still need offices, and the remaining 60% (ie. 31% in open-plan offices and 29% in bullpens) are in un-partitioned work-spaces. In addition to these, there are also the community-type spaces mentioned above.

While irregular floor-plate configurations for the skyscraper can contribute to creating a wider variety of internal spaces in the sky, the designer must constantly endeavour to re-invent the skyscraper's floors to create new forms for the internal life of the occupants. The skyscraper office floor must be more than just a 'concrete tray in the air'. Design efforts must be directed to replicate, as far as possible, the conditions at ground level.

The external wall and its openings can be designed to enable the occupants to experience the varying seasons of the year, especially in climatic zones where the seasons are evident and culturally important. This may be achieved through variable external-wall performances or by having openable panels which do not interfere with the comfort of the occupants.

c Pressurisation of service-cores and the use of fire-rated elevator-car doors so that the elevators can discharge directly to the tenant's space (NB: efficiency can increase by at least as much as 4 to 10 %).

d Natural ventilation for all elevator lobbies, staircases and toilets to reduce the need for mechanical pressurisation ducts which will further improve the efficiency of the building.

e Addition of 'skycourts' and terraces as 'sun-shading' which may improve on the permissible plot ratio and give additional marketing features to the building and improve net areas.

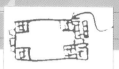

As employee interaction becomes increasingly more important, the design of the public zones where this can take place requires greater attention. For instance, the ground-level entrance lobby and all typical lobbies might be enlarged beyond the minimum provision between elevator openings, becoming zones for social interaction. The office elevator lobby could be more spacious and contain equipment and furniture similar to that in the elevator lobby of an upmarket hotel (eg. to contain public phone, lounge seats, and, on certain floors, even a concierge).

skycourts and interstitial spaces

Attempts to depart from a hermetically-sealed floor might be directed towards adding layers of 'transitional spaces' between the inside area and the outside of the skyscraper. Notwithstanding the high wind-speeds occurring at the upper levels of the tall building, which can reach occasional maximum wind-gusts of 50 m/sec (even in non-typhoon zones), the introduction of 'skycourts' (both private and communal) would enhance the well-being of skyscraper occupants.

'...the driving force of life anywhere is contact with the environment and with your neighbours. Design of tall buildings which recognises this will create a life in the sky superior to the ground with an added dimension of spatial awareness.'

TONY FITZPATRICK
OVE ARUP & PARTNERS

f Toilets located near the main elevator lobby (and not near the rear staircase) to avoid the need for central corridors in most internal layouts.

g Provision of optimum floor-plate area in relation to marketability and the building's footprint as is permitted by the site configuration.

h Deployment of zoned-elevator configuration so that space above the lower zone elevator can be reclaimed for rentable space.

Skycourts are large terraced areas that can be both private and communal and are located in the upper parts of the tall building. In the bioclimatic skyscraper, they provide a transitional spatial layer that serves as an intermediary between the inside and the outside of the building, providing the occupants with a choice. By providing such choices, these skycourts change the user's aesthetic perceptions of the office floor, replacing the hermetically-sealed environment that remains uniform regardless of season. The user can now choose to enter these intermediary spaces from the totally enclosed office space, giving the individual greater control over access to fresh air and views to the outside.

Skycourts also provide communal-interaction spaces for non-work-related uses such as lunch and relaxation. Where located as private terraces, executives can convert them to executive washrooms, pantries and personal landscaped gardens-in-the-sky abutting their offices. These skycourts could be used to hide secondary supplementary heating, ventilation and air-conditioning (HVAC) systems; besides also serving as evacuation and refuge-zones for the entire floor in the event of emergencies, thereby contributing to a safer building.

Exit to these skycourts might be through sliding full-height glass doors. By being full-height, these doors allow a better quality of natural light to enter the office space. However, with openable full-height doors, the skycourts can also act as natural ventilation ports. The sliding doors regulate the extent of natural ventilation permitted to enter the office space in the event of air-conditioning break-down. Further natural ventilation control can be supplemented by adding another layer of louvred-shutters in the event of exceedingly high winds. Furthermore, as openings at the facades of the skyscraper, the skycourts reduce the vortices at the facades. If their edges are lined with planter-boxes, they can also add greenery and organic planting material to the facades of the skyscraper.

i All balconies are built of steel (to be considered as 'grills') so as to avoid their calculation as part of the permitted plot ratio.

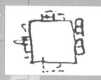

j Use of single package air-conditioning/ heating units to reduce plant-room requirements, thereby increasing efficiency.

k Provision of unisex toilets (ie. combine toilet facilities with indi- vidual wash basin as one toilet unit thereby reducing toilet provision and increasing efficiency).

Further ways to improve the interior life of the skyscraper are to connect these skycourts by external stairs and ramps so that occupants can have an alternative access to the upper floors besides the internal staircases. Atriums can also be added to improve the quality of natural light to the inner spaces. The variety of internal spaces might be further improved by the addition of mezzanine floors or the addition of interconnected executive half-levels.

These skycourts also serve as flexible zones to permit the future addition of executive washrooms or kitchen spaces.

atria, air-spaces
and wind-scoops

In the bioclimatic skyscraper, solar heat gain through the windows is reduced by shading the 'hot' sides of the building using deep recesses in the external wall. These may take the form of totally recessed windows, balconies or small-scale courtyards on the upper-floors such as 'sky-courts' (see pages 77-79).

The use of multi-storey recessed 'transi- tional spaces' represents another way of shading the 'hot' sides of a tall building. Positioned either centrally or peripherally, such huge transitional air-spaces or atria perform the same role as the verandah in traditional vernacular architecture – mediating between inside and outside. The building occupants can hence enjoy access to such semi- enclosed spaces.

'Interior life in the sky ... involves looking down instead of up,
and inward instead of outward. High-rise living has many
of the characteristics of flight, with the addition of space
and solidity.'   MARTIN PAWLEY

Such semi-enclosed spaces need not be totally enclosed from above: the tops of atriums can be shielded by a 'louvred-roof' and solar-shading to encourage wind-flow to the inner areas of the building. These devices may even be extended over the entire face of the building to create a multi-storey atrium that acts as a wind-scoop to direct natural ventilation to the inner parts of the building, as well as for the exit of hot-air resulting from the 'venturi effect' (thermal conditions permitting). (The 'venturi effect' is when warm air rises through convection.)

By organising the building's internal passageways to be perpendicular to the atrium space and to lead off from this space, the passages act as 'conduits' for ventilation and breezes into the internal office space. The air-flow from outside to inside can be controlled with adjustable louvres at the window-openings.

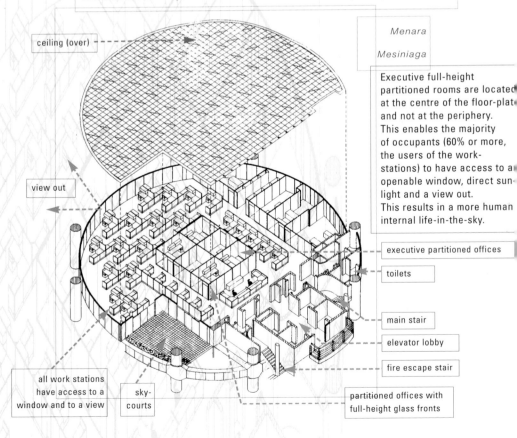

ceiling (over)

Menara

Mesiniaga

Executive full-height partitioned rooms are located at the centre of the floor-plate and not at the periphery. This enables the majority of occupants (60% or more, the users of the work-stations) to have access to an openable window, direct sunlight and a view out. This results in a more human internal life-in-the-sky.

view out

executive partitioned offices

toilets

main stair

elevator lobby

fire escape stair

all work stations have access to a window and to a view

sky-courts

partitioned offices with full-height glass fronts

The typical skyscraper can be considered to consist of the following internal spaces:

- LIFT LOBBIES
- TOILET AREAS AND OTHER WET AREAS
  (EG. EXECUTIVE WASHROOMS, KITCHENS, ETC)
- MAIN STAIRCASE
- ESCAPE STAIRCASE
- MAIN USER SPACES (NRA)
- TRANSITIONAL AND INTERSTITIAL SPACES (EG. CORRIDORS, PASSAGEWAYS, BALCONIES, TERRACES, ATRIA, ETC)

For these internal spaces in the bioclimatic skyscraper, the following are the design criteria:

LIFT LOBBIES

- Naturally ventilated (eg. openable windows at minimum 25% of floor area)
- Naturally sunlit
- View of the locality/awareness of place
- Can be space which is open to the sky (ie. can be partially enclosed by external walls as in a recessed transitional space)
- Direct experience of climate and diurnal seasons of the locality (ie. openable windows, doors with access to terrace/balcony, etc)

TOILET AREAS AND OTHER WET AREAS
(eg. executive washrooms, kitchens, etc)

- Naturally ventilated (eg. 0.2 sq m openable windows minimum per WC or urinal and free uninterrupted passage of air)
- Natural sunlit space
- View of the locality/awareness of place

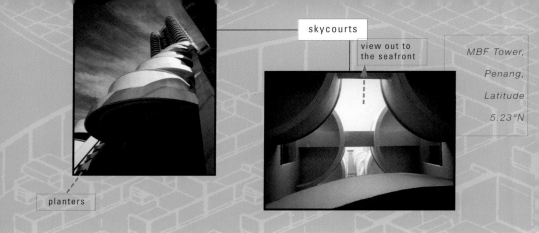

skycourts

view out to
the seafront

planters

MBF Tower,

Penang,

Latitude

5.23°N

MAIN STAIRCASE

- Naturally ventilated (eg. 1 sq m window area per floor)

- Naturally sunlit space

- View of the locality/awareness of place

- Can be space which is open to the sky, ie. enclosed or unenclosed (NB. Protection from rain/snow/etc frequently requires it to be enclosed and since stair is often used for access between floors, a greater level of weather exclusion may be needed)

ESCAPE STAIRCASE

- Naturally ventilated (eg. 1 sq m window area per floor)

- Naturally sunlit space

- View of the locality/awareness of place

- Can be space which is totally open to the sky (ie. unenclosed stair since it is used primarily for escape purposes)

MAIN USER SPACES

- Can be air-conditioned or heated spaces but designer has to provide the option of natural ventilation (may be through choice on non-peak days/hours or through necessity in the event of break-downs). Window area of 5% per 10% of the clear floor area for free uninterrupted passage of air

- Naturally sunlit space (if a deep plan floor-plate is not permitted or required, maximum inhabitant workstation depth to window area should preferably not be deeper than three times the floor-to-ceiling height)

- View of the locality/awareness of place

- Provision of views out to give users experience of the changing seasons of the year

82

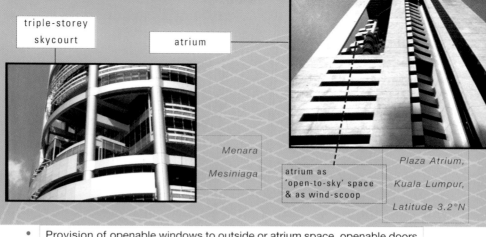

triple-storey skycourt

atrium

Menara Mesiniaga

atrium as 'open-to-sky' space & as wind-scoop

Plaza Atrium, Kuala Lumpur, Latitude 3.2°N

- Provision of openable windows to outside or atrium space, openable doors to terrace/skycourts, provision of terraces and balconies, and variable external configuration to cope with changing seasonal condition, etc

- Provision of user access to transitional spaces to external environment (eg. terraces, balconies, skycourts, etc)

- Access to vegetation/planting (eg. for greater reconstruction of conditions at ground level and the fresh air and oxygen/carbon dioxide absorption benefits of extensive planting)

- Provision of visual contact and relationship with lower floors

- Provision of executive toilets/washrooms/kitchenettes

- A more 'domestic' configuration of commercial spaces (eg. 'living-room' analogy to interior design and space planning)

- Lower density of users per square metre

TRANSITIONAL SPACES (EG. BALCONIES, TERRACES, SKYCOURTS, ETC)

- Located at the transitional spatial zone between the inside of the building and the external environment

- Naturally ventilated

- Naturally sunlit space

- Totally 'open-to-the-sky' space (ie. no enclosing walls) enabling users to have direct contact and experience of the climate of the place

- Opportunities for greening/landscaping

- Creation of visual contact and relationship with lower floors

1925 Ergonomics

WH Leffingwell wrote 'Office Management, Principles and Practices', suggesting ways to make the office worker more comfortable. In this first ergonomic study, he recommended that chairs and desks be designed with human physiology and work requirements in mind.

Menara Mesiniaga

study model

rooftop plaza & pool   skycourt

The above indicates how the regular range of internal spaces in a commercial skyscraper might be modified to create an alternative bioclimatic environment. However, further efforts need to be directed by the designer towards an alternative configuration of the skyscraper where there is a meshing of these internal elements (while, of course, remaining commercially viable) if a new architecture is to emerge.

Through these, the designer can transform skyscraper design from simply being a series of stacked multi-storey concrete trays in the air to a village in the sky of colonised spaces with an environmentally interactive community.

The office skyscraper of the future may well become more and more like a hotel with better designed public areas, more comfortable private areas, butler services with service elevators, wash rooms and communal recreational facilities. Its building management might even become more similar to that of a hotel, with 'back-of-house' providing ordered meals and other amenities to offices, similar to room service.

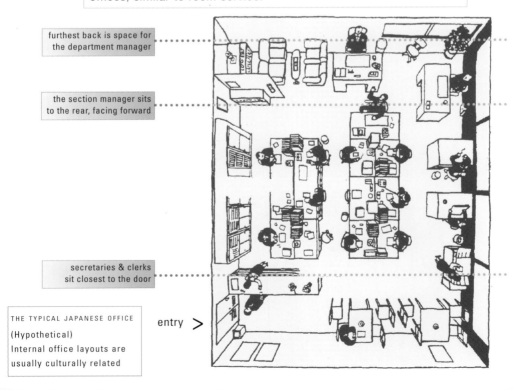

furthest back is space for the department manager

the section manager sits to the rear, facing forward

secretaries & clerks sit closest to the door

THE TYPICAL JAPANESE OFFICE
(Hypothetical)
Internal office layouts are usually culturally related

entry >

skycourts

recessed
strip
windows

banking hall

Menara Budaya,

Kuala Lumpur,

Latitude 3.2°N

MBF Tower

Steel staircase at
level 1

1964
Systems furniture

Herman Miller introduced its Action Office
Furniture in the United States. This furniture
system was based on office operation
principles, and its relationship to the
organisation that it serves.

internal
partitioning strategy

Strategies in internal partitioning depend on the organisation occupying the space. Partitioning should allow for various tenancy situations as well as different type of office organisations (see page 71).

As most office users would like control of natural ventilation and access to a window, the preferred office partitioning strategy should place the enclosed rooms in the middle of the office floor while rooms on the periphery can have full-height glazing to give a full view out. In this way the majority of the office workers (ie. those in the work-stations) will have visual and physical access to natural sunlight and to openable windows resulting in a more humane office environment.

The depth of the floor-plate is also an important design consideration, as we have seen (see pages 69 and 70). In some countries where sunlight is considered vitally important (eg. temperate climatic zones) the access of the office worker to it is a key consideration, resulting in limits on distance from external windows. These criteria generally result in shallower floor depths. For larger floor plates requirements, the designer may need to incorporate a light-well or atrium in the centre of the floor.

atrium as transitional space between the elevator lobby and the NRAs.

Plaza

Atrium

Wisma Kencana, Kuala Lumpur, Latitude 3.2°N

sky-garden

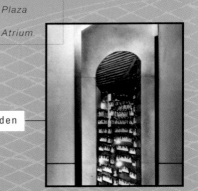

the changing nature of the workplace

At the same time the nature of work itself in the office skyscraper is changing. These changes are largely motivated by advances in information technology (IT), along with the increasing power of the personal computer microchip, which is doubling in power around every eighteen months or so. As computers become smaller, cheaper, more portable and more ubiquitous, a curious phenomenon has happened: work begins to uncouple from the workplace.

People have started to work more at home, on planes, in airports and in other people's offices. In the process, organisations have begun to reinvent the ways in which their own office environment supports work, especially as information technology has made human work less a matter of repetitive pen-pushing and more a case of cognitive decision-making.

The new work patterns and management concepts that have emerged have significant implications for designers and architects, facility managers and users, and include such concepts as: home-working, telecommuting, the office-hotel, hot-desking, the virtual office, mobility, empowerment, teams, cross-training, re-engineering, de-layering, out-sourcing, contingency, etc. Hence, over the last decade (perhaps more than any other time since the advent of mass-production) the way people work has been profoundly redefined. The entire aesthetic of the internal office workplace in the skyscraper has to change.

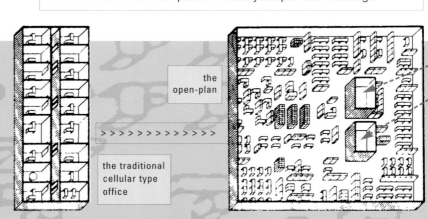

the open-plan

the traditional cellular type office

> > > > > > > > > > > >

service-core area

elevator core area

> > > > >

ventilating voids

MBF Tower,
places in the sky

study model of sky-
courts at facade

Empowerment and employee self-reliance seem to be gaining hold in corporation management systems. In those companies that are flattening out their management hierarchies and gradually decentralising decision-making, workers are gaining greater control over what they do. Self-direction has superseded the doctrine that workers do only what they are told. High performers are rewarded with higher pay. Flexible human resource management strategies free workers to pursue the more fulfilling combinations of varied work, family life, and other interests.

In the 1980s, the corporate office had the users cabled right into their desks, imprisoned within a systems approach to layout and furniture, as wires ran though the wall and panels of micro-architectural furniture. Wire-management and raised-floors were the catchwords of the period.

87

In the early 1990s, cellular phones began to free users from wire-management. The computer became cordless. Now users are faced with the prospect of the cable-less office thanks to new technologies such as CLANs (cordless local area network) that aim to make central areas of the skyscraper office cable-free. The dominant technology for this, whether microwave, radio or infra-red signal, has yet to be determined.

Hence the office and skyscraper of the future may well be cordless. This combination of a more fluid company structure and work practice questions the need for conventional, rigidly-planned office spaces as we know them today, and the need for office buildings entirely.

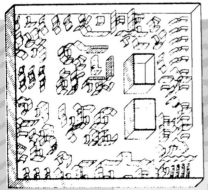

the
Bürolandschaft
(the village/club office landscape)

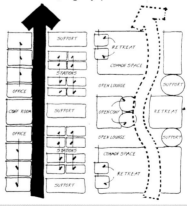

corridors with permeable boundaries allow people to see what's going on as they move through the building, create opportunities for contact and communication, and transform a boring highway into a lively stimulating journey

| 1900 | 1955 | 1960 | 1965 | 1970 |

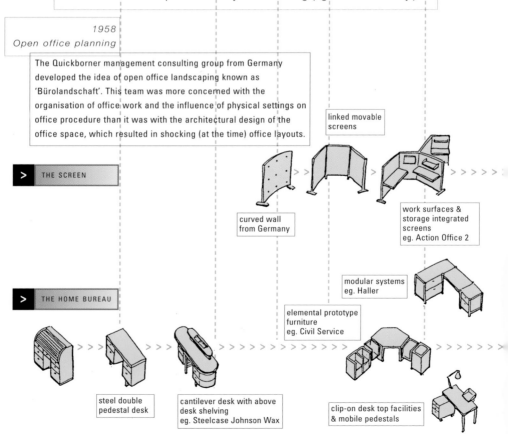

> THE LIBRARY WALL

demountable partitions

storage wall with work surface

enclosed cell with storage wall & screens

the non-workplace

Flattened corporate hierarchies leave many employees less in need of over-the-shoulder supervision. This suits telecommuting (working out of home/car/other people's office, etc), office-hotelling (unassigned work-stations instead of personal offices), and the virtual office (working through modems). With these concepts, workers can tap into the office database from their laptops at home or teleconference from a cellular phone as they are travelling (eg. on the freeway.)

88

1958
Open office planning

The Quickborner management consulting group from Germany developed the idea of open office landscaping known as 'Bürolandschaft'. This team was more concerned with the organisation of office work and the influence of physical settings on office procedure than it was with the architectural design of the office space, which resulted in shocking (at the time) office layouts.

> THE SCREEN

linked movable screens

curved wall from Germany

work surfaces & storage integrated screens eg. Action Office 2

modular systems eg. Haller

> THE HOME BUREAU

elemental prototype furniture eg. Civil Service

steel double pedestal desk

cantilever desk with above desk shelving eg. Steelcase Johnson Wax

clip-on desk top facilities & mobile pedestals

1975	1980	1985	1990 - 2000

> >

humanizing the work-
place by adding
colour & interest
eg. Olivetti Synthesis
Knoll Stephens

increasing informality
eg. Pianeta Ufficio

the office as
club house

tiled workspace
eg. Ethospace

telecommuting

Wherever these workers are, with computer groupware, digital phone lines and wide-ranging cellular networks, they can be a node on the corporate computer network. Telecommuters represent the fastest-growing portion of the work-at-home set. It is projected that in the USA about half of the office workers will be working from home in the year 2000. The push to telecommute has gained momentum through US government incentives to reduce air-pollution (through car travel), corporate efforts to cut office space costs, and the need to hire key talent.

Affordable desk-top video-conferencing means that more office workers can beam in as needed. Current software enables telecommuters to use video, share documents and surf the Internet (ie. simultaneously carry voice, video and data through multi-media software).

The main problem of telecommuting is supervision. However, video-conferencing solves a major part of this problem.

89

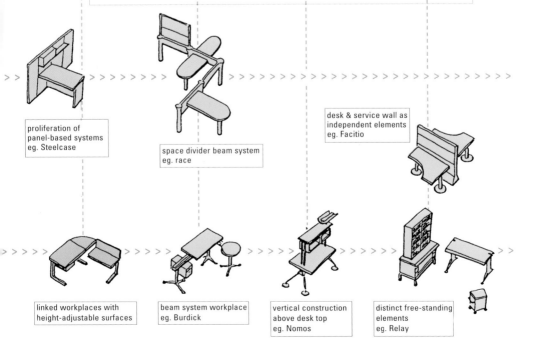

> >

proliferation of
panel-based systems
eg. Steelcase

space divider beam system
eg. race

desk & service wall as
independent elements
eg. Facitio

> >

linked workplaces with
height-adjustable surfaces

beam system workplace
eg. Burdick

vertical construction
above desk top
eg. Nomos

distinct free-standing
elements
eg. Relay

office hotelling

Office-hotelling is where, say, up to ten people share a single desk in a fully equipped office on an 'as-needed basis'. Employees must reserve in advance. In this way, many accounting firms, for instance, have slashed their office requirements, reducing the overall office density figure (ie. sq m NRA per employee).

Accompanying this approach are attitudes to information filing where group and personal filing are combined. Files are taken to desks in portable trays, personal filing is kept to a minimum, and desks are kept clear.

90

the new workplace

It is likely that not all offices in the future will be singularly telecommuting or hotelling. A composite system may evolve in that an organisation may have the following categories of workplaces: **conventional partitioned offices (for executives), permanent work-stations (for administrative staff), grouped and shared 'hot-desks' for consultants, 'touch-down' desks (for other staff visiting the office for brief periods) and meeting rooms.**

Consultants are encouraged to be where the work is: at the client's premises. When back at HQ, their 'hot-desking' more than doubles the use of desk-space. This cuts down the amount of office space needed per employee, even when offset by the increase in meeting rooms and social rooms, and rooms for customers to work in.

the new role
of the office skyscraper

One of the greatest challenges to the new models of office management is whether workers will have enough contact with one another. Telecommuting can result in isolation and sensory deprivation through working alone. Many enjoy the pageant of the office, the civilized parade of people who have got up and dressed each morning to present themselves to their colleagues: the new tie, the fancy braces, the unusual hair-colour. Corporations provide their employees with much of their social life, particularly if they are working eight to twelve hours a day. They are unlikely to find such a large group of men and women roughly their own age with similar backgrounds, interests and aspirations anywhere else.

Working in a common environment affords workers the opportunity to understand better why people react the way they do. They learn social skills from interaction.

Loss of regular interaction can also make it difficult to transmit corporate culture and to stimulate motivation.

Teleworking by definition is solitary and deprives the worker of the social intercourse of office life: the critical factor against it is human loneliness. A large part of the employee's communication and learning is not technically through their jobs but through talking with colleagues. If they are cut off from these opportunities, they will not have the kind of informal communication and learning necessary.

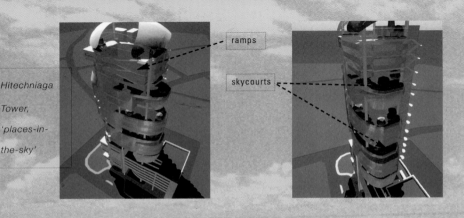

Hitechniaga Tower, 'places-in-the-sky'

ramps

skycourts

Those forced to telecommute and work from home may feel that they no longer have a place in the organisation. They may feel that they are losing access to both informal knowledge and explicit knowledge, of seeing how others solve business problems. These feelings may also lead to loss of company loyalty and commitment.

Thus it may be argued that the future of the workplace will be a non-workplace where no office buildings are needed. However, while new concepts of workplace prevail, we contend that these are not likely to eliminate the necessity for the office buildings as headquarters. The key question in office skyscraper design in the future is to effect and sustain the high level of human and social interaction that needs to take place at work despite the new found mobility.

Office skyscrapers in the future may evolve to become more like hotels with 'hot-desking' as we have seen. A new generation of office layouts and office equipment might be needed: it is likely that the office would be modular and open.

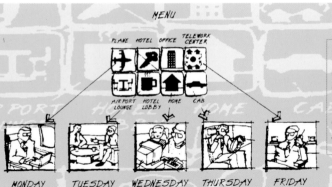

Integrated workplace strategies provide an array of workplace options for those working remotely

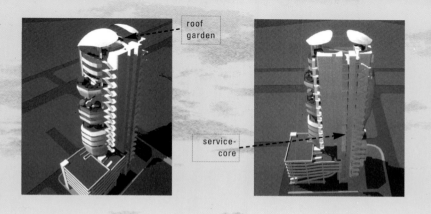

roof
garden

service-
core

There will be a gradual shift from the office 'as factory with low interaction and accessibility' to the 'transactional office' based on project teams and a high degree of interaction and access.

In the future, the new office environment will probably be more like a London Gentleman's Club, an upmarket five-star hotel, or a Viennese coffee-house where social conversation, refreshment, recreation, private contemplation, relaxation and work all take place in a seamless setting.

The main workspaces will probably have sofas and social interactive facilities such as a pool table, diner-style booths, and a snack-bar. There will be spots for one-to-one meetings, and, of course, space for large communal gatherings, brainstorming sessions and seminars. There will be carrels and work-stations in which the employees can plug-in their personal portable PCs, faxes and make phone-calls. There will be special conference and project rooms with computers and phones.

Personal space will probably be in the form of lockers. Each employee will have a locker for his personal effects and will be issued with a laptop and cellular phone-cum-portable fax; or 'an office-box', a portable piece of equipment that combines all these functions.

Ironically, as this becomes a reality, the office environment as a place for interaction and community will probably become even more important to management and employees alike.

93

> 'Crime used to be confined to the streets. Now we have our offices on the eleventh floor systematically ransacked by a gang that works on specific floors of skyscrapers across the city. We feel helpless against these acts which seem to happen in split seconds. The streets feel safe.'
>
> PROFESSOR LEON VAN SCHAIK

People who work away from the office look forward to the social stimulation of the office environment. They want to exchange ideas after hours, sitting in front of the computer or out in the field. Nothing can replace the important body-language interactions and the eye-to-eye affirmations and analysis that happen only through person-to-person meetings, something which is particularly important for forming relationships, for certain business transactions and negotiations, and for motivation.

94

NEW OFFICES ARE RAPIDLY BECOMING:

- **MEETING PLACES** as much as workplaces, places for group interaction, which are not just at ground level but are interspersed throughout the skyscraper

- **PLEASANT PLACES** which attract and retain the shrinking number of new graduates joining the ranks of the skilled workers

- **FLEXIBLE SPACES,** far more space efficient and adaptable, reducing both capital and running costs

- **HUMANE PLACES,** often smaller and nearer home (or even at it) but still part of a global communications network, combining recreational activities at the upper levels of the skyscraper with the conditions similar to that at the ground-plane

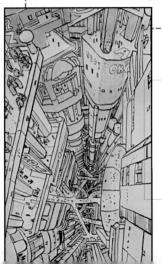

'Places in the Sky and Skybridges'
Drawing by Moebius from
The Long Tomorrow
by Dan O'Bannon

'Life in the sky constitutes, paradoxically, a distancing from nature. The generation of children raised in skyscrapers all want to play in virtual worlds.' AKIRA SUZUKI

In addition to these future directions, an agenda of requirements for the internal occupants of the bioclimatic skyscraper might be:

- control of fresh-air and air-movement
- access to openable windows and potential for natural ventilation
- a view out
- access to greenery
- access to transitional spaces
- provision of communal spaces
- greater linkages and accessibility
- provision of places-in-the-sky
- reception of natural sunlight
- control of lighting level
- greater comfort and furnishing
- ability to change internal arrangements and furniture and equipment
- provision of relaxation areas both indoors and out
- greater space per person
- better heating/cooling
- ability to adjust temperature
- less noise and distraction
- better amenities
- provision of recreational facilities
- awareness of place
- awareness of seasons of the year
- re-creation (in the sky) of conditions as in the ground plane.

'Living away from the ground seems unnatural, and yet can be
quite exhilarating. We are above 'the madding crowd' and can
observe without being observed...but it remains impossible to
wander in a skyscraper and thus it is the interior arrangement
of each floor which determines the social order in a way quite
different to that found in traditional buildings.'

PROFESSOR BRYAN LAWSON

96

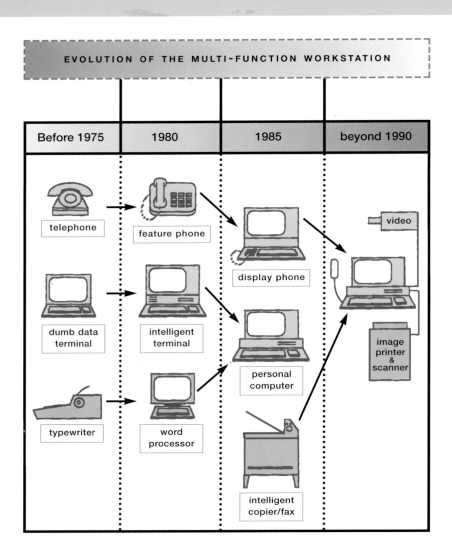

EVOLUTION OF THE MULTI-FUNCTION WORKSTATION

| Before 1975 | 1980 | 1985 | beyond 1990 |

telephone

feature phone

display phone

video

dumb data terminal

intelligent terminal

personal computer

image printer & scanner

typewriter

word processor

intelligent copier/fax

vertical
landscaping

- symbiotic relationship with other building parts
- increased organic mass
- sun-shading
- air-filtration shields
- facade microclimate-cooling through evapotranspiration
- improved air quality through photosynthesis (oxygen production)
- wind-breaks
- wind-speed reduction
- occupants aesthetic well-being

'A paradise in the sky and a multi-national market on the ground, blanketed in acid rain. This is the setting of Do Androids Dream of Electric Sheep? *In* Metropolis *a forced labor camp lies beneath the city.'*

AKIRA SUZUKI

vertical landscaping

Landscaping and planting at the upper parts of a skyscraper are crucial to the aesthetic well-being of its users as well as being an important ecological issue for this intensive building type.

The design issue in the bioclimatic skyscraper is how to incorporate diverse planting and vegetation vertically in a building that has discontinuous floor-planes stacked on top of one another, and which are significantly removed from the ground plane (where the earth's vegetation and fauna are located).

Conceptually, we might regard the skyscraper simply as a vertical extension of the ground plane into the air. We must ensure that the usual hard and soft landscaping that are traditionally applied at the ground plane extend (by landscape design) vertically in the skyscraper.

The essential proposition here is that the skyscraper's living and work places 'in the sky' remain as much in contact with the earth's biological components as possible. In this regard, our bioclimatic design approach must seek to recreate as much as possible the ecological living conditions existent at the ground level in the upper planes of the skyscraper, as well as achieving greater connectivity of the location's biotic components (eg. through spiraling linkages between floors) and the existing biologically-dense ground plane.

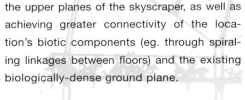
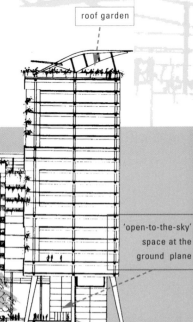

roof garden

JA Tower,
Kuala Lumpur,
Latitude 3.2°N

preservation of vegetation at the ground plane

'open-to-the-sky' space at the ground plane

SECTION

the future facade of the
skyscraper may be
full-planted with vegetation

the ideal green high-rise

VERTICAL LANDSCAPING

Vertical landscaping is the greening of the skyscraper. It involves the introduction of planting and vegetation and the other vital ecosystem components into the tall building, in addition to the introduction of landscaping at the ground plane. In the bioclimatic skyscraper, the vertical landscaping improves the micro-climate at the facades of the building, makes use of planting as wind-breaks in skycourts (similar to its use as wind-breaks in the ground-plane), absorbs polluting carbon dioxide and carbon monoxide and creates oxygen through photosynthesis, improves ecosystem biodiversity as well as enhancing the aesthetic well-being of the occupants.

99

Greening of Buildings
8% cooling-load savings
from 10% increase in
vegetated areas

planting trellis

vertical
landscaping
devices

roof garden

skycourts

planter boxes

planting mound

WEST ELEVATION

rationale:
counteracting
biological imbalances

In any ecosystem, the climate of the locality is held to be its predominant influence even though other biotic factors such as flora, fauna and soils are also important. However, in most urban locations all that remains of the site's earlier ecosystem is probably only the top-soil of the upper geological strata, and a much simplified and reduced fauna-complement made up of humans!

Architecture, in particular the skyscraper, is a massive *concentration* of an inorganic mass onto a small location. This concentration totally imbalances the ecology of the locality. To counteract this, the designer must introduce as much compatible organic matter in the form of diverse planting and landscaping (even including acceptable compatible fauna) into the skyscraper both internally and externally. This is to compensate for and to match the imbalance. The intention is to counter the intensive inorganic mass of the built structure.

JA TOWER

Although soft-landscaping strategies for low- and medium-rise buildings are relatively well-developed (eg. common solutions include using planter-boxes and roof-planting), they are notably less advanced in the case of tall buildings.

Traditionally, landscape planting is laced horizontally. However, in the case of the tall building, a vertical approach or 'vertical landscaping' is needed. Vertical landscaping is simply plant and other organic material integrated vertically with the tall building.

101

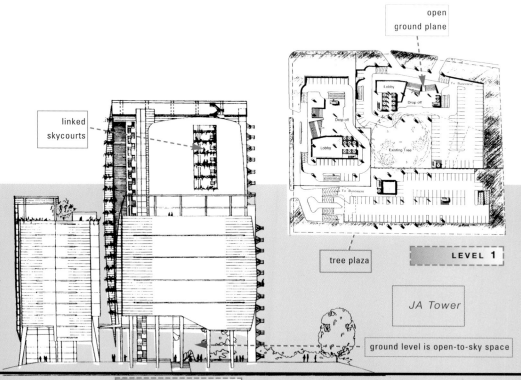

linked skycourts

open ground plane

tree plaza

LEVEL 1

JA Tower

ground level is open-to-sky space

SOUTH ELEVATION

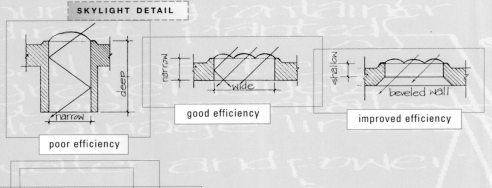

deep

narrow

narrow

wide

good efficiency

poor efficiency

shallow

beveled wall

improved efficiency

benefits

What are the benefits of vertical landscaping? By introducing planting and organic matter to the face, the interior spaces, skycourts, ground plane, facades and other surfaces it benefits the skyscraper as follows:

- The inorganic mass concentrated onto the site by the intensive built-form of the skyscraper is counteracted by organic material, improving the ecology of the area.

- The ecological value of increasing the amount of plant material in the tall building is that it increases the site's biological diversity, thereby contributing to its likely ecological stability.

- The introduction of planting has aesthetic benefits for the users of the buildings and results in improving morale and work productivity.

- The use of planting at the faces of the building enhances the aesthetics of the skyscraper as a foliaged structure.

- The planting, besides providing shading to the internal spaces and to the external walls, also minimises heat reflection and glare into the building, thereby providing effective micro-climatic responses at the faces of the building.

102

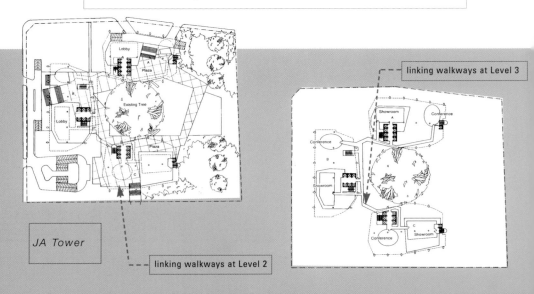

JA Tower

linking walkways at Level 3

linking walkways at Level 2

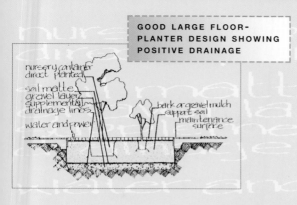

GOOD LARGE FLOOR-PLANTER DESIGN SHOWING POSITIVE DRAINAGE

nursery container direct planted

soil matte
gravel layer
supplemental
drainage lines

water and power

bark or gravel mulch support soil maintenance surface

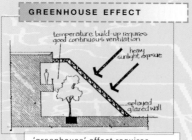

GREENHOUSE EFFECT

temperature build-up requires good continuous ventilation

heavy sunlight exposure

splayed glazed wall

'greenhouse' effect requires adequate ventilation to offset heated and stratified air in space.

- The evaporation processes of the plants can also be an effective cooling device to the face of the building.

- Plants absorb carbon dioxide and carbon monoxide (especially from external vehicular emissions), and give out oxygen through photosynthesis, thereby creating a healthier and cooler micro-environment within and around the facade of the building.

- Plants can act as visual screens and sound diffusers, especially at the skycourts, to reduce the sound and smells of the city below.

- Plants help soften the hard architectural surfaces and provide texture to nondescript surfaces.

- Plants can serve as wind-breakers (to supplement lower-shields) at skycourts.

103

structural loading

It is possible to create good planting effects with as little as 600 mm of soil; this could include trees up to 5,000 mm tall, if the soil depth can be increased locally with, say, 300 mm of topsoil overlying a 50 mm thick drainage layer to give a saturated density of only 650 kg per sq m. Vertical landscape design calls for the integration of two factors: first, the organic requirements of living plants; and second, the integration of these requirements into the total skyscraper architectural concept.

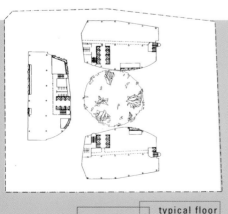

JA Tower

typical floor

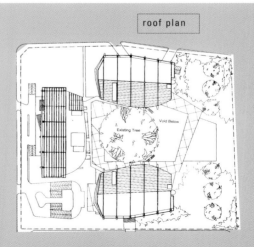

roof plan

Void Below

Existing Tree

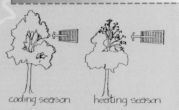

cooling season   heating season

natural lighting

Direct daylight to the planting is highly encouraged as is energy-efficient and pleasant ambient lighting. However, it must be carefully designed and calculated if it is to be the primary lighting source for interior plant material. Limitations of skylights or vertical glazing must be realised in terms of actual light intensity falling on plant material (see detail).

Natural light is dependent upon building latitude, season, altitude of the sun, weather conditions and cloud cover. Depending upon the season, geographical location and building orientation, skylights and vertical glazing usually require some supplementary artificial lighting.

Minimal use of reflective or tinted glazing in the skyscraper window is recommended if daylight is planned for plants inside. There should also be good ventilation to eliminate stratified hot air.

Probably the most important factor for any plant is light, since the whole of its existence revolves about its ability to produce carbohydrates. It is interesting to note that in many urban situations, plants tend to grow rapidly. This is to be expected, for plants are unlikely to find such favourable conditions in any other landscape, ie. 300 mm to 1000 mm of good quality top-soil, regular irrigation, high root temperatures, and a high level of maintenance.

JA Tower

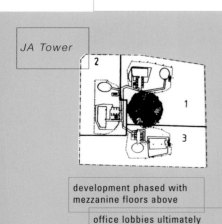

development phased with
mezzanine floors above

office lobbies ultimately
becoming interconnected

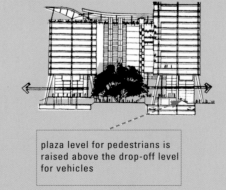

plaza level for pedestrians is
raised above the drop-off level
for vehicles

As a general rule, plant growth rates increase as root temperature rises. Studies show that in temperate climates it is common in winter for the soil of a roof garden to be at least 3°C if not 5°C higher than in the surrounding landscape. This increase in root temperature has a considerable effect on the vigour of the plants, as they start to grow earlier in the spring and their growth is sustained longer into the autumn.

planting roots

Most roots develop in a horizontal manner. This is to be expected, as in natural situation the top soil is not more than 300 mm to 400 mm thick and is frequently much shallower, and it is at this layer that most nutrients are to be found.

Roots will penetrate a membrane in the planter box or roof deck that has been fractured but they will not drive their way through a continuous layer. A single sheet of polythene buried in the soil is impervious to normal root activity, so a roofing membrane backed by concrete slab should be generally adequate.

skycourts create attractive landscape areas within the office floors

existing rain tree is preserved as the focus of the development. Site maintained as green area with views under buildings to the rain tree

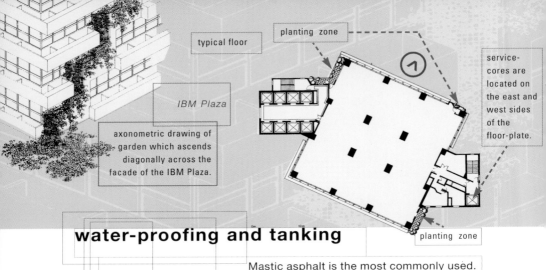

typical floor

planting zone

IBM Plaza

service-cores are located on the east and west sides of the floor-plate.

axonometric drawing of garden which ascends diagonally across the facade of the IBM Plaza.

planting zone

water-proofing and tanking

Mastic asphalt is the most commonly used. Others include: reinforced elastomeric bitumen, polyvinyl chloride sheet and ethylene propylenediene monomer. The tanking must be carefully detailed and installed because repairs are hard to effect once plants are in place. Testing of roof gardens before the planting involves flood-testing which might last for several days.

planting irrigation

Irrigation is vital in the planted skyscraper because of the high degree of exposure and the limited soil depths. Supply has to be consistent as the landscape only has to dry out once and many of the more common landscape plants will die.

Plant watering is preferably done manually. If manual systems are used, a water supply outlet should be provided nearby (eg. preferably no greater than say 30 m from planting area).

However, a gravity-fed drip system controlled by stop-cocks can also be used with sprinkler heads laid inside the planter-boxes to feed water and fertilisers to the plants at designated times during the day (and more frequently during drier seasons). In cold climates, the supply must include a mixer for hot and cold water.

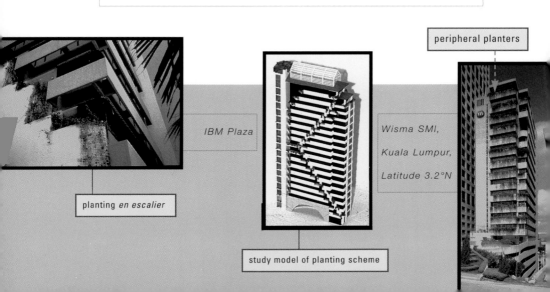

peripheral planters

IBM Plaza

planting *en escalier*

Wisma SMI, Kuala Lumpur, Latitude 3.2°N

study model of planting scheme

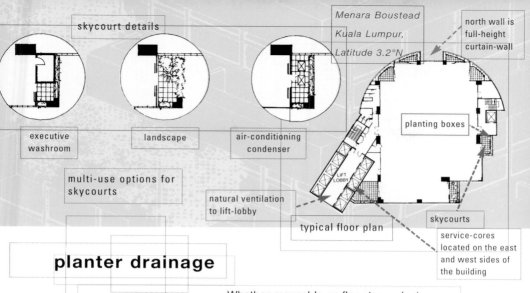

skycourt details

executive washroom

landscape

air-conditioning condenser

multi-use options for skycourts

Menara Boustead
Kuala Lumpur,
Latitude 3.2°N

north wall is full-height curtain-wall

planting boxes

LIFT LOBBY

natural ventilation to lift-lobby

typical floor plan

skycourts

service-cores located on the east and west sides of the building

planter drainage

Whether moveable or floor-type planters are used, drainage of excess water after the watering of soil mass is important. All planters should be specified or designed properly for this purpose. To avoid wetting the internal office carpets, moveable planters should have an excess-water reservoir in the bottom and should be sized so that the nursery containers fit easily into the planters. This permits easy withdrawal of a plant if excess water or other factors become a problem. Plants should never be direct-planted (ie. removed from nursery containers) into planters, as this only compounds the drainage problem.

In large floor-type planters, plants should still be left in their nursery containers, but direct-planted into a highly porous and well-draining support soil medium (such as peat, sand and bark combinations) which should be added after the excavation of the existing soil to a depth of 1.5 m. The support soil layer is impervious to water percolation. Auxiliary drainage lines tied to the building's drainage lines can facilitate positive drainage and prevent soil fungus problems caused by heavy retention of drainage water.

Drainlines should be laid in a gravel layer separated from the support soil by a fibre-glass soil-separator mat. If custom box planters or railing planters are designed, the designer must provide for excess-water reservoirs and ways in which the water can be extracted.

107

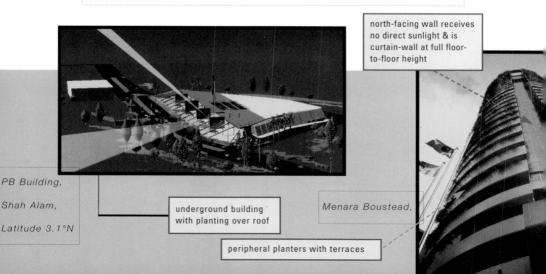

north-facing wall receives no direct sunlight & is curtain-wall at full floor-to-floor height

PB Building,
Shah Alam,
Latitude 3.1°N

underground building with planting over roof

Menara Boustead,

peripheral planters with terraces

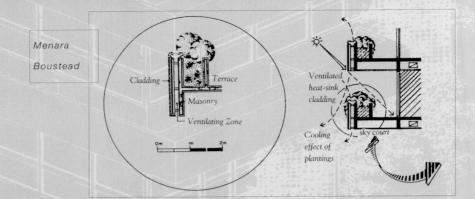

Cladding — Terrace
Masonry
Ventilating Zone
0m 1m 2m

Ventilated
heat-sink
cladding
Cooling
effect of
plantings
sky court

There might be two floor traps built into the planter boxes, one at the base and one at the top of the soil level to drain water over-flow from rainfall in the event that it does not percolate fast enough through the soil-mix and threatens to overflow onto the adjoining floor or terrace.

planting temperature

Most interior foliage plants thrive well in an environment similar to the human comfort range of 21.5°-24°C during the day (for light period) and prefer a 5°C cooler night (or dark-period). Excess temperatures either way will usually damage plant material. Hot stagnant air can dry up and dehydrate the foliage, and rapid temperature changes of 0°- 4.5°C can also damage plants. The temperature should never be allowed to fall below 0°C.

effect of heating, ventilation and air-conditioning

In most interior spaces, the carbon dioxide levels are normally high enough to require only adequate ventilation to replenish the carbon dioxide used in photosynthesis and to prevent stagnation of air around foliage.

Ventilation is also required to prevent heat build-up around foliage in high light (ie. the 'green-house effect') and possible foliar burn.

Air-conditioner-cooled air and/or heating-air usually neither harms nor helps plants, as only the ventilation has any effect on the plant, unless the air is extremely cold or hot. Cold or hot air may harm the plants, so plants should not be placed in the direct path of the airstream from the supply-grills. This is especially important if the HVAC system is in a heating cycle as the hot air will burn the foliage (see diagram on page 104).

108

Menara
Boustead

physical biological continuity

Physical continuity between planting is generally held as important for encouraging species diversity and migration, thereby contributing to a more stable urban ecosystem.

A variety of different indexes have been used by ecologists to describe the health of an ecosystem and, whilst it should be recognised that these sometimes contradict one another ('one man's flower being another man's weed'), most see a high level of species diversity as desirable.

To achieve physical continuity in 'vertical landscaping' in the skyscraper, we can have a system of linked and stepped planter-boxes organised as 'continuous planting zones' up the faces of the building. Vertical landscaping can make use of trellises (for vertical growth) and porous planters. These permit a certain amount of species-interaction and migration to take place and can be linked to the ecosystem at the ground level.

The alternative option would be to separate the planting into unconnected boxes. However, this can lead to species homogeneity which necessitates regular human maintenance to keep it ecologically stable.

Of the three possible relationships between built systems and planting – juxtapositioning, intermixing and integration – integration is clearly preferrable.

'the super-skyscraper presents opportunities for landscaping, not just with planting terraces, but on a really grand scale...super glades of trees...the botanical atria...'

PROFESSOR IVOR RICHARDS

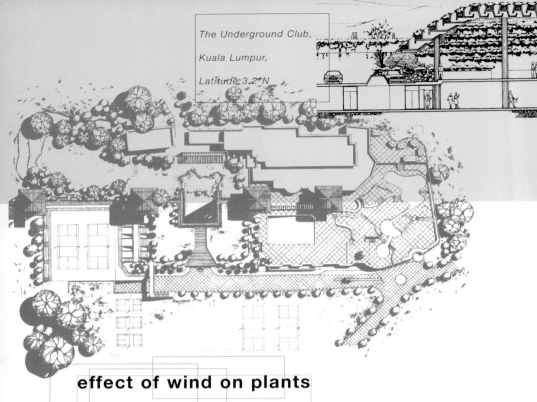

effect of wind on plants

110

One of the growing plant's problems on and around urban structures is the high degree of exposure. At roof level, it is common for wind speed to be more than double that experienced at ground level. Protection from the wind is necessary through sliding louvre-panels acting as wind-breakers.

the

vegetated

facade

'We still have a remarkably conventional view of how the high-rise city could be. Each skyscraper is a tower sitting on the ground, with only one point of contact at its base, but this does not really have to be so. In fact, we can take the ground up into the skyscraper to form a kind of 'virtual ground'. In fact, this is already common in dense cities where high-level walkways may cross roads under which tunnels exist. It is just that our minds still tell us the ground is one single surface. Skyscrapers could be connected at any level we choose.'

PROFESSOR BRYAN LAWSON

chapter five

wind **+**
ventilation

'The wind is either
an unwelcome intruder,
or a tool which is
there for free, and
should be used.
The sensation of
natural cooling, and the
perception of the wind
through movement,
is both desirable
and exhilarating.'

MELANIE RICHARDSON
DEREK TROWELL

wind and ventilation

The wind speeds around the upper parts of the skyscraper can be excessive as they increase with the building's height. In the bioclimatic skyscraper, we need to take advantage of this free energy where practical and to make use of the high wind speeds for natural ventilation purposes – to increase the rate of fresh air changes into the building for improved micro-climate cooling and a healthier internal environment.

Some of the key considerations of wind and natural ventilation for the skyscraper are discussed here.

112

Menara UMNO,

Penang,

Latitude 5.24°

boundary layer

As the wind strikes a building it is affected by the climatic conditions of the geographical area, the surrounding terrain, and the effects of other buildings adjacent to the site. The terrain starts influencing the wind several miles upwind from the building site and creates a wind profile, which describes the shape and the gradient of the wind, including turbulence and eddies in the boundary layer. The boundary layer is a layer of air sometimes hundreds of metres above the ground that separates laminar flow from uniform flow.

All air above the boundary layer is moving in uniform flow and is unaffected by the roughness or character of the ground surface terrain. Air below the boundary layer is in laminar flow and contains turbulence, gusts and eddies. Laminar flow increases with altitude as it approaches the boundary layer. The issue for the designer is how these affect the skyscraper. The answer is best ascertained through wind tunnel testing.

ventilation

Generally, ventilation means the supply of outdoor air to an indoor space. It is incorrect to define ventilation simply *as circulation of air within the space*. If a room has no openings, theoretically, there is no ventilation. For example, if all the windows and doors of a room are closed there is little ventilation even if the ceiling or wall fans are turned on.

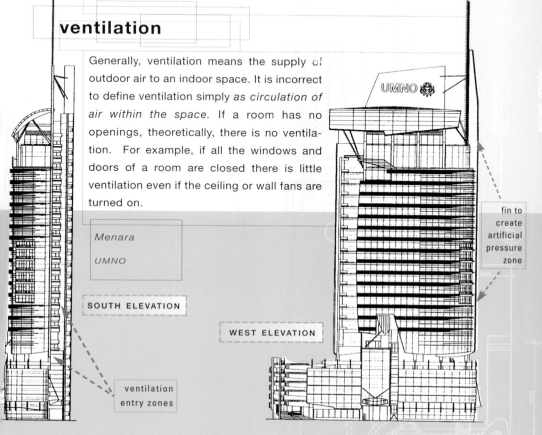

Menara

UMNO

SOUTH ELEVATION

WEST ELEVATION

fin to create artificial pressure zone

ventilation entry zones

UMNO

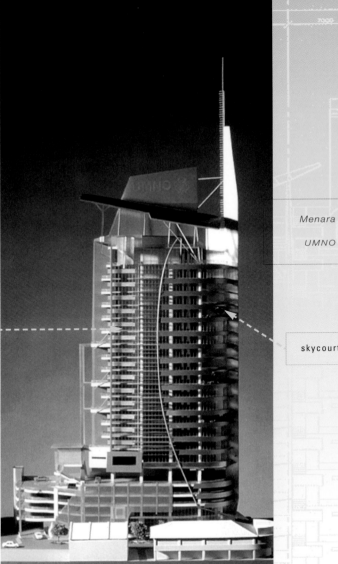

ventilation
zone

Menara
UMNO

skycourts

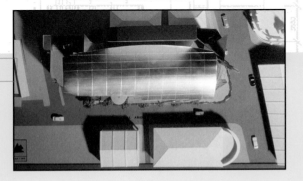

aerial

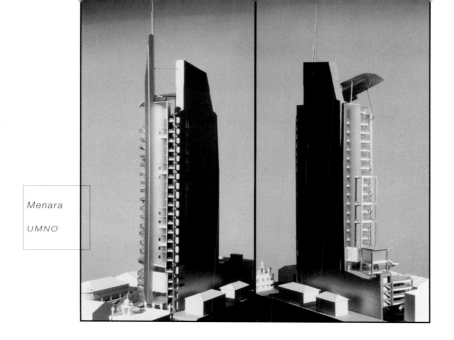

Menara

UMNO

effects of wind on
skyscrapers

The skyscraper in relation to the wind force is, in effect, a vertical cantilever beam. The response of a building to the mean wind velocity is to deflect laterally under a sustained lateral (directional) pressure, converted from the kinetic energy of the wind.

By its very nature, a skyscraper is an obstacle to the wind and deflects air along various streams. The deflected airstream can be channelled into the interior to ventilate spaces and to cool the building structure. In this regard, the wind can be both a positive and negative factor in skyscraper design. Depending on the shape of the building, steady wind velocity can also cause vortex shedding in the wake of the structure.

'Wind is at once the enemy and the potential friend. Enemy since it seeks to shake and destroy; technology must be harnessed to use active damping to resist these forces at minimum cost. But it can be a friend: constant air movement at height can be used to ventilate, pollution-free, at minimal cost. High-frequency wind turbines can generate power for the building's basic systems.'

TONY FITZPATRICK
OVE ARUP + PARTNERS

Wind, therefore, affects the skyscraper's structural design and the design of its cladding, so the accurate determination of the wind loads by wind engineering is important both for safety and comfort.

Wind, which acts on the vertical surface of the building, is a more critical factor in the skyscraper than in low buildings and has many implications for structure (see page 124).

Besides wind loading, wind-induced motions in the skyscraper have proven to be a problem for some of the more slender towers, affecting occupant comfort. Gusting, which is a random phenomenon, causes the structure to oscillate off the mean deflected shape in a manner which can only be predicted by statistical means.

There are also secondary problems, such as wind-induced leakages, whistling, cladding and out-rigger 'rattling' to be considered and resolved.

However, on the beneficial side, wind can provide the bioclimatic skyscraper with natural ventilation opportunities and wind-induced energy as supplementary sources of energy to the building's electrical systems.

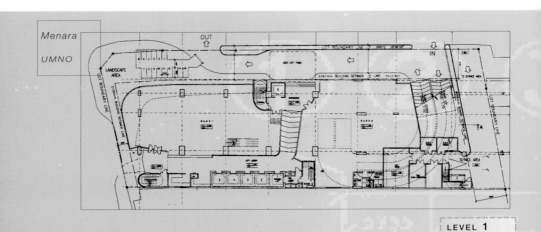

Menara UMNO

LEVEL 1

wind engineering

Wind engineering emerged as a separate identifiable branch of engineering expertise for skyscrapers in the 1970s and 80s. It covers a number of disciplines including: aerodynamics, structural dynamics, meteorology, wind tunnel technology, instrumentation, statistics, computational fluid dynamics, air chemistry and architecture. It currently places heavy reliance on scale model simulations in wind tunnels and, in some instances, on computational fluid dynamics (CFD) models.

117

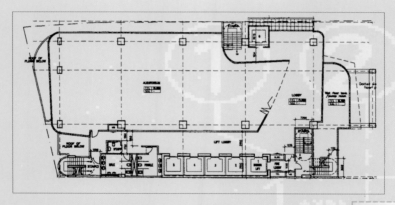

LEVEL 8

wind tunnel
testing

The wind tunnel simulation is considered by many to be accurate and allows detailed information on loads, local wind velocities, dispersion of air pollution and wind-induced vibration effects to be obtained through appropriate instrumentation of the model.

An important part of the wind tunnel study is scaling up the results to full scale. The principles of dynamic similarity are employed to do this (and also to establish the validity of the model test in the first place). Strict dynamic similarity implies that certain non-dimensional parameters have the same value on the model as at full scale (eg. the use of pressure coefficient in the equation of local surface pressure, reference static pressure high above the ground, air density and gradient wind velocity).

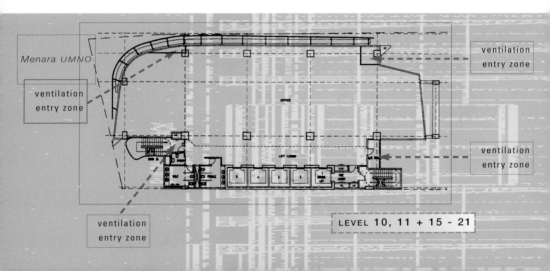

Menara UMNO

ventilation entry zone

ventilation entry zone

ventilation entry zone

ventilation entry zone

ventilation entry zone

LEVEL 10, 11 + 15 - 21

wind statistics

An important part of wind engineering is obtaining reliable wind statistics for the locality (eg. the 'wind-rose'). Only by combining wind tunnel data with such statistics can the frequency of occurrence of critical loading conditions be determined. Usually the wind tunnel laboratory obtains the meteorological records and undertakes this analysis as part of the wind tunnel study. In areas subject to special types of storm, such as the typhoon, it is important to assess how many of these storms are represented in the data. For example, at any one location with a wind record of twenty years, there may not have been a sufficient number of typhoon occurences recorded to reliably estimate winds over a fifty year period. In these cases, it is necessary to undertake computer simulations to artificially generate a sufficient statistical database. The Monte Carlo simulation, which uses extensive historical data on tracks, central pressure drop, and maximum winds, is one example of this.

119

Menara

UMNO

entrance

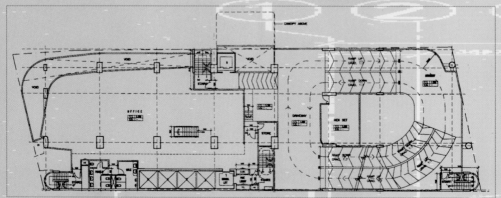

LEVEL 2

exterior wind loads on cladding and wind tunnel tests

The skyscraper's outer wall or skin must be designed so that it will neither buckle under wind pressure nor develop leakages from wind-driven rain (see Chapter 6).

The wind loads on the exterior cladding of buildings are typically positive (pushing inward) on a wall facing into the wind and negative (sucking outward) on walls parallel to the wind and on the sheltered downwind face. Building codes provide estimates of the magnitude of these loads for simple rectangular-shaped buildings in uncomplicated surroundings. However, buildings such as these are the exception rather than the rule: in reality, the shape of the sky-scraper is often far from a simple rectangle and is typically surrounded by other structures in complex arrangements. This leads to extremely variable loading patterns on the exterior cladding and, as described previously, wind tunnel tests have become a standard method for obtaining the detailed loading patterns.

The net load on any exterior panel is the difference between the pressure acting on the outer surface and that acting on its inner surface. Thus, although the bulk of the load comes from the exterior wind pressure, internal pressures, as well as external, must be determined through the wind tunnel test.

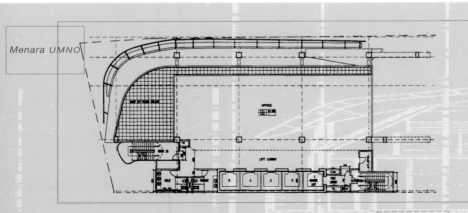

Menara UMNO

LEVEL 25

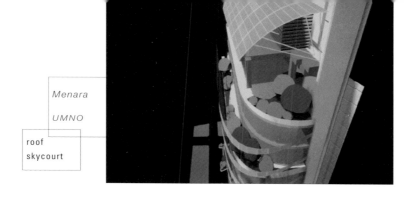

One of the advantages of a detailed wind-tunnel study of wind pressures is that the localised 'hot spots' of very high suction are identified, and can therefore safely be designed for. At the same time, it may be found that for a large portion (eg. 95%) of the building surface, the wind pressures are quite moderate, introducing the possibility of some savings (eg. in aluminium stiffening, brackets, glass thickness, etc).

The nature of wind currents is such that they will cause negative pressures to build up on the leeward side of the building. These negative pressures often cause more damage than the positive pressure on the windward side. The architectural ramification of this phenomenon is the necessity of designing a cladding system that will permit inside and outside pressures to equalise themselves (eg. using double-skin 'rain-check' systems or notches in the framing). Glass failure during a wind storm is usually due to negative pressure: the glass or panel is 'sucked' from the building, and hazardously falls onto the street below.

The required resistive strength of the panel or glass is affected by its location on the building. Since wind speed and pressure increase with altitude, if the glass panels are kept uniform in size, they will need to be increased in thickness as their height above the ground increases.

121

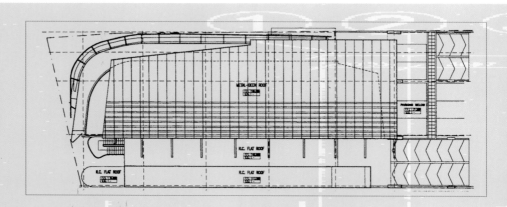

ROOF

building motions

Building motion due to wind forces arose as a design problem in the USA after several tall buildings experienced problems. Essentially, if the building moves too much, its occupants become uncomfortable or alarmed. For many skyscrapers it is now often motion criteria rather than strength requirements that govern the design. Excessive motion downgrades the quality of the building making it less marketable to tenants.

In the 1970s and 80s, an informal rule-of-thumb for acceptable horizontal acceleration was that the peak acceleration sensed by occupants of the top floors should not exceed 2% of gravitational acceleration more often than once in ten years. Recently, it has been held that other motions such as tortional deflections and velocities may be of equal or greater importance.

China

Haikou

Tower #2

The controlling parameters that designers have at their disposal for limiting building motion are: overall shape, mass, stiffness and damping. The most common approach is to have the right combination of stiffness and mass. The more of these qualities the better, but they entail increased costs and in earthquake areas increased mass can be counter-productive since it raises earthquake loadings. Motion reduction by design includes provision for voids in the upper parts of the building (as 'skycourts') to let the wind blow through. An alternative method is to use viscoelastic dampers or tuned mass dampers and sloshing liquid dampers.

wind on pedestrians

Skyscrapers can also redirect strong winds that exist high above the ground and bring them down to ground-level, creating uncomfortable or even dangerous wind environments for pedestrians. Wind-blown plazas, for instance, deter people from using them and affect the commercial success of a project or buildings nearby. A number of cities now have by-laws requiring that new skyscrapers have the ground-level winds around them examined prior to receiving approval, to avoid creating problems in adjacent streets and plazas.

China Haikou Tower #2

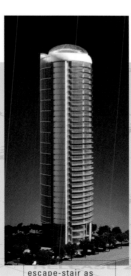

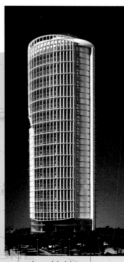

2-zoned
elevator system

escape-stair as
ventilation orifice

solar-shield

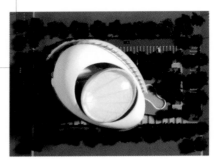

winds and structure

As we have seen, wind is a more critical issue in the skyscraper than in low structures. It exerts a great force, particularly on the upper floors of the skyscraper. Therefore, floor structural systems must be designed to transfer the wind loads from the exterior walls into the structural resisting components of the building (eg. central-core, 'bundle-of-tubes', etc) where the building walls and/or columns will in turn transfer the wind forces down to the ground.

124

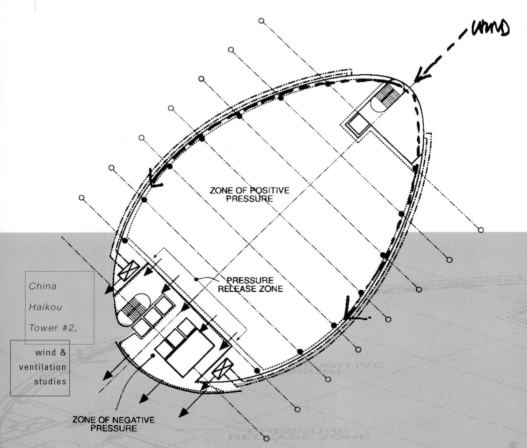

China

Haikou

Tower #2,

wind &
ventilation
studies

ZONE OF POSITIVE
PRESSURE

PRESSURE
RELEASE ZONE

ZONE OF NEGATIVE
PRESSURE

WIND

natural ventilation

Natural ventilation is desirable for the following reasons:

- for increased comfort in hot-humid periods

- for health reasons to provide sufficient oxygen and maintain pollutants at agreeable levels

- for the better perceptual satisfaction of building occupants

- for energy conservation through the reduction/elimination of mechanical means of ventilation

China Haikou
Tower #2

wind &
ventilation
studies

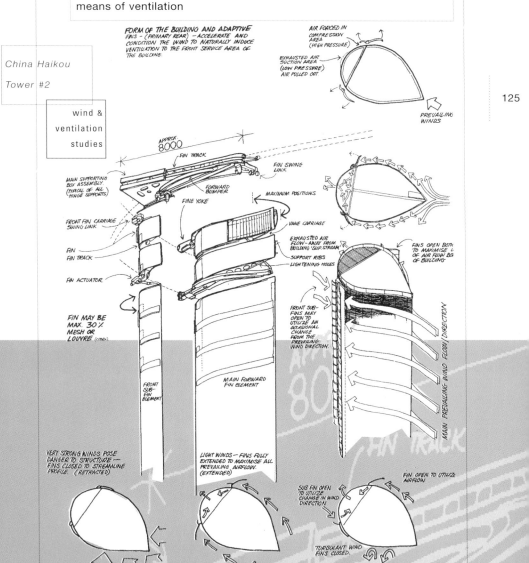

ventilation rate

The ventilation rate – measured in either air-changes per hour or cubic metres or air supply per hour – depends on the activities of the occupants and the volume of the space or floor area per person (see table on page 130). When smoking takes place in a building, the ventilation rate is significantly increased.

Studies of building occupants show a high level of dissatisfaction with existing ventilation (whether it be natural or mechanical), while noise, lighting and smoking feature less strongly (in Duffy et al, 1993). Evidently, 'fresh-air' buildings with potential for natural ventilation and lighting are high on the building occupants' list of preferences. For instance, in the tropics, natural airflow is one way to remedy the hot sticky conditions of a hot humid climate, as it is in temperate zones during the summer. Free air movement around the occupants and throughout the building increases the evaporation process and hence the degree of comfort. The exchange of indoor air with fresh outdoor air provides cooling and the moving air can also act as a heat-carrying medium.

While absolute calm may be encountered in practice, measurements have shown that air movement near ground level is usually in excess of 0.8 to 1.6 km/hr.

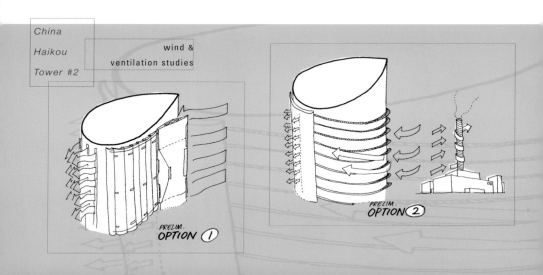

China
Haikou
Tower #2

wind &
ventilation studies

PRELIM.
OPTION ①

PRELIM.
OPTION ②

BEAUFORT SCALE	DESCRIPTION	MEAN WIND SPEED RANGE (M/S)	EFFECTS AT 10M
B0	calm	0 - 0.2	
B1	light air	0.3 - 1.5	No noticeable wind
B2	light breeze	1.6 - 3.3	Wind felt on face
B3	gentle breeze	3.4 - 5.4	Wind extends light flag
B4	moderate breeze	5.5 - 7.9	Raises dust and loose paper. Hair disarranged, clothing flaps
B5	fresh breeze	8.0 - 10.7	Limit of agreeable wind on land
B6	strong breeze	10.8 - 13.8	Umbrellas used with difficulty. Force of the wind felt on the body. Noisy, frequent blinking.
B7	near gale	13.9 - 17.1	Inconvenience felt when walking, difficult to walk steadily. Hair blown straight.
B8	gale	17.2 - 20.7	Generally impedes progress, walking difficult to control. Great difficulty with balance in gusts.
B9	strong gale	20.8 - 24.4	People blown over by gusts. Impossible to face wind; earache, headache, breathing difficult. Some structural damage occurs; falling roof tiles, tree branches, etc. Hazardous for pedestrians.
B10	storm	24.5 - 28.4	Seldom experienced inland. Trees uprooted; considerable structural damage occurs.

In the case of the skyscraper, outdoor breezes can be used not only to ventilate elevator lobbies but also to pass through the whole building for structural cooling. The higher wind speed at upper parts of the skyscraper can be used as a useful cooling element. To some extent, convective cooling through the stack effect can be explored to the advantage of the building height during calm periods.

In the bioclimatic skyscraper, natural ventilation of elevator lobbies, staircases and toilets eliminates the requirement by the fire authorities for mechanical pressurisation of these spaces, thereby lowering initial capital costs and subsequent operating costs (see Chapter 2).

Wind-speed increases with height and is generally recorded at an anemometer height of ten metres above the ground.

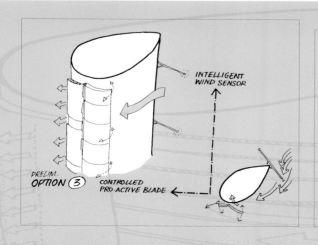

PRELIM.
OPTION ③   CONTROLLED PRO-ACTIVE BLADE

INTELLIGENT WIND SENSOR

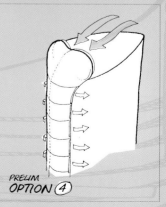

PRELIM
OPTION ④

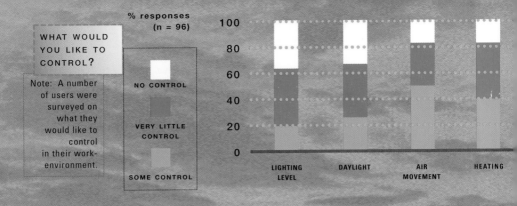

% responses
(n = 96)

WHAT WOULD
YOU LIKE TO
CONTROL?

Note: A number
of users were
surveyed on
what they
would like to
control
in their work-
environment.

NO CONTROL

VERY LITTLE
CONTROL

SOME CONTROL

LIGHTING
LEVEL   DAYLIGHT   AIR
MOVEMENT   HEATING

adjustable openings and sieves

The external walls of the bioclimatic sky-scraper should be regarded more as a 'sieve' than as a sealed skin. They should function as a permeable membrane with adjustable openings. Ideally, the skyscraper's external walls should act like a filter that has variable parts to control cross-ventilation, provide solar protection, regulate wind-swept rain, and discharge heavy rain.

For good, natural cross-ventilation to be an effective substitute for air-conditioning (with around 30 air-changes per hour), the best arrangement for windows is as full wall-openings on both the windward and leeward sides, with adjustable or closing devices which can assist in channelling the air flow in the required direction following the change of wind. Ideally, openings should be as large as possible, though the high velocity of winds at the upper floors of the tall building can make this impractical. A recessed window with means of adjusting the through-flow of wind and wind-swept rain would provide an alternative to air-conditioning when desired.

For natural ventilation and sunlight to work, the depth of the furthest work table should not be more that one and a half times the floor-to-floor height (6 m from the external wall). The minimum width of air-wells should be 2 m (depending on climatic zone) to be effective.

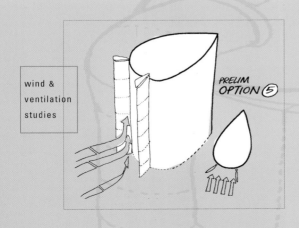

wind &
ventilation
studies

PRELIM
OPTION 5

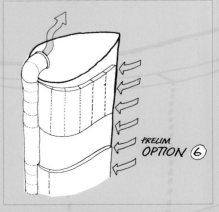

PRELIM
OPTION 6

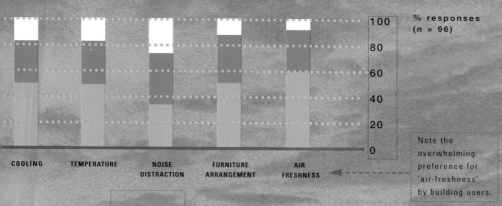

100
80
60
40
20
0

COOLING   TEMPERATURE   NOISE DISTRACTION   FURNITURE ARRANGEMENT   AIR FRESHNESS

Note the overwhelming preference for 'air-freshness' by building users.

external materials and thermal insulation

The roof design of the skyscraper is of less importance than in the low and medium-rise building since its external wall area already exceeds its roof area. Furthermore, the height of the building means that any overhangs of the roof affect only the upper few floors. However, the absorption of direct solar heat by the roof and the structure of these top floors needs to be considered. In the case of the tall building much of the roof is usually occupied by mechanical plants which offer some insulation

Roofs and walls in the tall building should be constructed of low-thermal-capacity materials with reflective outside surfaces where these are not shaded. The roof should be of double construction and provided with a reflective upper surface. The use of a good thermal insulation layer is recommended.

129

The major thermal forces acting on the outside of the tall building are a combination of radiation and convection impacts. The radiation component consists of incident solar radiation and of radiant heat exchange with the surroundings. The convective heat impact is a function of exchange with the internal air and may be accelerated by air movement. The exchange effect may be increased by diluting the radiation over a larger area through the use of curved surfaces such as vaults, domes, atria, louvred or irregularly surfaced roofs, which will at the same time increase the rate of convection transfer.

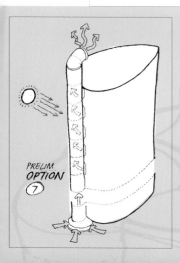

PRELIM OPTION 7

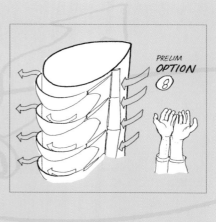

PRELIM OPTION 8

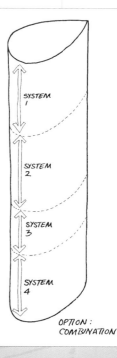

SYSTEM 1

SYSTEM 2

SYSTEM 3

SYSTEM 4

OPTION: COMBINATION

MINIMUM FRESH AIR SUPPLY	the provision of outside air to air-conditioned space should not exceed more then 30% of the rates below	
TYPE OF BUILDING/OCCUPANCY	MIN FRESH AIR SUPPLY M³/HR/PERSON	M³/HR/FLOOR AREA
1 • restaurant & dance halls	17	10
2 • offices	13	1.2
3 • shops, supermarkets & department stores	13	2.3
4 • lobbies, concourses & corridors	13	0.9
5 • classrooms, theatres & cinemas	8.5	6.0
6 • factories & workshops	13	1.8
7 • bedrooms & apartments	13	-

Wall surfaces which have direct solar insulation (especially the east and west sides) should be shaded. Their cladding material's insulation and 'time-lag' characteristics should be taken into consideration. External materials used might be those that are effective heat-sinks (eg. aluminium composites) or those designed to have a 'double-layered' ventilating space.

Another very effective protection against radiation impact, especially in external wall design, is the selective absorptivity and emmissivity characteristic of a material, especially under hot conditions. Materials which reflect rather than absorb radiation, and which release the absorbed heat as thermal radiation more readily, bring about lower temperatures within the building.

130

natural ventilation

Fresh-air buildings are currently the preferred norm. **Natural ventilation is the use of fresh air of sufficient volume and air-change to ventilate enclosed spaces without the use of mechanical means.**

Ventilation conditions inside a building have a direct influence on the health, comfort and well-being of the occupants. We all respond to air purity and motion, and to the indirect influences of ventilation on the temperature and humidity of the air and indoor surfaces. During hot periods natural ventilation can provide comfort by accelerating the conduction of heat and increasing the rate of evaporation around the occupants, as we have already seen.

CHINA HAIKOU TOWER #3

west elevation

'Chicago was not a windy city before they built the skyscrapers.' ANDREW ALLSOP
OVE ARUP & PARTNERS

In designing for natural ventilation, we need to be aware that airflow through and within an internal space is stimulated by two means: the distribution of pressure gradients around a building, and thermal forces caused by temperature gradients between indoor and outdoor air. The distribution of pressure zones is the result of wind being deflected around, within and above the building.

On the sides facing directly into the wind, high pressure zones are created. These areas are elevated above atmospheric pressure. Those areas where the velocity of the air is at its lowest, forming a suction effect, are called low pressure areas.

Thermal force ventilation is caused by the different densities of air. The warmer or less dense air tends to rise by convection, the 'venturi effect'. This creates a vacuum, drawing air in to replace the rising air. If openings are located at the bottom and top of an internal space, then convective natural ventilation is stimulated. However, in most hot, dry areas this method of ventilation is not sufficient to give thermal comfort.

In the bioclimatic skyscraper, the provision of natural ventilation opportunities in all the elevator-lobbies, staircase and toilet areas eliminates the need for the mechanical ventilation of these areas, as well as the need to comply with the requirements from the Fire Authorities for mechanical pressurisation of these spaces in the event of a fire. This lowers the initial costs of the building as well as reducing energy consumption.

131

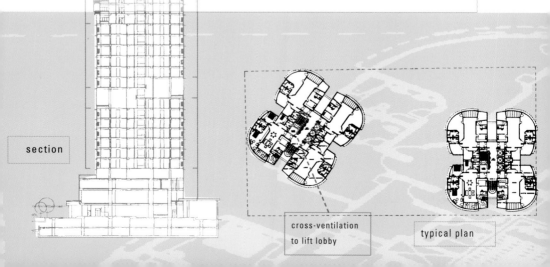

section

cross-ventilation
to lift lobby

typical plan

three functions of ventilation

Ventilation has three distinct functions. These are: *health ventilation* which maintains air quality in the building by replacing indoor air with fresh outdoor air; *thermal comfort ventilation* which provides thermal comfort by helping the heat exchange from the body to the surrounding air; and *structural cooling ventilation* which is a means by which the structure is cooled when the indoor temperature is higher than the outdoor temperature (as an energy conservation benefit).

health ventilation

In buildings, the quality of air is determined by the working and living processes (such as cooking, keeping warm, etc) which takes place within them. The function of health ventilation is to provide the air quality necessary for the removal of odours, carbon monoxide and any other by-product of the occupants' working and living processes.

132

Outdoor air, on average, is composed of 21% oxygen, 0.03-0.04% carbon dioxide, 78% nitrogen, 1% inert gases (primarily argon) and between 5 to 25 g of water vapour per m^3 of air. Expired air contains about 16.3% oxygen, 4% carbon dioxide, 79.7% nitrogen and other gases (mainly ammonia), and 45 g of water vapour per m^3. Bacteria and odour-producing organic materials are given off by the body in addition to those that result from personal habits (ie. smoking and diet). It should be remembered that human oxygen requirements depend primarily on the metabolic rates of the individual and may directly affect other discharged gases from the body. In most cases, the carbon dioxide and oxygen variations in buildings are rarely above 1%. The level of carbon dioxide should not rise above 2-3%, and the level of oxygen should not drop by more than 3-4%.

China Haikou

Tower #3

over 60%
external
exposed
surface area
to each
apartment unit

plan A

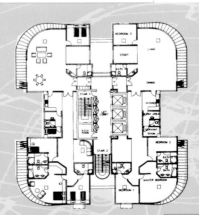

plan B

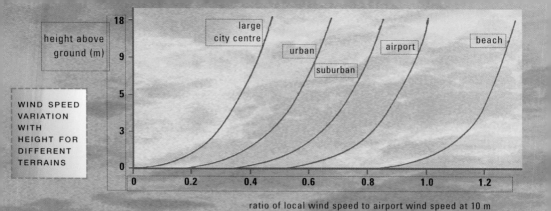

WIND SPEED VARIATION WITH HEIGHT FOR DIFFERENT TERRAINS

height above ground (m)

large city centre

urban

suburban

airport

beach

ratio of local wind speed to airport wind speed at 10 m

It is difficult to establish a requirement for dealing with odour levels. It should be assumed that the ventilation rate be adjusted for each activity occurring within a building so that any perceptible odour is eliminated. Spaces where cigarette smoking and cooking take place, as well as bathrooms and gymnasiums, require higher rates of air change than other places.

The perception of odour is directly related to air temperature. Researchers have studied the effect of ventilation rate on odour level and found that a temperature reduction from 30.5° to 21.5°C causes a reduction in the perception of odour levels. This temperature difference is equivalent to increasing the air supply from 0.14 to 1.5 m^3 minimum per person. Bacterial content is not affected by changes in ventilation rate from 0.03 to 1.5 m^3 minimum per person.

Ventilation requirements need to be carefully determined for areas that have no direct connections with the outside such as windows.

In the energy cycle, carbon monoxide is the result of incomplete combustion of fossil fuels. This can also occur on a smaller scale in heating and cooling appliances. When carbon monoxide comes into contact with the bloodstream through breathing, it reacts with the haemoglobin in the blood to deprive the body of oxygen, ultimately causing asphyxiation. Hence ventilation should be sufficient to eliminate any possibility of a saturation of carbon monoxide in the air. The best solution is to eliminate the need for fossil fuels in the first place.

133

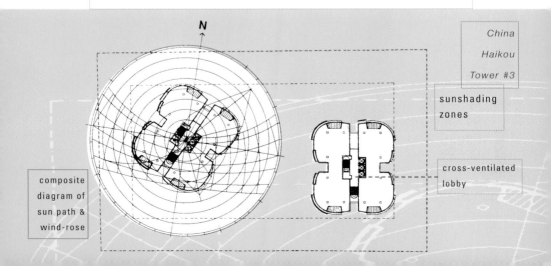

N

China

Haikou

Tower #3

sunshading zones

cross-ventilated lobby

composite diagram of sun path & wind-rose

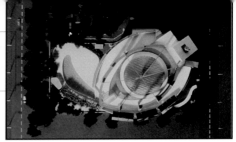

China Haikou
Tower #1

thermal comfort ventilation

The purpose of thermal comfort ventilation is to remove the physiological and psychological discomforts which arise from high temperature and uncomfortable indoor conditions. In very few cases, it is possible for natural ventilation to be distributed homogeneously throughout a space when high-velocity flow rates are involved. In terms of thermal comfort, the velocity of airflow, rather than the number of air changes, is paramount. It is important that a satisfactory number of air changes occur where odours are involved, but when rapid heat conduction is primary, a high-velocity airflow is more important. Thermal comfort ventilation may also be employed during the cooler months. The purpose of this is to force fresh air to the ceiling level where it can settle to the warmed floor. This can also facilitate energy conservation. Thermal comfort ventilation is discussed more thoroughly in the following sections.

structural cooling ventilation

Ambient air temperature is most directly affected by the heat absorption capabilities of the surrounding surfaces. This also applies to indoor air temperatures. Structural cooling ventilation deals primarily with reducing the temperature of the indoor surfaces. These temperatures fluctuate according to the average exterior surface temperatures. This, in turn, is the result of external surface colour, thermal resistance and orientation. These temperatures are expressed as deviations from the maximum outdoor temperature. The results of tests suggest a relationship between ventilation and external colour.

134

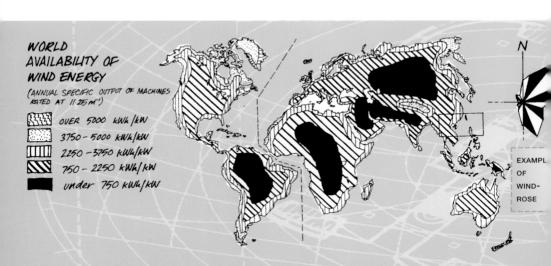

WORLD
AVAILABILITY OF
WIND ENERGY
(ANNUAL SPECIFIC OUTPUT OF MACHINES RATED AT 11.25 m²)

OVER 5000 kWh/kW
3750 - 5000 kWh/kW
2250 - 3750 kWh/kW
750 - 2250 kWh/kW
under 750 kWh/kW

N

EXAMPLE OF WIND-ROSE

The quantitative effect of ventilation varies with the surface material and its thickness, especially when the exterior surface is grey. The cooling effect of ventilation on the maximum temperature tends to be greater when the walls are thinner. For example, grey painted walls appear to be more affected by ventilation than lightweight walls of the same thickness.

There are cases where ventilation may actually rise inside due to a light exterior surface and thermal resistance of a wall retarding the absorption of solar radiation. The shading of windows and their size are important elements to consider. When the wall colour is dark, ventilation reduces the daytime temperature of the internal surface, which affects the internal air temperature. This, of course, is relative to the thermal resistance of the wall and its thickness, and to the magnitude of change that ventilation can effect.

Ventilation requirements vary with the general climatic and microclimatic conditions during different seasons. These requirements should be determined prior to specifying the location of openings, mechanisms to be used in the openings, and the general orientation of the internal spaces.

In cold, dry regions where it is important to minimise the intrusion of outside air, humidified air is often preferable. Ventilation is sometimes required during the summer months. Humidity is undesirable for providing cross-ventilation along the NE-SW axis and the south and west should be consciously avoided for humidity control. All windows should have two or three layers of glazing for winter protection.

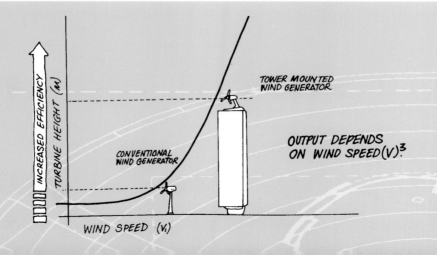

China Haikou

Tower #1

In areas where the winter months are very humid and not quite cold enough to require high thermal insulation, the rate of ventilation should be reduced so as not to lower the indoor temperature. In temperate regions (eg. North America) openings should generally allow for summer breeze penetration (generally from the southwest). Openings should be limited in the northern and western directions.

In hot areas such as the tropics, ventilation is important to remove moisture from the skin and to aid heat conduction. It is the velocity of the air that is critical, rather than the volumetric air flow. Natural ventilation is a very important element of design in these areas. In hot, humid areas the velocity should approach 2-3m/sec during the hotter period. In a hot, dry climate it is advisable to reduce the ventilation rate to a minimum during the daytime. Windows should be open during the night but during the day the velocity can even be lower than in cold climates. The open windows at night will allow ventilation to offset the increased temperatures on material walls and reduce the air temperature. The evening velocity may only be 1-2m/sec.

The criteria for ventilation are determined by the exterior wall colour and thermal resistance, the type of internal activity, and the climate of the location. The air velocity of natural ventilation is determined by temperature and humidity requirements. Ventilation effects may fluctuate within a space, necessitating an internal structuring of activities by the varying air velocities.

136

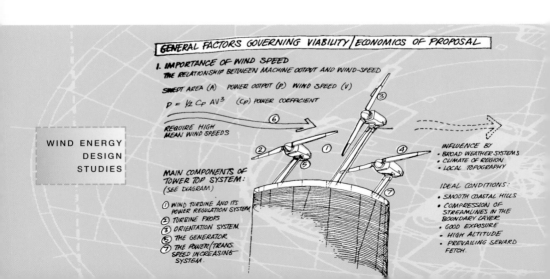

WIND ENERGY
DESIGN
STUDIES

GENERAL FACTORS GOVERNING VIABILITY/ECONOMICS OF PROPOSAL

I. IMPORTANCE OF WIND SPEED
THE RELATIONSHIP BETWEEN MACHINE OUTPUT AND WIND-SPEED

SWEPT AREA (A)   POWER OUTPUT (P)   WIND SPEED (V)

$P = \frac{1}{2} C_P AV^3$ (C_P) POWER COEFFICIENT

REQUIRE HIGH
MEAN WIND SPEEDS

MAIN COMPONENTS OF
TOWER TOP SYSTEM:
(SEE DIAGRAM)

① WIND TURBINE AND ITS
   POWER REGULATION SYSTEM
② TURBINE PROPS
③ ORIENTATION SYSTEM
⑤ THE GENERATOR
⑦ THE POWER/TRANS.
   SPEED INCREASING
   SYSTEM.

INFLUENCE BY
· BROAD WEATHER SYSTEMS
· CLIMATE OF REGION
· LOCAL TOPOGRAPHY

IDEAL CONDITIONS:
· SMOOTH COASTAL HILLS
· COMPRESSION OF
  STREAMLINES IN THE
  BOUNDARY LAYER
· GOOD EXPOSURE
· HIGH ALTITUDE
· PREVAILING SEWARD
  FETCH.

window orientation, size and airflow patterns

Airflow through a space is dependent upon the pressure distribution around the building, the orientation of the inlet, the sizes of the openings, and the inertia of the outside air. This section deals primarily with orientation and sizing of openings, and their effects on inducing various airflow patterns. The following section will focus on the location and type of openings.

Window orientation is very important to ensure even distribution of air motion throughout the space. Quite often, with a direct axis between inlet and outlet, the flow of air will go directly to the outlet if the inlet is perpendicular to the direction of the prevailing wind with little effect upon the other areas of the room. When windows are on opposite walls and the prevailing wind is oblique (45°) to the opening, higher velocities occur within the space when the inlet ratios are 1:1, 2:1, 2:2, 2:3, 3:2, 3:3. It is not recommended to have the inlet larger than the outlet. Where the windows are located on adjacent walls the higher velocities will occur when the wind is perpendicular to the opening.

When tests were done on rectangular models it was found that wind shadows existed. Careful design of the openings and placement of internal walls can alleviate this. What happens is that the inside flow enters (unless scooped, such as by a casement window) and tends to follow its inertial direction until the pressure difference at the outlet causes it to change direction. This data is important for areas that have a westerly or easterly prevailing wind in the warmer months. Orientation requirements would conflict if the wind had to be perpendicular.

2. IMPORTANCE OF SCALE

A GENERAL AND PROGRESSIVE IMPROVEMENT IN THE COST/UNIT ENERGY OUTPUT CAN BE EXPECTED WITH INCREASING SCALE.

3. RATE OF MACHINE OUTPUT

WIND POWER IS MOST LIKELY TO BE ECONOMIC IN:

- RELATIVELY SMALL MACHINES FOR SPECIFIC SITE APPLICATIONS WHERE THE RELATIVELY POOR ECONOMICS OF SMALL UNITS CAN BE OFFSET BY HIGH ON-SITE ENERGY COSTS.

- LARGE MACHINES FOR NETWORK / BUILDING COMPLEX CONNECTION WHERE FULL OPPORTUNITY OF THE ECONOMICS OF SCALE AND FREEDOM OF SITING CAN BE CAPITALISED UPON.

WIND GENERATION — FURTHER ASPECTS:

- GLOBALLY WIDESPREAD AVAILABILITY / TECHNOLOGY.
- RELATIVELY SMALL AREA OCCUPIED BY PLANT
- POSSIBILITY OF LOW ENVIRONMENTAL IMPACT.
- A STEADY MOVE (SCALE, LOCATION, APPLICATION) TO COST COMPETITIVENESS WITH CONVENTIONAL SOURCES.
- POSSIBLE ENERGY GAIN OF 50:1 OVER PLANT LIFE.

DESIGN CHOICES
(SEE DIAGRAM)

1. TURBINE TYPE OR CONFIGURATION
2. TURBINE DIAMETER
3. THE CHOICE OF FIXED OR VARIABLE PITCH BLADES.
4. NUMBER OF BLADES IN TURBINE
5. THE CHOICE OF FIXED OR VARIABLE TURBINE SPEED
6. LOCATION OF THE TURBINE UPWIND OR DOWNWIND.
7. SYSTEM STIFFNESS

Now the orientation direction can be towards the south-east or south-west and still assist natural ventilation. For example, the farmers of Quebec, Canada (Latitude 46°N) orient their houses on an east-west axis so that the smallest areas bear the brunt of the prevailing winter wind. This orientation facilitates an easy adaptation to the prevailing summer wind.

Window size has a significant role in determining airflow velocity in cross-ventilated situations. In rooms where windows are only on one wall, there is little or no effect. In order for air to enter a room, it must be able to leave. In cross-ventilated spaces the increased size of the openings has an influential effect when both the inlet and the outlet are increased simultaneously. It should be noted that the rate of velocity falls off as the windows get larger. The average indoor velocity has a direct relationship to the size of the smaller opening through the maximum velocity that is achieved by manipulating the relative sizes of the inlet and outlet.

Most apartment and office skyscrapers have only one external wall, with sometimes more than one window. In this case, the ventilation must be induced by other means than that occurring in cross-ventilated rooms. The air velocity inside these rooms is approximately one-third to a quarter what it is in cross-ventilated rooms with the same total area of openings. The rooms with only one external wall must have artificial pressure zones created. This can be done by vertical projections from the wall (eg. fins). Higher indoor velocities occur when the wind is oblique to the window. This can have important design implications in rooms with two windows with vertical projections between them.

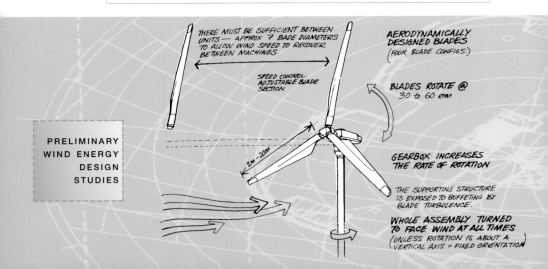

PRELIMINARY
WIND ENERGY
DESIGN
STUDIES

THERE MUST BE SUFFICIENT BETWEEN UNITS — APPROX 7 BLADE DIAMETERS TO ALLOW WIND SPEED TO RECOVER BETWEEN MACHINES.

AERODYNAMICALLY DESIGNED BLADES (FOUR BLADE CONFIGS.)

SPEED CONTROL ADJUSTABLE BLADE SECTION

BLADES ROTATE @ 30 to 60 RPM

2M - 20M

GEARBOX INCREASES THE RATE OF ROTATION

THE SUPPORTING STRUCTURE IS EXPOSED TO BUFFETING BY BLADE TURBULENCE.

WHOLE ASSEMBLY TURNED TO FACE WIND AT ALL TIMES (UNLESS ROTATION IS ABOUT A VERTICAL AXIS = FIXED ORIENTATION)

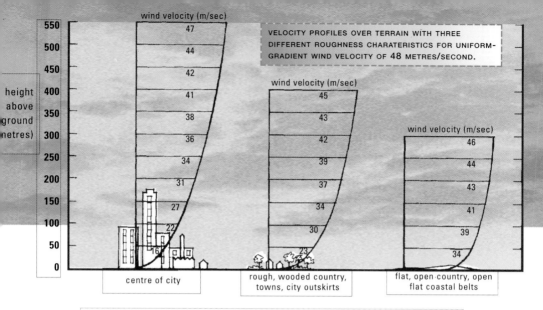

VELOCITY PROFILES OVER TERRAIN WITH THREE DIFFERENT ROUGHNESS CHARATERISTICS FOR UNIFORM-GRADIENT WIND VELOCITY OF 48 METRES/SECOND.

centre of city

rough, wooded country, towns, city outskirts

flat, open country, open flat coastal belts

Artificial high and low pressure zones are created, inducing the air to enter one window in the high pressure area and leave by the low pressure area. If projections are located on both sides of the windows, the entire effect is lost.

Cross-ventilation offers the optimum situation for natural ventilation. Since cooling is the primary reason for using cross-ventilation, the airflow should be directed to the level of human activity rather than towards the ceiling or above the head. The location of the outlet and the type of physical mechanism used in the inlet will determine the airflow pattern. An important design consideration is that, in most cases, the maximum velocities occur in a room when the outlet is larger than the inlet. Maximum airflow occurs when the outlet and inlet are the same size, but for cooling, maximum velocity is more important. The average velocity is a direct function of the total area of the windows. Tests have shown that in terms of orientation, higher indoor velocities occur when the wind is oblique to the inlet window.

139

- PRIMARY SOURCE — **WIND**
  MOVEMENT OF AIR STIMULATED BY HEATING OF THE SURFACE OF THE EARTH BY THE SUN.

- OUTPUT DEPENDS ON:
  AREA SWEPT BY BLADES; CUBE OF WIND SPEED.

- PHYSICAL SIZE:
  BLADES 2M → 20M

- PEAK OUTPUT:
  1 to 600 kW — DEPENDING ON SITE AND SIZE

- ANCILLARY EQUIPMENT:
  SPEED CONTROL THROUGH ADJUSTABLE SECTIONS IN BLADES; MECHANISM TO KEEP BLADES FACING WIND. POWER CONTROL AND CONDITIONING TO MATCH LOAD.
  THE TECHNOLOGY IS FLEXIBLE AND MODULAR — CAN BE APPLIED TO ANY SCALE.

IMPORTANT CONSIDERATION IS THE INTERACTION BETWEEN THE NATURAL VIBRATIONS OF THE STRUCTURE AND THE FREQUENCY OF ROTATION OF THE BLADES.

- NOISE
  NOISE COMES FROM MOTION OF BLADES — MEASURED IN dB(A).

- COSTS
  TO BUILD — £1000 per kW
  TO RUN — 2p per unit (1 kW hour)

- ERECTION
  THE WIND TURBINE IS QUICK TO INSTALL — MEDIUM SIZE TURBINE CAN BE ERECTED IN ONE DAY.

TYPE OF OCCUPANCY USE OF ROOM	SENSIBLE HEAT FOR OCCUPANTS WATTS	MINIMUM AREA OF OCCUPIED FLOOR SPACE PER PERSON SQ M	AREA OF OPENABLE WINDOWS PER PERSON CROSS VENTILATION		
			ONE-SIDED VENTILATION	TWO SETS OF VENTILATION IN SERIES	THREE SETS OF VENTILATION IN SERIES
RESIDENTIAL (APARTMENT & FLATS, CALCULATED ON LIVING AREA)	65	15	10.6 SQ M	0.55 SQ M	0.61 SQ M
BUSINESS (OFFICE, HOTEL SERVICE AREAS, CALCULATED ON USABLE AREA)	75	10	12.2 SQ M	0.64 SQ M	0.71 SQ M

It has been shown that the inlet and outlet do not necessarily have to be located on opposite walls to induce airflow. Airflow pattern is directly determined by the design of the inlet and the horizontal location of the outlet. The inlet can act as a nozzle, directing up and down and determining the maximum cooling effect. Ceiling height does not directly affect the airflow pattern. If the ceiling is slanted, warm air rising can flow along the ceiling to an outlet which will draw in fresh air through an inlet, though this effect of thermal ventilation is not powerful enough to offer comfort during the warmer months. The depth of the room also has little effect as long as airflow can occur between inlet and outlet.

In a design where a double-loaded corridor exists, the corridor may act as a plenum. The outlets can open onto it. If the corridor supplies air, sufficient obstructions must exist to distribute the air though not inhibit its flow.

The 'venturi effect' (see page 131) has both advantages and disadvantages. In rectangular rooms that are oriented so that the inlet and outlet are opposite each other on the smaller wall surfaces, the direct airflow will fill the entire room. In rooms that are square or where the inlet and outlet windows are on the larger wall surfaces then the effect will only cool the area located between the windows and do little for the surrounding surface area.

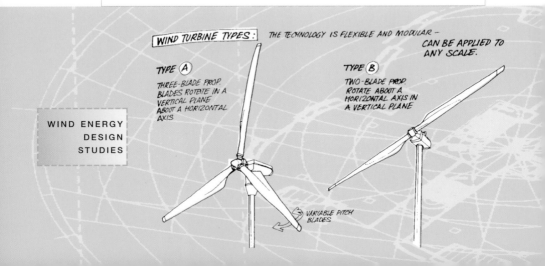

WIND ENERGY DESIGN STUDIES

WIND TURBINE TYPES: THE TECHNOLOGY IS FLEXIBLE AND MODULAR – CAN BE APPLIED TO ANY SCALE.

TYPE (A)
THREE-BLADE PROP. BLADES ROTATE IN A VERTICAL PLANE ABOUT A HORIZONTAL AXIS

TYPE (B)
TWO-BLADE PROP. ROTATE ABOUT A HORIZONTAL AXIS IN A VERTICAL PLANE

VARIABLE PITCH BLADES

TYPE OF OCCUPANCY AND USE OF ROOM	SENSIBLE HEAT FOR OCCUPANTS WATTS	MINIMUM AREA OF OCCUPIED FLOOR SPACE PER PERSON SQ M	* AREA OF OPENABLE WINDOWS PER PERSON CROSS VENTILATION		
			ONE-SIDED VENTILATION	TWO SETS OF VENTILATION IN SERIES	THREE SETS OF VENTILATION IN SERIES
SCHOOL CLASSROOMS	65	1.5	10.6 SQ M	0.55 SQ M	0.61 SQ M
HOTEL BEDROOMS DORMITORIES AND SELF-CONTAINED SINGLE ROOM FLATS (CALCULATED ON LIVING AREA)	65	3	10.6 SQ M	0.55 SQ M	0.61 SQ M

* area of openable windows is calculated on the assumption that window sashes cause little friction to airflow with the external wind speed of 0.4 m/s and an indoor temperature of 0.5°C rise

The rate of airflow can be determined from the equations given below:

Q = KAV (WHEN CROSS-VENTILATION IS USED)

Q = RATE OF AIRFLOW, M^3/HR.

A = AREA OF INLETS, SQ M.

V = WIND VELOCITY, MPH

K = A VALUE DEPENDENT UPON THE OUTLET TO INLET RELATIONSHIP

$\dfrac{\text{AREA OF OUTLET}}{\text{AREA OF INLET}}$	K
1:1	3150
2:1	4000
3:1	4250
4:1	4350
5:1	4400
3:4	2700
1:2	2000
1:4	1100

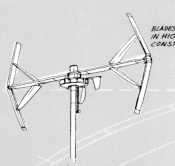

TYPE Ⓒ TERMED 'DARRIEUS' BLADES IN FORM OF 'H' ROTATE ABOUT A VERTICAL AXIS IN A HORIZONTAL PLANE. PROP. ATTACHED AT CENTRE OF CROSSPIECE.

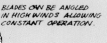

BLADES CAN BE ANGLED IN HIGH WINDS ALLOWING CONSTANT OPERATION.

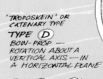

HIGH POWER COEFFICIENT

'TROPOSKEIN' OR CATENARY TYPE
TYPE Ⓓ
BOW-PROP — ROTATION ABOUT A VERTICAL AXIS — IN A HORIZONTAL PLANE.

TYPE Ⓒ and Ⓓ'S OMNI-DIRECTIONAL FEATURE AVOIDS THE NEED FOR YAW CONTROL AND INCREASES ENERGY CAPTURE. THE GEARBOX AND GENERATOR CAN BE POSITIONED NEARER THE GROUND. THE ONCE PER REV. REVERSING GRAVITY LOADS ON BLADES, WHICH ARE A FEATURE OF HORIZONTAL AXIS TYPES, ARE AVOIDED WITH EXTENDED FATIGUE LIFE.

• THE BEST SIZE OF MACHINE TO USE IS NOT YET CLEAR

• THE LARGER THE MACHINE — THE GREATER THE NOISE AND VIBRATION.

$Q = KA\sqrt{H(T_I-T_0)}$ (WHEN VENTILATION IS BY THERMAL DIFFERENTIATION)[14]

Q = RATE OF AIRFLOW, M^3/HR

A = AREA OF INLETS, SQ M

H = HEIGHT BETWEEN INLETS AND OUTLETS, METRE

T_I = AVERAGE TEMPERATURE OF INDOOR AIR AT HEIGHT H, °C

T_0 = TEMPERATURE OF INDOOR AIR, °C

AREA OF OUTLET / AREA OF INLET	K
5	745
4	740
3	720
2	680
1	540
3/4	455
1/2	340
1/4	185

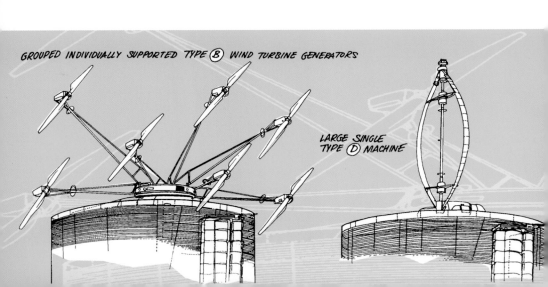

GROUPED INDIVIDUALLY SUPPORTED TYPE Ⓑ WIND TURBINE GENERATORS

LARGE SINGLE TYPE Ⓓ MACHINE

EFFECT OF WINDOW SIZE IN ROOM WITH CROSS-VENTILATION ON AVERAGE AIR VELOCITIES (% of external wind velocity) (Source: B Givoni, *Man, Climate and Architecture*, Van Nostrand, NY, 1974)						

INLET WIDTH	OUTLET WIDTH	WINDOWS IN OPPOSITE WALLS		WINDOWS IN ADJACENT WALLS	
		WIND PERPEND	WIND OBLIQUE	WIND PERPEND	WIND OBLIQUE
1:3	1:3	35	42	45	37
1:3	2:3	39	40	39	40
2:3	1:3	34	43	51	36
2:3	2:3	37	51		
1:3	3:3	44	44	51	45
3:3	1:3	32	41	50	37
2:3	3:3	35	59		
3:3	2:3	36	62		

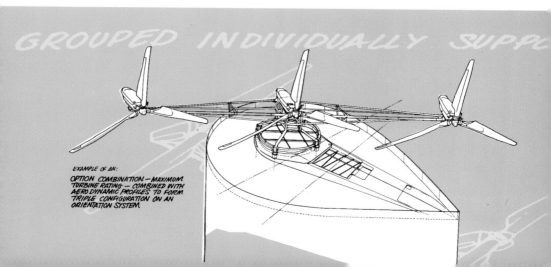

GROUPED INDIVIDUALLY SUPP

EXAMPLE OF AN:

OPTION COMBINATION — MAXIMUM TURBINE RATING — COMBINED WITH AERO DYNAMIC PROFILES TO FORM TRIPLE CONFIGURATION ON AN ORIENTATION SYSTEM.

EFFECT OF WINDOW LOCATION AND WIND DIRECTION ON AVERAGE AIR VELOCITIES (% of external velocity)			
DIRECTION OF WIND	WIDTH OF WINDOW		
	1/3	2/3	3/3
PERPENDICULAR TO WINDOW	13	13	16
OBLIQUE IN FRONT	12	15	23
OBLIQUE FROM REAR	14	17	17

Summary

- Depth of the room has little effect.
- Ceiling height has little effect.
- Vertical projections can induce ventilation when properly placed between two windows on the same external wall.
- When windows are located on adjacent walls an inlet perpendicular to the prevailing wind is best.
- When the inlet and outlet are directly opposite each other, having the inlet oblique to the prevailing wind gives a more distributed effect.
- Maximum velocity occurs when the outlet is larger than the inlet.
- The inlet and the horizontal placement of the outlet determines the air-flow pattern.

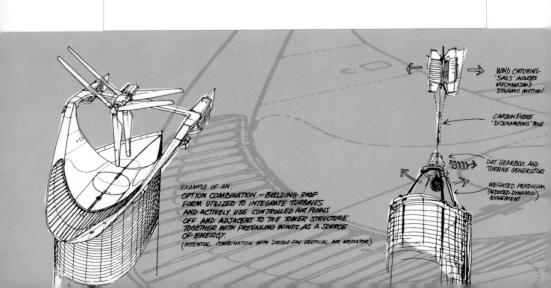

EXAMPLE OF AN:
OPTION COMBINATION – BUILDING ROOF FORM UTILIZED TO INTEGRATE TURBINES AND ACTIVELY USE CONTROLLED AIR FLOWS OFF AND ADJACENT TO THE TOWER STRUCTURE TOGETHER WITH PREVAILING WINDS AS A SOURCE OF ENERGY.
(POTENTIAL COMBINATION WITH DOUBLE-FIN VERTICAL AIR MEDIATOR)

WIND CATCHING 'SAILS' INDUCES MECHANISMS DYNAMIC MOTION.

CARBON FIBRE 'DISCHARGING' POLE

DAT. GEARBOX AND TURBINE GENERATOR

WEIGHTED PENDULUM (INDUCED DYNAMIC MOVEMENT)

NOTE:
ALL SKETCHES
SHOW
WINDOW AS
SEEN FROM
OUTSIDE

single-hung

double-hung

horizontal sliding

SIMPLE OPENING

window location and type

The vertical location and type of inlet is more critical to control than the respective characteristics of the outlet. The vertical location of the inlet has only a slight effect on the airflow pattern, if any. The vertical location of the inlet can control both the velocity and direction of the airflow. There is a drastic reduction in wind speed when the inlet is located below the average windowsill level. When the inlet is located this low it can reduce the velocity by as much as 25% in comparison to the mainstream velocity in a cross-ventilation situation. The overall average velocity is only affected slightly. As air strikes a vertical wall, a force component is formed that tends to move parallel to the surface. When an opening is located in the wall, the amount of air entering that opening is dependent upon the pressure inside, the force component which varies with the surface area, and the design of the inlet.

145

As a result of this force component, the openings in the upper storey of the skyscraper generate completely different results to those in the first few storeys. The force component tends to flow up, or at times down, the faces of the skyscraper. If the room has a window with an adjustable sash, the amount and direction of air can be regulated. This force component is an important consideration when designing overhangs or balconies for rooms also requiring natural ventilation.

NOTE:
ALL SKETCHES
SHOW
WINDOW AS
SEEN FROM
OUTSIDE

casement

folding

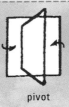
pivot

VERTICAL-VANE OPENING

146

In skyscrapers, the force components split up so that part flows down the face and part flows upward. Balconies and sun-hoods over the inlet window directly affect the ventilation. Overhangs located well above the inlet tend to strengthen the downward force component giving a favourable direction to the incoming air when wind is perpendicular. A sun shade with no slots tends to allow the upward component (even though it is small due to the limited surface area below the opening) to determine the direction of the entering airflow. When the sun-shade or sun-hood has a sizeable gap between it and the building surface, the downward component is allowed to influence the direction of the airflow.

In some cases, when there are too many balconies or extended horizontal sun-hoods, the force component breaks up before actually striking the surface of the inlets (when the wind is perpendicular), and the wind simply goes over the building. If the surface with all the balconies is oriented oblique to the wind, it is possible that the wind will be channelled underneath them, only to be caught by casement-type windows. This is only theory, and a great deal of research is still necessary.

Different types of inlet windows produce different airflow patterns and affect the distribution of various velocities throughout the space. Strip windows, for instance, were found to give a more even distribution of airflow throughout a space than single 'punched in' type windows. Of course, even the strip windows require the proper kind of sash to direct the flow into the living zone. A study of various window types was carried out by Thoe R Holleman at the Texas Engineering Experiment Station in 1951. The wind patterns were traced with smoke but no velocity recordings were made. The results of the test on the double-hung type of window indicated that the airflow came in on a horizontal level in each case studied: one sash open, both top and bottom open maximum, and both open minimum. These results suggest that this type of window has to be located at the level at which the effect is desired.

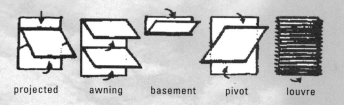

projected   awning   basement   pivot   louvre

HORIZONTAL-VANE OPENING

With horizontal sliding windows, the same effect occurred with the incoming air travelling at a horizontal level under all conditions. Thus this type of window should also be located at the height where the airflow is desired. In the vertical-vane opening windows tested (casement, folding, vertical pivot) the air could be adjusted to flow right or left though its vertical flow could not be adjusted, other than by locating the opening at the height where the air was desired. When the projected sash window was tested, it was found that the air was directed at a horizontal level when the sash was fully opened and directed upward when the sash was anything less than fully opened. The jalousie type produced a laminar effect as it flowed through the opening. Any upward (and any downward) angle could be adjusted to a maximum of 20°.

The awning and horizontal pivot type windows gave a horizontal direction to the airflow when opened all the way, and an upward angle to any opening less than full. The basement window directed the air only upward. It appears that all the horizontal-vane opening windows (except possibly the jalousie type) need to be located below the level where the air is desired. With so few types of windows able to satisfy the needs of natural ventilation, it is clear that window design is an area that needs much consideration and work.

The results indicate that to obtain desirable comfort conditions from natural ventilation the following are necessary:

- to have a movable sash which can adjust the breeze downward
- to slot sun-hoods properly into the plane of the building's external wall and permit downward forced air to flow into the space
- not to locate the inlets below average window sill level

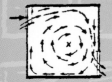  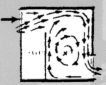 

division of interior space

Whenever an incoming airflow is forced to change direction within a space, the energy inherent in the inertia of the flow is appreciably depleted. This occurs when the width of a building is greater than the depth of its rooms. It is necessary that each room be ventilated with respect to the other rooms. With the proper location of interior partitions, a greater area of space can be naturally ventilated with only a moderate reduction in velocity. The larger the internal opening between spaces, the less the reduction in velocity. It should also be noted that the closer the internal partition is to the outlet, the more satisfactory the ventilation will be. It is preferable for the upwind room to be larger. Furniture, equipment and shades or curtains can affect the airflow. It should be remembered that the main airstream can often be eight times as powerful as the cartwheeling eddies.

148

influence of landscape

The height, width and density of landscape elements can influence the air movement within a structure. Studies done at the Texas Engineering Experimental Station by Robert F White indicated that the foliage mass of a tree serves as a direct block to the passage of air and that the air velocity underneath a tree is measurably increased with respect to surrounding flow velocities. Planting was found to change the direction of airflow entering the building. Shrubs tend to give airflow a diminishing downward appearance and an eddy is created behind the shrub. Also illustrated was the effect of a tree (10 m high, with an 8 m spread starting 2 m from the ground), on the airflow pattern, and how a tree hedge combination causes a reversed airflow within the structure.

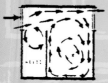   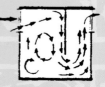

summary of
site planning considerations

Streamlines of air are pushed above the level of building tops causing eddies behind the building, relative to its size and height. Any building located in an eddy is dependent upon its velocity, which is generally very low. Airflow along streets is an important consideration. Where thermal convection from the air layer closest to the building surface is to be used for natural ventilation, the amount of solar radiation on the surface is important (to heat up the air so it will rise). Surrounding buildings may shade these surfaces if orientation is not carefully considered. Care should be taken to analyse the wind patterns of the surroundings either by building a model and testing with smoke tracings in a wind chamber or on site with anemometer readings. Accurate predictions on the effects of airflow on and created by the new structure can then be made. A new structure should be built with consideration for the other elements of both the natural and built environment.

wind
generators

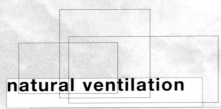

natural ventilation

- A building's ventilation has a direct effect on the human body through air purity and temperature control.

- Ventilation serves three functions: to maintain the air quality (health ventilation); to increase thermal comfort by aiding heat conduction from the body (thermal comfort ventilation); and to cool the indoor surface temperature (structural cooling ventilation).

- Airflow through a building is dependent upon the forces of wind pressure creating high and low zones; when openings are placed in each of the two areas, airflow is induced.

- It is possible to induce airflow in rooms with openings only on the windward side by creating artificial pressure zones through vertical projections.

- Airflow patterns are the result of inlet location and design, and external building elements.

- More than one space within a room may be ventilated with the smaller space closer to the outlet.

- Landscape can alter or aid airflow through a building.

It has been shown that the use of natural ventilation in the bioclimatic skyscraper can contribute significantly to energy savings, to 'humaneness' of design, and to a 'healthy building'. However, it is important to establish from the start to what extent natural ventilation is required and for what design objectives.

As already discussed, these design objectives might seek to address: health (ie. through provision of the required level of air-changes and fresh air intake); energy conservation (eg. structural cooling); or comfort (eg. reduction of humidity through cooling breezes). Natural ventilation for structural cooling purposes does not constitute a 'naturally ventilated building'.

For the skyscraper, the service-core and elevator shafts are important not only for structural reasons and their role as buffers for heat and climatic variation, but also as potential locations for natural ventilation orifices. During design, the determination of their location on the plan might also be assisted by the wind-rose of the locality. This depends upon the design objective.

The designer may need to adopt separate natural ventilation systems for the public areas (ie. the elevator lobbies, staircases and toilet areas) and the private areas (ie. the net useable floor areas).

'...too dangerous they say, but when one night our champagne glasses were swept off the tables by a gust of wind and dashed against the swimming pool on the tenth floor, it seemed only to add to our happiness – we need to be in the elements.' PROFESSOR LEON VAN SCHAIK

In addition to this, it is important to remember that wind performs exponentially differently as the height of the building increases. The designer may need to develop further separate systems for different levels of the building to cope with the variations both vertically and across the different faces of the skyscraper. One approach is to divide the building into separate design zones (say three zones or more). This is best done after a wind-tunnel test has made the distribution of wind pressures on the building surfaces apparent. This is also the strategy adopted by the glazing and curtain-wall designers to determine the glass thicknesses and structural-stiffenings required for the cladding design. It is evident that a composite set of natural ventilation systems is needed for different parts and heights of the bioclimatic skyscraper.

Reliable wind-rose information for the locality (over the entire year) is essential to ascertain the shaping of the floor-plan; to determine floor depths, points of entry and dispersal for natural ventilation; and to design vent openings and directional fins to create artificial pressure zones at points of entry (if required). The design of vents at the point of incoming air depends on whether the natural ventilation is 'general' or simply 'supplementary' (eg. useful in the event of heating and/or air-conditioning shut-down, etc), or on any of the design objectives stated earlier.

chapter six

external wall + cladding

'the skin of the skyscraper is its interface with the world ...light, shade and air: it is necessary to admit or reject all in differing amounts at different times. The intelligent skin, sensing the internal needs of the skyscraper, can control all these and provide a source of power as well. Beauty is the bonus.'

TONY FITZPATRICK
OVE ARUP & PARTNERS

- solar buffer
- solar gain
- wind break
- cross-ventilation
- views

the external wall
of the
bioclimatic skyscraper

Cladding is the external wall or fabric-covering which wraps the building. It is of primary importance in the bioclimatic skyscraper where it acts as an enclosing filter between the building's interior and exterior.

The role of cladding is a complex one and the following objectives need to be considered in its design:

- energy efficiency (ie. the building's skin should contribute to the reduction in energy consumption)
- provision of central daylight to reduce direct and reflected glare
- minimisation of water penetration and condensation
- provision of a choice of colours, textures and finishes
- compatibility with automated window-cleaning equipment
- ability to accommodate building movement
- minimisation of loading on the structural frame
- minimisation of maintenance requirements

Depending on the climatic zone, the design considerations for these components in the bioclimatic skyscraper include solar-insulation and reduction (eg. through shading devices in the cladding), solar glare reduction, rainwater collection or discharge, wind and natural ventilation, orientation and buffering, view, and relationship with the ground plane at different heights.

154

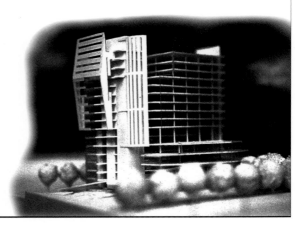

SJCC

(Subang Jaya

City Centre)

Block A,

Petaling Jaya,

Latitude 3.1°N

variable facade
cladding system

Passive solar architecture is a consequence of applying passive solar design principles. These include the effective management of solar radiation at the facade and natural heating/cooling sources which influence the building envelope (ie. cladding system) to minimise internal heating, cooling and daylight energy requirements for the occupants' comfort. This is possible through strategies such as: appropriate orientation; managing direct heat gain and daylighting (window and shading); managing indirect heat gains (thermal control in opaque systems); ventilation; thermal mass as heat-sink or source; and other more novel techniques for manipulating indoor comfort.

The bioclimatic building might be regarded as being 'materials led'. The designer has to be careful in the choice and placement of materials from the window and shadings to thermal mass, insulation and openings for ventilation. The 'fifth facade' – or roof – should also have thermal controls (thermal insulation) for thermal comfort as well as prevention of unnecessary heat gain/loss.

155

The skyscraper's envelope provides the potential for energy savings through the manipulation of the solar control and thermal elements:

SOLAR CONTROL	THERMAL CONTROL
• window-to-wall ratio (WWR)	• insulation in walls
• window properties	• multiple glazing
• shading systems	

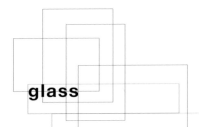

glass

The most basic form that glass takes within the construction industry is that of the 'window', an element described as a section of an envelope that is transparent through which light and/or air can be admitted.

To follow the history of architecture is to trace the development of the window. It is directly related to climate, to technology, and to a natural desire to experience light and air. Just as the trees of the forests stretch out their branches, jostling for their share of sunlight and fresh air, so we turn our faces to catch the last of the sun's rays. In our burgeoning metropolises, our concrete jungles, this yearning is no less apparent. Imagine the city without light, the building without windows.

Such has been the window's evolution that architects no longer perceive it as a mere opening but design in terms of totally glazed enclosures, a system now more commonly recognised as curtain-walling (or glazing that is not structurally load-bearing).

The window has emerged as an envelope (even encasing entire structures) that is highly engineered, taking into account energy considerations, environmental forces and protection from the climate in its design.

The need to provide an external envelope to protect man from the elements was first answered by the primitive hut which utilised natural materials. As buildings developed, glass was gradually introduced and with the dawn of the Industrial Revolution and the evolution of mass-produced iron and glass, the use of the window became widespread. As technology became more advanced a distinction began to be made between the exterior enclosure and the main building structure: this finally emerged as the curatain wall in the 1950s.

SJCC

Block A

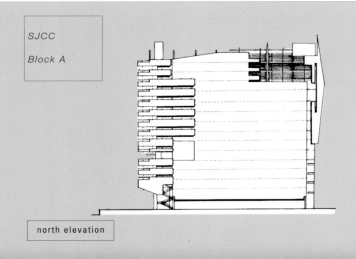

north elevation

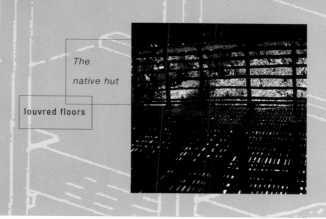

Until this period, buildings had remained fairly low-rise, reaching twenty storeys or so. However, the advent of lightweight 'sheath' glazing systems enabled architects to build super-tall skyscrapers of fifty to eighty storeys or more. As the external wall was no longer required to support the floor loads, the main structure could reach unprecedented heights whilst the secondary glazing support system (or skin) was merely required to provide the user with panoramic views, natural light and opportunities for natural ventilation. This had previously been unimaginable with load-bearing masonry structures. Thus glass has been an important component in the evolution of the modern high-rise building.

In the twentieth century architects explored new building types, materials and methods of design. The accelerated rate with which they did so resulted in a misunderstanding of material applications and led to a lack of design competence causing the inevitable failure of building envelopes. It is the problem of the appropriate application of materials and technology that still confronts architects today.

The designer must not only examine types of glass, he must also select the type of system and its framing materials, seals and gaskets, and specify the criteria for water penetration, air leakage, thermal movement, fire protection, and thermal, light and sound transmission. He must analyse the abilities of the materials to resist deterioration, caused in particular by high temperatures, humidity and elements such as acid rain or pollution in cities.

157

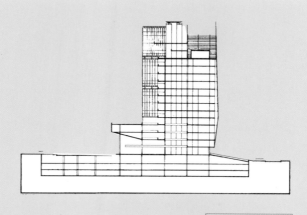

section A-A

SUEP
(Taipan
Crest)
Kuala Lumpur
Latitude 3.2°N

wall sunshading

Pan Global
Tower,
Johore Baru,
Latitude
1.27N

This amounts to a somewhat daunting task on the face of things, with even the selection of glass based on several considerations, not just the aesthetic. Glazing design must take into account the type and thickness of the glass in order to meet wind-load requirements, resist potential dangers (such as breakage of the glass under impact or from rapid temperature changes), and minimise solar heat gain and cost.

external wall glazing systems: unitised, semi-unitised and stick

158

External wall systems may either completely envelope the main structural body of the building, referred to as a *sheath-wall,* or may be contained within the structure by beams and/or columns, known as a *panel-wall.*

The panel-wall, or infill system, is identified mainly by the exposure of the structure and this provides the main disadvantage over the sheath system in selection. The different way in

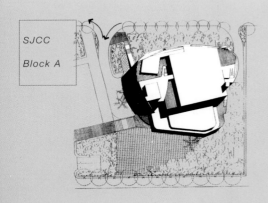

SJCC
Block A

roof plan

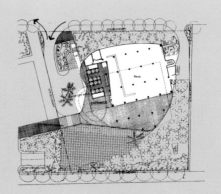

level 1 (ground)

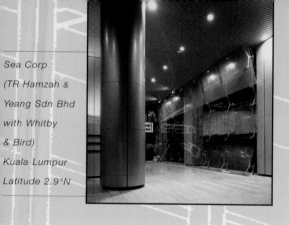

Sea Corp

(TR Hamzah &

Yeang Sdn Bhd

with Whitby

& Bird)

Kuala Lumpur

Latitude 2.9°N

lobby
structural glass

cast-iron
brackets

which the structure and the glass react to changes in climate is problematic and great care must be taken in the design and construction of the exposed elements to prevent deterioration of the system.

Assembly procedures further classify the external wall systems into three basic types.

The oldest method of assembly is the *stick system*. Usually the mullions and transoms (vertical and horizontal supports) are delivered to the site as loose elements. The mullions are installed first followed by the transoms and then the glazing elements. The main advantage of this system is its degree of on-site dimensional adjustment, allowing for varying degrees of tolerance in the main structure. Aesthetically, the general appearance externally is one of a grid-like framework.

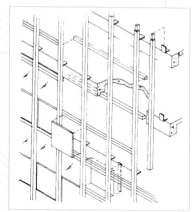

stick system

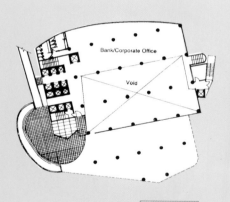

level 2

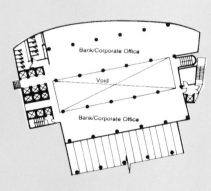

level 4

louvred walls in traditional building

The *unitised system* is popular for a number of reasons, primarily because a panel is pre-assembled and pre-glazed in the factory prior to its delivery to the site. This permits tighter quality control minimising on-site problems with sealants. This system also has the added advantage of reduced construction time on-site as the erection process is sequential, floor by floor, which means that floors can be fully sealed and protected from the elements for other trades to begin work. The aesthetic advantage over the stick system is the possiblity of producing a four-sided structurally-glazed unit. This enables the envelope to appear 'frameless' as the glass is held in place by structural silicone on all four sides, the framing being internal. The stick system can only accommodate a two-sided structurally-glazed system so either the horizontal transoms or the vertical mullions can be seen externally.

The *semi-unitised system* is a composite of the stick and unitised. The mullions and transoms are delivered to the site in a loose form as in the stick system, but the glass is pre-glazed in the factory into aluminium frames and on delivery is fixed to framework which is already erected. Thus the erection time is longer and the system still carries quality control problems, though not as many as the stick system.

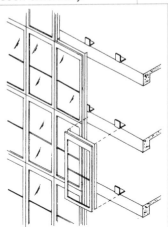

unitised system

SJCC Block A

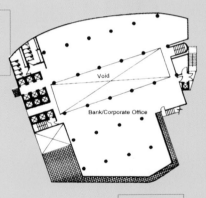

Void

Bank/Corporate Office

level 5

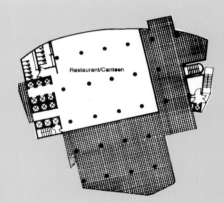

Restaurant/Canteen

level 6

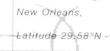

New Orleans,

Latitude 29.58°N

jalousies in

traditional

architecture

glass selection

The selection of a form and external wall system significantly determines the overall character of the building. The envelope can be an intricate combination of exposed elements or a sheer wall appearing to cling to the main structure. Either way, the selection of the most appropriate cladding material will affect not only the hue and tone of the facade but also its performance.

A wide variety of glass types is available for the designer, offering many colours, finishes and thicknesses. However, each option carries drawbacks, and various design criteria have to be considered before selection.

Glass can be categorised into two main classes – *float* and *safety* – within which there are subdivisions including: *heat-strengthened glass, tempered glass, tinted float glass, laminated glass* and *reflective glass*. However, there are also many forms of decorative glass available, though these are often limited to interior applications.

Annealed float glass is a low distortion transparent glass manufactured by floating a ribbon of molten glass over a bath of molten metal. The ribbon is gradually cooled in an annealing layer then washed, dried and cut. Due to its flatness and smooth surface its quality of either clear transmitted or reflected images is high, with approximate maximum sizes of 10m in length, 3m in width and up to 19mm in thickness. Its clarity enables diverse uses including general window construction for houses, shops and office buildings, glass screens, display windows and picture frames.

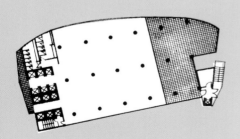

level 13

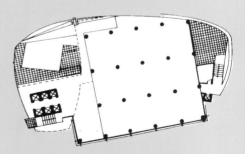

level 14 (penthouse 1)

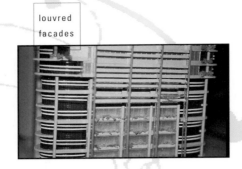

louvred glasses

louvred facades

blinds

sun-shading at the insides of the building

However, this same clarity becomes a disadvantage in a high-rise scenario when further design parameters are applied. Criteria such as light transmittance, wind-loading, and thermal stress and transmittance need to be considered before selection. The high level of light transmittance of float glass is equalled by its low thermal performance. This can be moderated by tinting the float glass. Tinted glass or heat absorbing glass is coloured by the addition of small amounts of iron, nickel or cobalt, resulting in either blue, green, grey or bronze. Not only does this colouration offer more individuality to building facade and a greater degree of privacy to the user, it also absorbs some of the heat from the sun whilst still permitting a high level of light penetration and minimising excess glare.

162

Thermal transmittance is measured by the shading coefficient of the glass combined with its U-value. All manufacturers of glass provide shading coefficient figures to enable the designer to make the correct or the most appropriate selection for the building. Effectively, the darker the tint of the glass, the lower the shading coefficient as less heat is transmitted through the pane, therefore giving a lower temperature internally on average. Shading coefficients should be selected in collaboration with the mechanical and electrical engineer to determine the design of the cooling systems. As more sunlight is allowed into the building the requirements for cooling capacity increase to maintain human comfort parameters which will become costly due to increased energy consumption in the overall running of the building.

SJCC

Block A

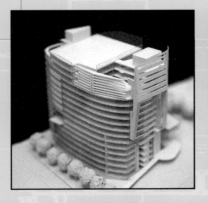

BMTR #5
Beijing,
China
Latitude
39.55°N

study
model

Although tinted float glass moderates solar heat gain, its shading coefficients are high in comparison with heat reflective glass. Heat reflective glass is achieved by plating metal oxide onto the surface of float glass. By plating the metal oxide onto heat-absorbing or tinted glass, the combined properties improve energy-saving efficiency. Certain tinted glass panels allow up to 70% of the sunlight to penetrate the interior, although tinted reflective glass is able to reduce this amount to 30%. In some instances from 10 to 40% of the sunlight can be reflected back into the environment and heat is absorbed (by heating the glass). The remaining amount of reflectivity has become a major cause for concern as the built environment has become more dense. Some building authorities have placed restrictions on the percentage of reflectance permissible to minimise heat build-up in surrounding buildings and to reduce the dangers of blinding passing motorists. Typically 25% reflectance is preferred.

The selection of heat-absorbing glass and heat-reflective glass to meet thermal and light transmission parameters in design may result in a moderately effective solution to these criteria, but may also result in complete failure in others. In climates where solar heat gain is severe, thermal stress properties on glass are a parallel consideration. Heat sources, particularly the sun, can create differences in temperature between the centre and edges of the glass.

163

heat-absorbent and heat-reflective

The difficulty with heat-absorbent glass is that it retards the initial transmission of solar radiation to the interior. However, solar heat is built up in the glass pane and is eventually re-radiated into the interior. Double-glazing does little to the transmission of radiation if the internal glass is clear glass, and the re-radiation is within the spectrum of clear-glass transmission.

Heat-reflective glass, either coated or laminated by means of adhesive film, is more effective to reflect solar radiation away from buildings. However, reflected solar heat may cause 'heat pollution' of neighbouring buildings as they receive the reflected solar radiation.

Another problem with reflective glass is glare. There is concern that motorists may be affected by the glare. In some cases, even though the image of the sun is not directly in the zone of vision, veiling or luminescence may occur and the contrast between the 'task' and the 'background' is reduced. The phenomenon may impair motorists' vision.

164

recessed panels

Glass panels that are either set back or partially covered by balconies, awnings or solar screens so that portions of the panel are in shade are subject to thermal shock or stress. As the area of the glass in shade resists the expansion of that in direct sunlight, tensile stress occurs around the edges of the glass with the potential to cause thermal cracks. Likewise, glass that is placed as a spandrel panel must be strong enough to resist the heat load of the spandrel cavity. Therefore, a toughened glass such as tempered, heat-strengthened or laminated glass has a higher performance level than tinted or reflective float glass.

heat-strengthened glass

Heat-strengthened glass is manufactured by heating annealed glass nearly to its softening point then cooling it faster than the normal rate to place the outer surfaces and edges in compression, and the interior in tension. It has approximately twice the strength of annealed glass and should be specified where thermal stresses are high. (Annealed glass is manufactured by heating and cooling gradually, it shatters into sharp fragments when broken.)

tempered glass

Tempered glass, manufactured in the same way but cooled with air more rapidly than heat-strengthened glass, has three to five times the bending and impact strength of annealed glass, and approximately three times the resistance to rapid temperature changes. However, when selecting tempered glass where increased glass strengths are required for the spandrel and vision areas of the skyscraper, it is advisable to specify that the glass is heat-soaked before erection. Fully tempered glass composition often includes small quantities of allowable imperfections which may cause spontaneous breakage. Tempered float glass is classified as a 'safety glass'.

165

Due to the small blunt particles tempered glass shatters into when broken under severe impact, it is less hazardous than the large knife-like shards resulting from most other glass panel breakage. It is ideal in areas where human impact is a concern, including elements such as glass balustrading, shop fronts, escalator side panels, and frameless glass screens. In a high-rise envelope when spontaneous breakage occurs, the glass will not usually remain in its frame. This becomes a hazard to anyone or anything at ground level. Heat soaking, however, causes the imperfect glass to spontaneously break under a controlled situation thereby minimising the risks to human life. If heat strengthened glass should break, the pieces will be large and tend to remain in the frame but it is not a safety glass.

Heat-strengthened or tempered glass, combined with tinted and reflective glass, produces high levels of performance for thermal stress, and thermal and light transmission. Careful evaluations must also be made of the risk of human injury, especially in a highly dense urban environment.

louvred –
edge to
floor edge

Jakarta Airport,

Jakarta

Latitude 6.10°S

louvred wall

laminated glass

Laminated glass is perhaps the most effective of all available glass types in meeting the requirements of these criteria. It is formed by applying heat and pressure to seal in a transparent or coloured adhesive polyvinyl butyl film between two or more sheets of glass. When laminating two pieces of float glass together the impact resistance is equal to that of float glass. But should the glass break the adhesive interlayer holds all the glass in place providing optimum safety whilst maintaining many of the parameters of good external wall design: withstanding the elements, preventing access by intruders or vermin, and preventing injury to occupants.

166

laminated tempered glass

Laminated tempered glass has such strength that its applications include bullet-proof glazing, large aquariums and swimming pools. Additionally, the polymer-based interlayer can be supplied in any colour desired; by overlaying interlayers the possibilities are infinite. The interlayer's inherent damping properties are effective in controlling sound transmission and reducing heat transmission and excess glare whilst still permitting light transmission, effectively filtering harmful ultraviolet rays. However, considerable care must be taken in the manufacture and installation of a laminated panel. Continued moisture penetration resulting from damaged or incomplete perimeter edge treatment can cause delamination of the panel and the interlayer to turn white.

wind-load and testing

In selecting any glass type, wind-load pressures on the external envelope must be evaluated. The resistance of glass to wind pressure varies depending on the nature of the pressure, the environment at the time of exertion, the type, size and thickness of the glass proposed, and the type of supporting system selected.

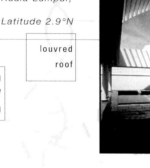

Roof-Roof House,

Kuala Lumpur,

Latitude 2.9°N

louvred
roof

louvred clothing
by Sonny San/
Cilla Foong

The cladding or the exterior surface of any building must resist thousands of cycles of wind-loading everyday. During storms, it is buffeted by gusts from various directions, and over a long period of time the skyscraper's structure and the external cladding must continue to withstand these forces without losing strength or weather-resisting qualities.

We have already seen how the wind, as it strikes the skyscraper, is affected by the climatic conditions of the geographical area, the surrounding terrain, and the effects of other buildings adjacent to the site (see Chapter 5).

Wind-loadings can be analysed as statistical variations, which will include events that can be expected over a period of time. This means the design wind load on the facade of the skyscraper must anticipate a statistical recurrence of an event over a fifty- or one hundred-year period, which may represent the life of the building. The likelihood of a wind or storm occurring can be interpreted from recorded meteorological data of the local area. By assuming a fifty- or one hundred-year recurring interval of peak statistical wind loads, one can expect a reasonable design factor.

In determining the appropriate design, wind pressures should be tested by an approved wind tunnel testing laboratory by means of a test model incorporating all existing and proposed surrounding buildings to ensure against adverse effects.

It is not enough to rely solely on wind speed data supplied by the meteorological department. Data supplied is indicative of the basic wind speed for any given area but does not take into consideration the effects of surrounding buildings, detail design, or the height of the proposed building. By carrying out the boundary layer wind tunnel test at the early stages of design the interaction of wind and the external envelope can be determined.

167

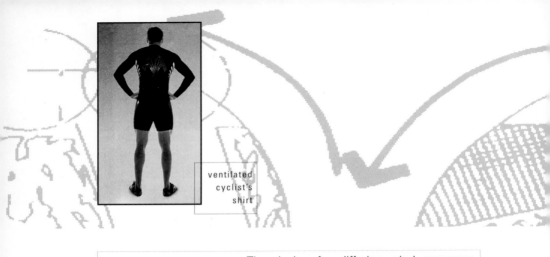

The design for differing wind pressures across the building facade may allow for a certain thickness of float glass for large areas of the system, but may require fully tempered or heat strengthened glass for localised 'hot spot' areas. Combining different glass types and thicknesses is generally aesthetically unacceptable. It is important to incorporate data determined in the wind tunnel testing to ensure the appropriate resistance to peak positive wind pressures and peak negative wind pressures of the selected glass. If the selected glass is unable to resist negative wind pressures, which generally occur at corners and edges of the building, the panels will be forced out of the frame system, endangering the occupants and people below.

Pre-construction testing of a mock-up sample area of the facade will inevitably highlight any weaknesses in the selection and design of any system. This form of testing, preferably performed on a mock-up of the actual building, will also determine whether systems are able to meet the specified performance levels. The most frequently tested performance characteristics are:

- Resistance to air infiltration/exfiltration
- Resistance to water penetration (static air pressure difference)
- Resistance to water penetration
  (cyclic static air pressure difference)
- Structural performance (deflection) (static air pressure difference)
- Structural performance (deflection)
  (cyclic static air pressure difference)
- Field test of water penetration
  (uniform or cyclic static air pressure difference)

Successful testing at this stage will achieve longer lifespan, higher performance levels, and cost savings. Once the system is erected repair can be extremely difficult and very expensive. The architect should ensure that the framing system and cladding material selected undergo adequate testing, that they have a quality specification with good design and detailing achieved with the help of specialist facade consultants, and that they are guaranteed by the facade contractor against performance failure.

The selection of the most applicable system and material for a building envelope can only be achieved by analysing the design criteria – environmental, aesthetic, construction, regulation and cost implications – in the early stages of the design. The failure of a facade will be directly related to the lack of consideration of one or more of these criteria.

It is therefore important to ensure that the selected envelope meets the building codes, incorporating fire regulations and wind-load requirements, and that it remains structurally stable under conditions such as wind and earthquake, and meets budget constraints. The only way to reduce costs after initial selection is to reduce the quality or change the intended appearance which may disappoint aesthetically.

169

the future of glass
and glazed systems

Fundamentally, a building enclosure is still required to perform in the same manner as it was in the 1950s when facades for skyscrapers benefited from new technologies and opportunities to create light and airy spaces in the sky using glazed systems.

Complying with the acknowledged design criteria for the selection of a suitable material is difficult with some of the more popular options presented to the designer. Considering that the facade of any building is the one aspect permanently on display to the general public, meeting aesthetic criteria is important. However, this should rarely override other basic parameters in the design process. For example, the selection of granite and natural stone to provide a more solid external statement must be evaluated carefully against thermal stress, safety, weathering performance and light transmission criteria.

TYPE OF GLASS	SOLAR OPTICAL PROPERTIES		
	REFLECTANCE (%)	ABSORPTANCE (%)	TRANSMITTANCE(%)
CLEAR GLASS			
3mm sheet glass	7	8	85
6mm float glass	8	12	80
6mm wired glass	6	31	63
COLOURED PATTERN GLASS			
3mm green	6	55	39
3mm blue	6	32	62
3mm amber	6	40	52
HEAT-ABSORBING GLASS			
6mm grey glass	5	51	44
6mm blue green glass	5	75	20
6mm green	6	49	45
6mm bronze glass	5	51	44
6mm spectral float glass (bronze)	10	34	56
HEAT-REFLECTING GLASS			
(laminated: 6mm gold-coated glass)			
heavy-density coating	47	42	11
medium-density coating	33	42	25
light-density coating	21	43	36

The designer needs to recognise that although such materials may reduce heat transmission to the interiors their reaction to sunlight is vastly different from glass particularly in the amount of expansion and contraction undergone during rapid temperature changes. Thin granite veneers have suffered dramatic failures resulting from incomplete evaluation of concentrated stress and its relationship to the properties of the stone. Natural stone also suffers more directly from pollution, acid rain, staining and discolouration, marring the appearance of a building after a short period of time.

Yet it is the reduction in the amount of natural light admitted and the curtailing of possible panoramas inherent in the selection of solid materials that are the most disregarded design criteria in the current skyscraper envelope.

When faced with the potential of massive solar heat gain in fully glazed facades combined with the statutory overall thermal-transmission-value (OTTV) regulations of local authorities, designers of skyscrapers understandably seek out materials that may aid in heat transmission reduction.

The simplest way of reducing OTTV (which is an index of the thermal performance of the building) is to reduce the window-to-wall surface area ratios, the theory being: the less glass provided, the lower the degree of solar heat gain. However, OTTV's are not calculated only on the basis of window to wall ratio figures: reduced shading coefficients found in heat absorbing, laminated and reflective

TOTAL SOLAR HEAT GAIN (%)	DAYLIGHT TRANSMISSION (%)	HEAT : LIGHT RATIO (%)
87	90	0.97
84	87	0.96
71	85	0.83
56	49	1.14
72	31	2.32
66	58	1.14
60	41	1.46
43	48	0.85
60	75	0.80
60	50	1.20
66	49	1.35
25	20	1.25
41	38	1.08
63	63	0.84

glass will also affect the end result. Incorporating the glass type that provides additional shading coefficients to the equations will result in similar OTTV reductions without needing to reduce the area of glass in the facade.

The application of research, design and development in this field has produced a variety of devices to enable architects to specify fully glazed facades for skyscrapers, in particular the development of sunshades.

By integrating sunshades in the support system of the envelope in either the horizontal and/or the vertical plane, uninterrupted shadow can be cast on the glazed plane throughout the passage of the sun across the facade, thus reducing solar heat gain.

Technology is already available to harness the solar energy and convert it into electrical energy by utilising photo-voltaic solar cells. These systems convert sunlight directly into electrical energy without the need of moving parts, ensuring greater reliability and durability than the conventional solar thermal systems. Integrating these cells in adjustable sunshading devices will permit angle adjustments to the path of the sun powered by the cells alone whilst maintaining maximum visibility from inside. These cells can be laminated into glazed units or fabricated in metal. By combining sunshading elements and heat absorbing or fitted glass with orientation analysis, the designer can determine which facades of a building will be subject to greater thermal loads and thus which will require sunshading devices.

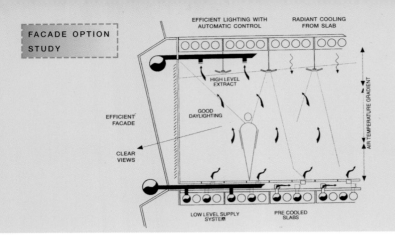

EFFICIENT LIGHTING WITH
AUTOMATIC CONTROL

RADIANT COOLING
FROM SLAB

HIGH LEVEL
EXTRACT

EFFICIENT
FACADE

GOOD
DAYLIGHTING

CLEAR
VIEWS

AIR TEMPERATURE GRADIENT

LOW LEVEL SUPPLY
SYSTEM

PRE COOLED
SLABS

Depending on the angle of incidence – the angle at which the sun strikes the glass – solar heat gain will vary. For instance, along the equatorial zone, the sun is at its lowest on the south side of a building in December and the north side of the building in June. As the angle of incidence at these times is at its lowest, sun-shading devices can be designed to cut out thermal transmission for north and south elevations which will also protect the envelope when the sun is at its highest and solar heat gain is greatest. In orienting large glazed facades towards the east or west, the sunshading becomes extensive and costly. If the opportunity is available at the initial concept stage to site the building with the core at these orientations, the designer is able to economise as the glazed north/south elevations will require less sunshading.

172

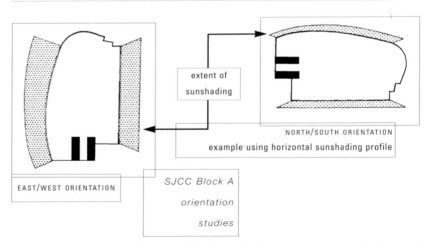

extent of
sunshading

NORTH/SOUTH ORIENTATION
example using horizontal sunshading profile

EAST/WEST ORIENTATION

SJCC Block A
orientation
studies

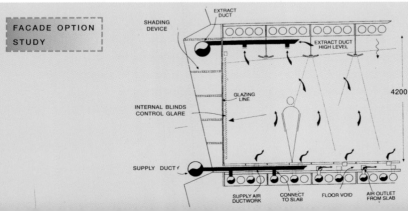

SHADING
DEVICE

EXTRACT
DUCT

EXTRACT DUCT
HIGH LEVEL

4200

GLAZING
LINE

INTERNAL BLINDS
CONTROL GLARE

SUPPLY DUCT

SUPPLY AIR
DUCTWORK

CONNECT
TO SLAB

FLOOR VOID

AIR OUTLET
FROM SLAB

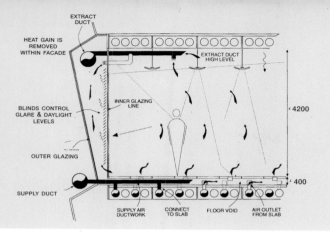

EXTRACT
DUCT

HEAT GAIN IS
REMOVED
WITHIN FACADE

EXTRACT DUCT
HIGH LEVEL

INNER GLAZING
LINE

4200

BLINDS CONTROL
GLARE & DAYLIGHT
LEVELS

OUTER GLAZING

400

SUPPLY DUCT

SUPPLY AIR   CONNECT   FLOOR VOID   AIR OUTLET
DUCTWORK   TO SLAB   FROM SLAB

Although sophisticated in its application, the sunshading device is still only one element in the control of solar heat gain. Further developments in glass technology are required if glass is to continue as the spirit of the skyscraper. Where sunshading is used, the glass should be protected effectively on the exterior, and not on the interior, as internal blinds only stop the light and not the heat.

Innovative designs for small patch-fitted glazed screens, overhead canopies, furniture and general interior applications prove the continued versatility of a product that externally seems unresponsive to the demands for effective solutions to widening design parameters. Glass will always be able to provide the most suitable building envelope in relation to the basic design criteria, but the present inadequate performance technology of the external envelope is evident in the 'band-aid' type of solutions available.

With the advent of intelligent mechanical and electrical services for buildings, technology has made rapid advances towards solving problems incurred by overall thermal transmission.

173

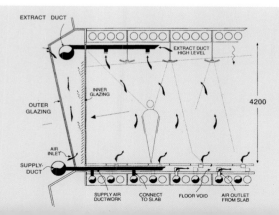

EXTRACT DUCT

EXTRACT DUCT
HIGH LEVEL

INNER
GLAZING

OUTER
GLAZING

4200

AIR
INLET

SUPPLY
DUCT

SUPPLY AIR   CONNECT   FLOOR VOID   AIR OUTLET
DUCTWORK   TO SLAB   FROM SLAB

'Greenpeace, we read, is targeting all designers
who don't make walls and claddings of their buildings
energy producing and/or conserving.
...bioclimatic skyscrapers get muscle.'

PROFESSOR LEON VAN SCHAIK

Imagine a future that has full-height flush-glazed facades which are frameless sheaths providing maximum natural light, able to withstand the external climatic elements and prevent access by intruders or injury to occupants, whilst also cooling the heat of the sun as its rays pass through to the interior.

seasonal variations

174

In the cold climatic zones, the facades of the bioclimatic skyscraper have to cope with cold winters, hot summers and the two mid-seasons – spring and autumn. The temperature variations are significant between winter and summer, and the facades need to be multi-faceted or multi-layered with adjustable/moveable functions that can accommodate different functions at different times of the year (see Shanghai Armoury Tower, Chapter 1).

One approach to the low-energy skyscraper is to seek to reduce the need for air-conditioning in the summer by using the benefits of night-time cooling, and to reduce heating and energy consumption in the winter by being less dependent on mechanical means and using as much solar heat gain as possible. Mid-seasons should be 'extended' through enhanced natural ventilation.

SHADING COEFFICIENTS FOR DIFFERENT TYPES OF GLAZING AND SHADING DEVICES

TYPE OF GLASS	POSITION AND TYPE OF SHADING	SHADING COEFFICIENT (SC)[a]
CLEAR GLASS		
3mm clear glass	none	1.00
6mm plate	none	
HEAT-ABSORBING GLASS		
6mm lightly heat-absorbing glass	none	0.51
6mm densely heat-absorbing glass	none	0.39
6mm heat-absorbing glass (green)	none	0.67
6mm heat-absorbing glass (blue)	none	0.55
HEAT-REFLECTING GLASS		
6mm heat-reflecting glass (gold)	none	0.24
3mm clear glass coated with reflective shield		
RSL 20	none	0.27
RSL 40	none	0.44
6mm plate glass with thin reflective film linings		
silver	none	0.24-0.28
gold	none	0.26-0.29
grey	none	0.32-0.39
photo-chromatic glasses	none	0.60-0.77
Translucent glass	none	0.57
EXTERNAL SHADES		
3mm clear glass	canvas roller blind	1.00
3mm clear glass	canvas awnings	0.25
3mm clear glass	completely shaded by fixed-type sun breakers	0.20
3mm clear glass	white louvred sun breaker blades at 45°	0.14
3mm clear glass	venetian blinds, light colour slat angle 0°	0.10
3mm clear glass	slat angle 45°	0.14
3mm clear glass	slat angle 90°	0.45
INTERNAL SHADING		
3mm clear glass	roller shades: white colour	0.40
3mm clear glass	roller shades: medium colour	0.62
3mm clear glass	heavy curtain white lining and folds	0.35
3mm clear glass	net curtain folds (dark)	0.75
3mm clear glass	venetian blinds, light colour slat angle 0°	0.50
3mm clear glass	slat angle 45°	0.63
3mm clear glass	slat angle 90°	0.78

[a] These are typical values only. Variations will occur due to variations in type and colour of glass, difference in treatments, cleanness of glass and shading devices.

> 'Cladding in the future will be as porous
> and perfect as human skin.'   MARTIN PAWLEY

sunshading of
tall buildings

Due to their height, skyscrapers are exposed more directly than other buildings to the full impact of external temperatures and direct sunlight. Therefore, their overall orientation has an important bearing on energy conservation.

The greatest source of heat gain can be that entering through the window. The direct radiation transmitted varies markedly with the time of the day and the angle of incidence.

In the hot-humid tropics, for instance, this remains fairly steady at about 50° and drops sharply at 60°. Main openings facing north-south minimise solar insolation and thus the building's air-conditioning load. If the site does not align with the sun's geometry on its east-west path, other built components of the skyscraper such as the service-core can follow the geometry of the site to optimise column grids in relation to basement and/or upper-floor car-park layouts, etc.

Unless important views lie elsewhere, the skyscraper's windows should face the directions of the least direct solar insolation in conjunction with the curtain-walling, if this is deemed aesthetically desirable.

Some floor-plate shaping adjustments or the incorporation of shading devices (eg. sunshades, recesses or balconies, etc) may be needed for those site locations which lie further north or south of the equatorial belt.

For aesthetic reasons, the fully glazed curtain-wall may be used on the non-solar facing facades, but on the 'hot' east and west sides some form of solar-shading is required, making due allowances for glare and the quality of light entering the spaces. For instance, the west wall in the tropics (and south-west in the higher latitudes) has the highest intensity at the hottest time of the day.

176

BP Tower,

Petaling Jaya

Latitude 3.07°N

the external wall
as an environmental filter
or sieve

The external walls of the bioclimatic sky-scraper should be regarded more as a 'sieve' than as a sealed skin (as mentioned earlier). These should function as a permeable membrane with adjustable openings. Ideally, the skyscraper's external walls should act like a filter that has variable parts to control good cross-ventilation, provide solar protection, regulate wind-swept rain, and discharge heavy rain. (See pages 120, 124, 128-29 for a detailed discussion of the position and placement of wall openings for cross-ventilation, and consideration of roof and wall design regarding solar heat absorption and reflection.)

Another result of the intermingling of international and regional solutions, of modern techniques and rural wisdom, was the brise-soleil or sun-breaker.

The brise-soleil was invented to make the principle of the 'free facade' tenable in hot climates.

In 1932, in a scheme for low-cost housing for Barcelona, Le Corbusier organised his dwellings as a tight-knit modern version of a casbah, and treated the facades to movable louvres and the roofs to thick turf protection.

honeycomb of protective louvres...

The thermal forces acting on the outside of the skyscraper include a combination of radiation and convection impacts. The radiation component consists of incident solar radiation and of radiant heat exchange with the surroundings. The convective heat impact is a function of exchange with the internal air and may be accelerated by air movement. The exchange effect may be increased by diluting the radiation over a larger area by the use of curved surfaces such as vaults, domes, atria and louvred or irregular surfaced roofs which will, at the same time, increase the rate of convection transfer.

Wall surfaces which have direct solar insolation should be shaded. Their cladding material's insulation and 'time-lag' characteristics should be taken into consideration. External materials used might be those that are effective heat-sinks (eg. aluminium composites) or be designed to have a 'double-layered' ventilating space.

Another very effective protection against radiation impact, especially in the external-wall design, is the selective absorptivity and emissivity characteristic of a material, especially under hot conditions. Materials which reflect rather than absorb radiation, and which release the absorbed heat as thermal radiation more readily, bring about lower temperatures within the building.

178

SKETCHES ILLUSTRATING THE PRINCIPLE OF THE BRISE-SOLEIL, LE CORBUSIER, LATE 1939

...modern equivalent of the wooden screen 'mashrabyas' of Arabic buildings or the brick louvred 'claustras' he had seen in Morocco.

Thus a new element was added to the 'free facade', but its regionalism was not so much cultural as climatic...

...this was a skyscraper clad with louvres on its most exposed facade.

Sunshading can be in the form of rectilinear design (in earlier buildings) – such as vertical fins – and horizontal projections, or a combination of the two, known as egg-crate. Le Corbusier invented the 'brise-soleil' to make the principle of the 'free facade' tenable in hot climates.

These devices are used for the purpose of reducing the heat-load of the building through its enclosing envelope, and to add character and style to the building facade.

These louvres can be fixed or movable. If fixed, the salient angle is dependent on the latitude of the site and the aspect of the window. The louvres can exclude summer sun and admit winter sun. They can be designed to exclude the sun all year round (eg. in the tropics). In the southern hemisphere, horizontal louvres with a diagonal section are suitable for the northern aspect as the sun angles are high, and vertical louvres are suitable for a window with a southern aspect due to low sun-angles to the east or west. Thus the diagonal louvres combine vertical and horizontal shading for complete exclusion of the sun. The tilt of the louvres may then be adjusted to admit sun during prescribed periods as desired, such as the winter of the temperate climate.

In a multi-purpose block for Nemours, the brise-soleil took on the character of deep-cut loggias and verandas

... the brise-soleil were integrated with the structure, creating a woven density of light and shade, as well as a vocabulary able to distinguish interior uses and to maintain unity and multiple scales simultaneously.

massive perforations...

GLASS TYPE	STANDARD THICKNESS mm	SUGGESTED APPLICATIONS
float glass (clear)	2 3 4 5 6 8 10 12 15 19	Windows in general construction, picture frames, furniture, table tops, etc. Internal partitions where safety is not a major concern.
tinted float glass (heat absorbing)	5 6 8 10 12	Windows in general construction, furniture, table tops, etc. Internal partitions where safety is not a major concern.
heat-strengthened glass	6 8 10 12	Curtain walls, internal partitions with a degree of safety required, shop fronts, display cases.
tempered glass (safety glass)	4 5 6 8 10 12	Curtain walls, large glazed screens, suspended and/or patch-fitted glazing systems, balustrading, escalator side panels, shop fronts, doors – generally areas where human impact safety is required.
laminated glass (heat-sealed panes of glass with one or more interlayers of polyvinyl butyl film safety glass)	6.38 to 24.38	Curtain walls, sloped or roof glazing, canopies, glazed screens (frameless), aquariums, zoo enclosures, swiming pools, generally areas that require maximum safety.
heat reflective glass	6 8 10 12	Curtain walls, glass screens.
ceramic fritted or screen printed glass	6 8 10 12	Curtain walls, glass screens, roof glazing.
mirror glass	2 3 4 5 6	Internal decoration only: walls, ceilings, colums, furniture, etc.
figured glass (transluscent patterned glass	3 4 5	Decorative applications: windows, shop displays, furniture, partitions.
decorative glass (opaque)	5	Internal decoration only: walls, ceilings, display systems, escalator side panels, table tops.
wired glass	6.8 10	Internal and external use in general construction. Vision panels to fire doors.

180

ADVANTAGES	DISADVANTAGES	REMARKS/NOTES
• maximum light transmittance • distortion free	• maximum heat transmittance • when broken, cracks into large 'knife-like' shards	do not use epoxy resin adhesive when joining glass to glass or other materials
• absorbs radiant heat from the sun to varying degrees thereby reducing heat transmittance	• reduced light transmittance with some colours • colour becomes darker as glass becomes thicker • when broken, cracks into large 'knife-like' shards	heat absorption causes thermal stress resulting in cracks particularly in thick plate glass.
• 2 times the strength of annealed glass • generally not subject to spontaneous breakage • high resistance to rapid temperature changes • when broken, large pieces will tend to stay in the frame	• this is not a safety glass • low wind pressure resistance	
• 3-5 times the bending and impact strength of annealed glass of the same thickness • high resistance to rapid temperature changes • shatters into small blunt pieces when broken. • large pane sizes giving optimum visibility • colour variety available	• no cutting, drilling or chamferring can occur after tempering • susceptible to spontaneous breakage • when broken, pieces will not remain in the frame	when specifying this glass ensure the inclusion of a heat-soaking process to minimise the likelihood of spontaneous breakage. Tinted tempered glass gives greater reductions in heat transmittance.
• maximum safety provided as it has a good resistance to penetration and remains in its frame when broken • intruder-resistant • great colour variety available • sound transmission reduction • ultra-violet ray filtration • heat transmission reduction • not subject to spontaneous breakage	• delamination can occur at edges • on-site cutting is not advisable • reduced light transmittance with some colours	laminated panels of tinted tempered glass or tempered reflective glass combine all the advantages of glazed systems required for high-rise facade systems
• high solar absorption thereby reducing internal cooling capacity requirements • reduced excess glare • greater degrees of privacy ensured • colour variety available	• reduced light transmittance • reflected sunlight and heat may affect surrounding buildings and passing motorists • subject to thermal stress	this glass can be used as tempered and laminated panels for better performance. When cleaning, some detergents can damage the coated surface
• fritting causes reduced heat transmission • lighter colours diffuse daylight • variety of patterns and colours available • greater degrees of privacy ensured	• all cutting, drilling and chamfering must be completed before screening	for external use the pattern must be on the inside
• surface patterns allow diffused daylight transmittance, thus giving privacy.	• transparency is increased when wet • figured surface attracts dirt more readily	
• greater colour variety • a protective coating ensures long lasting colours	• cannot be used in direct sunlight or externally, in environments of high temperature or humidity	further patterns can be created by sandblasting on the glass surface
• prevents and resists fire spread • a degree of safety given when broken • patterns available • intruder deterrent		

'Sealed boxes are really only appropriate for aeroplanes – buildings are an extension of the land and ought to be thought of as such. The facades of climatically designed skyscrapers will be fundamental in shaping the interaction between the building and its external environment, as well as creating an internal environment which feels comfortable, natural and fresh. Whilst creating this internal environment, the building facade should harness the forces of nature in the most cost-effective way. These forces include heat, light and wind.

The facade can be used to reject heat that is not required in the building, or to absorb it and redistribute it when it is.
Heat could be collected through heat-absorbing shading devices, ventilated glass walls, or heat absorbing fluids. Heat could be rejected by evaporative cooling on the surface, or insulated by the use of translucent insulating materials. It could be distributed through integral ductwork, glazed flues or fluid piping.

Light too can be used to improve the internal environment, and the facade can be used to reflect natural daylighting into the building. Various forms of glass including electrochromic glass and thermochromic glass can be used to control the amount of light in a space. Light can be used in the facade by the incorporation of photovoltaic cells.

Natural wind forces can be used, sometimes in combination with thermal forces, to improve natural ventilation. The shape of the building and the detailing of the facade can encourage the flow of air, which can help in cooling the building, as well as providing natural ventilation to the space behind.

Overall the facade of the future will be a more fundamental building block, both in low-rise as well as in high-rise buildings. It will take its full three-dimensional form, rather than its current two-dimensional form. It will contain systems and components to harness and utilise the forces of nature. It will also provide a route for M&E services and intelligent building systems in the vertical plane, rather than in the horizontal plane, as with current buildings. It will be a much more advanced and multi-functional component than we have today.'

NEIL NOBLE
OVE ARUP & PARTNERS

sub-structure + super-structure

'...the skyscraper's sub-structure
must enable future changes
and be programmed to respond to
the skyscraper's changes over a
period of, say, ten years...'
'...the skyscrapers's super-structure
must predict future changes
at the urban level. However,
huge cities are already growing in
a meaningless way as a result of
constant renewal combined with
explosive urban expansion.'

AKIRA SUZUKI

sub-structure and super-structure

The key structural design issues requiring close collaboration with structural engineers are the decisions regarding the floor-to-floor height and the size and layout of the vertical structural elements.

The size and layout of vertical structural elements generally comprises the service-core element and columns, and is greatly influenced by the structural requirements to resist lateral loads due to wind and/or earthquakes. These factors have significant overall cost implications.

The structural concept of the building depends in part on the floor-plate configuration and the approach to stiffening the building, since the skyscraper is essentially a 'vertical lever'.

Structure constitutes one of the largest masses in the skyscraper and has important bioclimatic implications in that it significantly affects the thermal performance of the building. It can, for instance, throw out the balance of any unadjusted heating and cooling systems. Structure can also be combined with low-energy systems for the building (eg. the use of a hollow floor structure for heated air during winter use).

The structure of the building should be considered integrally with its sub-structural design (eg. use of raft-foundations, basements as a pad, friction piles or end-bearing piles, etc) as well as with the building's uses (eg. the car-parking provision if within the tower or its base).

For instance, where the car-parking provisions are placed under or within the building, the structural grids used must permit an efficient car-park layout in relation to driveways, car-park bays and access ramps (eg. common car-park structural grids are 8.4 x 8.4 m). If possible the structural grids should also efficiently integrate with the skyscraper's internal sub-division modules (eg. one-office, two-office, three-office modules per column spacing, if an office building), ceiling-tile grids and window-mullion spacings, and grids for the GOPs (Grid Opening Points or Grommet for the Intelligent Building Systems outlets).

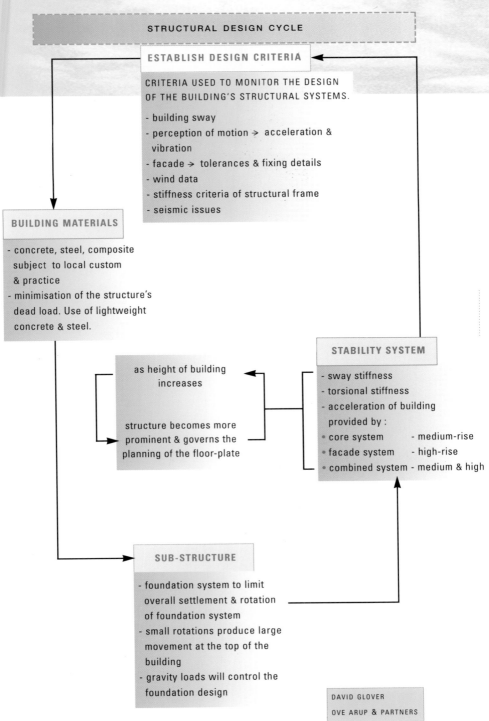

STRUCTURAL DESIGN CYCLE

ESTABLISH DESIGN CRITERIA

CRITERIA USED TO MONITOR THE DESIGN
OF THE BUILDING'S STRUCTURAL SYSTEMS.

- building sway
- perception of motion → acceleration &
  vibration
- facade → tolerances & fixing details
- wind data
- stiffness criteria of structural frame
- seismic issues

BUILDING MATERIALS

- concrete, steel, composite
  subject to local custom
  & practice
- minimisation of the structure's
  dead load. Use of lightweight
  concrete & steel.

185

STABILITY SYSTEM

- sway stiffness
- torsional stiffness
- acceleration of building
  provided by :
  • core system   - medium-rise
  • facade system   - high-rise
  • combined system - medium & high

as height of building
increases

structure becomes more
prominent & governs the
planning of the floor-plate

SUB-STRUCTURE

- foundation system to limit
  overall settlement & rotation
  of foundation system
- small rotations produce large
  movement at the top of the
  building
- gravity loads will control the
  foundation design

DAVID GLOVER

OVE ARUP & PARTNERS

The skyscraper's foundations and substructure design depends on the underground soil conditions which need to be determined by a soil test. This is best carried out along the column grid positions and core positions. Based on the soil test results, the calculated loading of the building on each column, and its anticipated overall structural performance, the engineer will determine the type of foundation system and/or systems (if composite system) to be used, the depth of piling for each column position, and the type of piling system.

On occasion, the outcome of the soil test may lead to the relocation or the adjustment of the structural grid or column positions (eg. if there is an underground 'lime-stone valley' where the central grid-line is located, these might be better shifted away from the uneconomical positions).

186

architectural design
considerations

Initial architectural decisions in skyscraper design are the structural grids of the floor-plate (particularly in relation to ceiling grids), car-parking integration, window mullion spacings, likely partitioned room-sizes, and range of tenancy situations and marketing preferences (eg. column-free floor preferences, etc).

Subsoil and water-table conditions influence piling design, sub-structural design, structural design, floor-plate design, the location of cores and structural columns, and basement provision. In some localities it may be necessary to improve soil (eg. sub-structural grouting).

Mandatory and market-preferred car-parking requirements may affect structural grids. This may require the use of transfer beams if the super-structure and sub-structural grids do not coincide.

The period of delivery from start to finish of the project may involve the consideration of a fast-track method of construction and building systems (eg. precast versus in-situ, rc frame vs steel-frame, etc), 'jump-start' construction, 'top-down' construction, and 'fly-form' shuttering which may also affect design.

The approach to the structure of the skyscraper depends on the floor-plate configuration (see Chapter 3). The structural grid (if there is one) determines the column positions and, with the ceiling-grids (eg. 600 sqmm), should also coincide with the window-mullion grids to help future internal partitioning.

Where the office skyscraper's internal partitioning meets with the external wall, it should meet the glazing mullion directly rather than in-between the window-panel (in which case the sound insulation of the room becomes problematic as the acoustical sealing of the gap between the partition's edge and the glazing in the middle of the mullion becomes difficult).

Where the skyscraper is above car-parking floors (whether in the basements or above ground) the designer should be economical when placing the car-parking and driveways between the columns. In determining the grids, the designer should also allow for the column's structural widths.

The vertical components of the structure are not usually complicated by the necessity of dealing with ducts, lights, sprinkler piping or other mechanical systems that must interface with the beams or girders of the floor structural system. However, the span of the structure between columns should also be considered in terms of the resultant beam depth and the ceiling voids. For instance, certain building regulations require that if ceiling voids exceed 1m, the voids need to be double fire-sprinklered thereby increasing costs.

188

Edge beam depths at the edge of the floor should also incorporate the requirements of the Local Authority's Fire Regulations. In some regulations there must be a fire stop of at least 1 m between the upper-floor and the lower-floor ceiling line to prevent fire transfer from the upper floor down to the lower floor.

If typical column-free office floor-plates are required, the spans may exceed the usual economical spans for concrete beams and special pre-stressed beams may need to be considered (eg. over 8 to 10 m clear span). However, these result in deeper beam depths and again these need to be co-ordinated with ceiling services and ducting requirements to achieve an acceptable ceiling-void and structural floor-to-floor heights which should generally be kept to a minimum. In some countries, the minimum floor to ceiling height for offices is 2.5 m up to 2.7 m. Commercial functions usually require a variety of ceiling heights ranging from 2.7 m to 3.7 m. Residential and hotel functions require ceiling heights of 2.4 m to 2.7 m.

The spacing of columns – if at the periphery of the typical floorplate – should help room partitioning into economical room grids (eg. three rooms per grid).

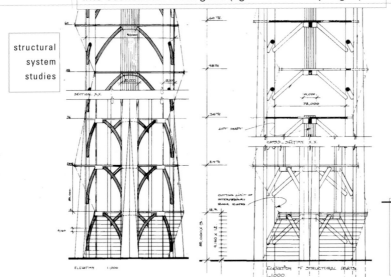

structural system studies

Tokyo-Nara Tower,

Tokyo,

Latitude 35.42°N

structure
and framing

The super-structure is that part of the structural system of the skyscraper above the ground. The sub-structure consists of the foundations, piling, ground-beams and pile-caps below the lowest floor level and basement. Structurally, the skyscraper is a vertical cantilevered beam and at each storey, the shear and overturning moment are known.

Conventionally, the beams, girders and joists are the principal horizontal structural framing members utilised in most skyscrapers. Columns and reinforced concrete-bearing walls are the common vertical structural supports. An important factor affecting structural design is to find out whether the column area is subtracted from the floor area in calculating the rental for the floor for that locality's market conditions. If the cross-sectional area of the columns are not a factor, the design of the columns should be directed towards economy of construction while achieving a sensibly sized column.

The ways that the horizontal and vertical framing members control and transmit the stresses to which they are subjected depends on the material that is used. The material also determines the size and proportions of the structural members.

The framing system is the skeleton of a building. Like any skeleton, it supports the rest of the structure. The horizontal components of most framing systems fall into two basic categories: one-way and two-way. Multi-way systems exist but are less commonly used than the other two systems. All horizontal framing systems distribute the loads and stresses that are placed on the building's floors until they can be picked up and transferred to the ground and foundations by vertical supports.

The design of tall slender buildings is usually constrained by the requirements to limit wind-induced drift and wind-induced accelerations. Excessive drift degrades the performance of the building envelope and interior finishes. Excessive wind-induced horizontal accelerations adversely affect occupant comfort.

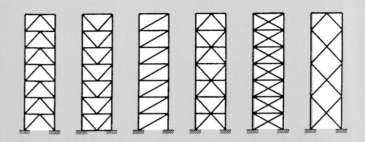

live and dead loads

The weight of the skyscraper's structure and that of all its permanently attached components, such as M&E equipment, fixed-in-place partitions and ceilings, are called dead loads. Superimposed loads produced by the building's use and occupancy are called live loads.

Live loads affect every floor in a skyscraper, and the amount of load is based on the type of use the floor is subjected to.

Many offices in skyscrapers require the use of heavy 'compactus' filing systems which by far exceed the conventional live-loads. Designers should allow for the provision of these or should pre-designate certain zones in the typical office floor for their placement.

cores and wind bracing

The service-core of a building is the area reserved for elevator, stairs, mechanical equipment and the vertical shafts that are necessary for ducts, pipes and wires (see Chapter 2). In addition, the core can contain washrooms and, in some instances, public lobbies and corridor space. The walls of the cores are also the most common location for the vertical wind-bracing. The core design and location are key to the bioclimatic skyscraper.

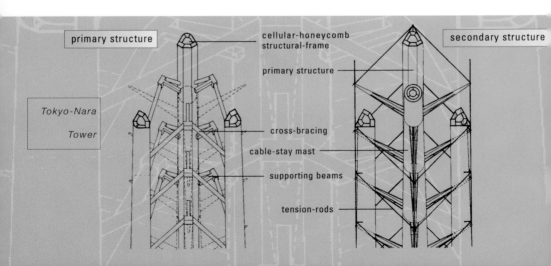

primary structure

cellular-honeycomb structural-frame

primary structure

secondary structure

Tokyo-Nara Tower

cross-bracing

cable-stay mast

supporting beams

tension-rods

portal frame

deep knee
brace

diagonal
brace

K-brace
(K = ⋏)

welded rigid
joints

double-height
k-brace

A braced bay is a line of columns tied together by a bracing system which causes them to act in unison.

Cental Plaza,
Kuala Lumpur,
Latitude 3.2°

K-bracing
as sun-
breakers

The service-core is the dominant component of the skyscraper. It is about 28% of the total structural cost of the building and takes up about 25% of the floor space. Its implementation is generally along the critical path of the building's construction programme, especially leading to the early completion of the elevator motor-room. This has to be completed before the elevator installation can take place.

By locating the wind bracing within the core walls, the designer is able to make use of a wall that is required for other purposes, such as to enclose stairs or elevator shafts. Thus dual use eliminates the need to create an additional wall that could interfere with the use of the building. However, in some structural solutions the core wall as sheer wall adds significant weight to the foundations and subsequently increases costs. A recent trend is the use of fire-rated gypsum-board core walls to reduce weight and costs, and to make use of other wind-bracing devices at the building exterior.

Typically, building cores are centrally located, but bioclimatically they should be placed so that they can be used as climatic buffers to the floorplates, ie. on the external wall. Other factors that influence the location of the core are its use and the circulation patterns of the building's occupants. Where the walls of the core are called upon to perform the additional structural task of providing wind-bracing, the core shafts must be located in the appropriate place to stiffen the building as a whole.

191

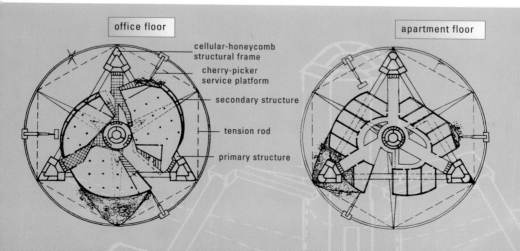

office floor

apartment floor

cellular-honeycomb
structural frame

cherry-picker
service platform

secondary structure

tension rod

primary structure

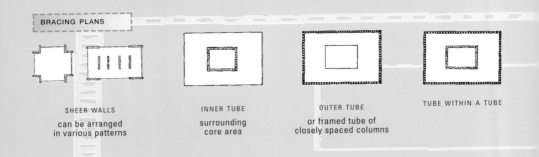

SHEER WALLS
can be arranged
in various patterns

INNER TUBE
surrounding
core area

OUTER TUBE
or framed tube of
closely spaced columns

TUBE WITHIN A TUBE

The taller the structure, the more critical the service-core location becomes. The other ducts and shafts that contain M&E services and distribution systems must be located in a manner that will permit a logical horizontal distribution of the M&E system at every floor level. The vertical shafts containing the exit stairs must be located in such a way as to conform to the maximum travel distances required for safe exiting of the building in an emergency.

Wind bracing may be combined with external bracing in very tall skyscrapers, forming what is called a tube-within-a-tube system. In such cases the core walls do not double for wind-bracing and dry wall construction may be used resulting in lower sub-structural costs, reduced wall thickness, and accelerated construction time. The fire-rating of these walls is in most conditions two hours.

Usually the cores are built first as the construction tower-crane is temporarily installed within the core as the skyscraper is built. The following are alternative ways of wall-forming for the core construction:

conventional system

This process is one of working off the last placed slab, setting up one side of a wall form-work to full height, then placing reinforcments, installing the wall form-work, tie systems, closing up the wall system, and then pouring the concrete. The form is left in place for a period of time. Next, the wall is stripped, the slab is formed and poured, and the process is repeated.

192

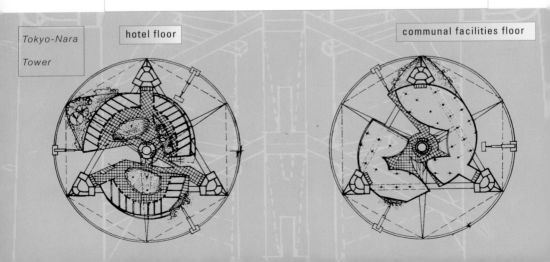

Tokyo-Nara Tower

hotel floor

communal facilities floor

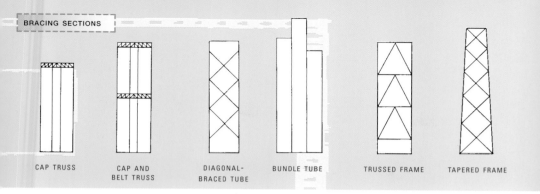

| CAP TRUSS | CAP AND BELT TRUSS | DIAGONAL-BRACED TUBE | BUNDLE TUBE | TRUSSED FRAME | TAPERED FRAME |

jump-form system

This is a system in which the builder runs the wall up ahead of the slabs. The jump form is a full floor height and operates pretty much in the same fashion as a conventional form except that it has hydraulic systems that move the forms up without the use of a crane. It has some advantages over the conventional system in that it can go up without bringing the slab system with it. On the other hand, it has many similarities with the conventional wall system in that the builder puts one side in place, places the reinforcements, closes the wall, places the concrete, lets it cure for a day or so, then moves the form system up again. The form system is supported on the new concrete.

slip-form system

The wall-forms are only about 1.2 m high. They are held together on a piece of equipment that looks like an inverted 'U' with some cross members. This 'yoke', as it is called, holds together the wall-form and also pulls it up as the concrete is placed. This whole system operates on a series of rods placed in the wall. A jack mounted on the 'yoke' rides up these rods, pulling the form system up. In this case, the form system itself is supported fully on the rods and therefore does not exert a load on the fresh concrete, which has to do nothing more than support its own weight.

193

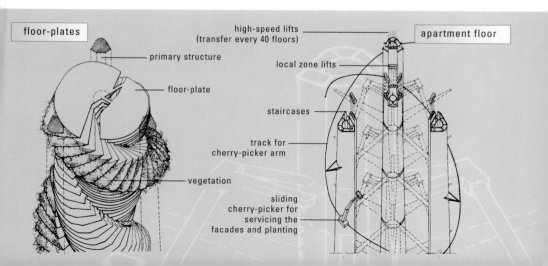

floor-plates

- primary structure
- floor-plate
- vegetation

high-speed lifts (transfer every 40 floors)

apartment floor

- local zone lifts
- staircases
- track for cherry-picker arm
- sliding cherry-picker for servicing the facades and planting

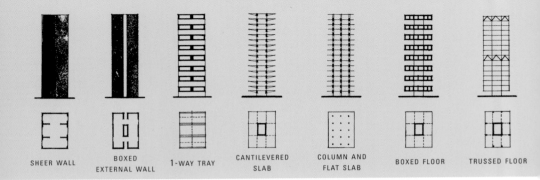

SHEER WALL   BOXED EXTERNAL WALL   1-WAY TRAY   CANTILEVERED SLAB   COLUMN AND FLAT SLAB   BOXED FLOOR   TRUSSED FLOOR

steel

Another technological innovation necessary for the development of the utilitarian skyscraper was steel-frame construction. Decorative towers of great height were nothing new, and many of them, including Cologne Cathedral and the Washington Monument, exceeded 150 m. However, when such structures are built of masonry, they need massive amounts of stone at the lower levels (and sometimes flying buttresses as well), and there is little usable interior space, at least in relation to the size of the lot required. This problem was solved with the invention of steel-frame construction (ie. the erection of a steel skeleton upon which non-load-bearing walls of a variety of materials could be hung).

Steel-frame construction was invented in Chicago. The Chicago Fire of 1871 levelled much of the emerging CBD, and architects and engineers in the United States gathered to participate in the reconstruction. Various ideas were tried in order to improve upon traditional building methods, including the use of interior cast-iron columns to brace the walls. The invention of the Bessemer process in the 1870s and the presence of the steel industry in Chicago may have spurred acceptance, since steel was becoming readily available and inexpensive.

Steel beams in the skyscraper are smaller than concrete beams and the total framing weight of steel per sq m of floor area is less than that of reinforced concrete even though steel

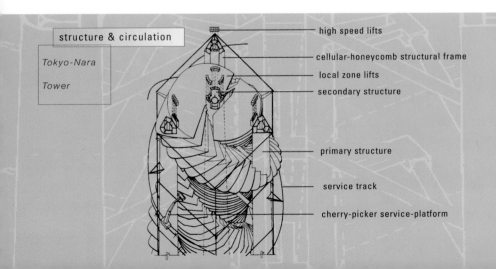

structure & circulation

Tokyo-Nara Tower

high speed lifts

cellular-honeycomb structural frame

local zone lifts

secondary structure

primary structure

service track

cherry-picker service-platform

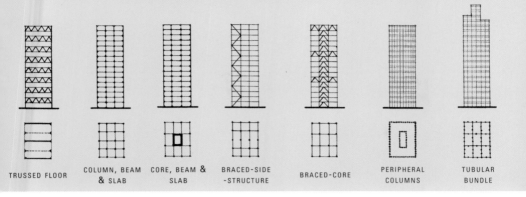

TRUSSED FLOOR	COLUMN, BEAM & SLAB	CORE, BEAM & SLAB	BRACED-SIDE -STRUCTURE	BRACED-CORE	PERIPHERAL COLUMNS	TUBULAR BUNDLE

itself weighs much more per cubic metre (7,852 kg for steel as opposed to 2,404 kg for concrete). This is because the cross-sectional area of a steel-framing member is much smaller than that required for a concrete member spanning the same distance and carrying the same load. However, a concrete column will be much better than a steel one for carrying load.

      With the use of steel construction a high level of precision is needed at the design and construction stages. In the case of concrete, lower levels of construction tolerances can be handled *in situ* whereas steel requires major cutting and adjusting in the event of dimensional discrepancies or sudden site adjustments.

195

concrete

      Concrete structures for skyscrapers are still the most popular in the developing world simply because of the lower cost of materials and labour, and the availability of skilled workers for its construction (compared to the precision and technical skills required for steel-frame construction).

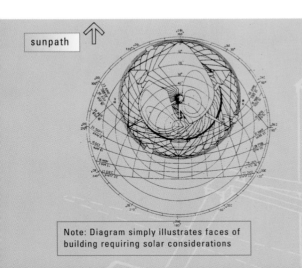

sunpath

Note: Diagram simply illustrates faces of building requiring solar considerations

structure

AVERAGES FOR STEEL-FRAME AND CONCRETE-FRAME SKYSCRAPERS:			
	BUILDING WIDTH/ BUILDING HEIGHT	USABLE AREA/ GROSS AREA (NRA/GFA)	TYPICAL BEAM DEPTH/SPAN
AVERAGES	RATIO	%	RATIO
STEEL-FRAME SKYSCRAPERS	1 : 4.2	77	1 : 21.8
CONCRETE-FRAME SKYSCRAPERS	1 : 3.4	73	1 : 19.6
ALL CASE STUDIES	1 : 3.8	75	1 : 20.7

Basic concrete is a mixture of cement, water, sand and gravel. Roughly 28 days are required for concrete to obtain its full strength and load-bearing capacity (unless additives are used). Normally concrete obtains sufficient strength within a week to support construction loads, thus permitting the forms to be removed and reused.

A distinct characteristic of cast-in-place concrete is its capability to behave as a nearly perfect rigid frame. Cast-in-place concrete structures are monolithic systems. The reinforcement detail of individual members consists of a series of steel bars extended over the joints into the adjacent members. This type of detailing provides the joint rigidity and continuity needed for a structural system to behave as a rigid frame. In contrast, most structures of steel can only partly satisfy the joint continuity, even though connecting elements such as bolts, rivets and welds are theoretically designed to maintain the continuity of the structure at joints.

Reinforced concrete is a combination of concrete and steel. The reinforcements, usually in the form of round steel bars or steel wires, are used in concrete members mainly to resist tensile stresses.

196

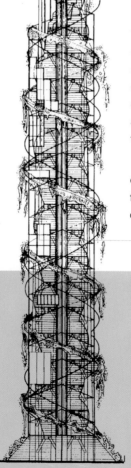

Tokyo-Nara Tower

cherry-pickers on spiral track

elevation

MECHANICAL EQUIPMENT & SHAFT AREA/ GROSS FLOOR AREA	HVAC SHAFT AREA/ GROSS FLOOR AREA	USABLE HEIGHT TOTAL FLOOR HEIGHT	GLASS AREA FACADE AREA	NO OF ELEVATORS NO OF FLOORS
%	%	%	%	RATIO
10.9	2.2	69	53	1 : 2.3
8.7	3.3	73	35	1 : 4.2
9.8	2.8	71	44	1 : 3.3*

*This table provides a broad rule-of-thumb in assessing the number of elevators to provide during the preliminary design stage (ie. 3.3 elevators per floor)

reinforcements

Reinforcement is also used to increase the member's compression resistance. These bars can be round, of varying diameters, grades and strengths. Steel may cost more than concrete, but it has a yield strength about ten times the compressive strength and about one hundred times the tensile strength of concrete.

Longitudinal steel bars resisting either tensile or compressive forces in a reinforced concrete beam are called main reinforcements. Stirrups are another type of reinforcement used in beams. The direction of the stirrups is transverse to the direction of the main steel, and they are bent in a box or U-shape. Similar reinforcement is used in columns, where it takes the form of ties. Secondary reinforcement is additional steel, usually used in slabs in directions perpendicular to the main reinforcement. The amount of steel generally ranges from 2% to 8% of the gross cross-sectional area of a column.

Concrete floors in concrete buildings can be categorised as follows:

- 2-way construction: flat plate, flat slab, waffle slab, and two-way slab
- 1-way construction: solid slab, pan joist, and beams and slab

For practical design considerations, columns are always required to resist a combination of axial load and bending moments. Column bending moments will necessarily exist as the result of direct loading.

Bioclimatically, concrete mass absorption and release of energy affects the performance of the building (eg. 'Trombe' wall, etc).

BUILDINGS USING HIGH STRENGTH CONCRETE

BUILDING	LOCATION	YEAR*	TOTAL STOREYS	MAXIMUM DESIGN CONCRETE STRENGTH N/MM²
PACIFIC PARK PLAZA	EMERYVILLE, CA	1983	30	45
SE FINANCIAL CENTER	MIAMI	1982	53	48
PETROCANADA BUILDING	CALGARY	1982	34	50
LAKE POINT TOWER	CHICAGO	1965	70	52
1130 A MICHIGAN AVENUE	CHICAGO	1965	70	52
TEXAS COMMERCE TOWER	HOUSTON	1981	75	52
HELMSLEY PALACE HOTEL	NEW YORK	1978	53	55
TRUMP TOWER	NEW YORK	1978	68	55
CITY CENTER PROJECT	MINNEAPOLIS	1981	52	55
COLLINS PLACE	MELBOURNE	1981	44	55
LARIMER PLACE CONDOMINIUMS	DENVER	1980	31	55
499 PARK AVENUE	NEW YORK	1980	27	59
ROYAL BANK PLAZA	TORONTO	1975	43	61
RICHMOND-ADELAIDE CENTRE	TORONTO	1978	33	61
MIDCONTINENTAL PLAZA	CHICAGO	1972	50	62
FRONTIER TOWERS	CHICAGO	1973	55	62
WATER TOWER PLACE	CHICAGO	1975	79	62
RIVER PLAZA	CHICAGO	1976	56	62+
CHICAGO MERCANTILE EXCHANGE	CHICAGO	1982	40	62++
COLUMBIA CENTER	SEATTLE	1983	76	66
INTERFIRST PLAZA	DALLAS	1983	72	69
900 N MICHIGAN AVENUE	CHICAGO	1986	15	97
SOUTH WACKER TOWER	CHICAGO	1989	79	83
GRANDE ARCHE DE LA DÉFENSE	PARIS	1988	79	65
TWO UNION SQUARE	SEATTLE	1989	58	115
PACIFIC FIRST CENTER	SEATTLE	1989	44	115
GATEWAY TOWER	SEATTLE	1989	62	94

* year in which high-strength concrete was cast
+ two experimental columns of 76 N/mm2 strength were included
++ two experimental columns of 97 N/mm2 strength were included

SOURCE: DRY,C, *HIGH PERFORMANCE CONCRETES FOR TALL BUILDINGS*, IN CTBUH, INTERNATIONAL CONFERENCE, RIO DE JANEIRO, 1994 | Pg. 635
CTBUH Report No.903.456

high-strength concrete

Concrete with design compressive strengths of 45 newtons per millimetre square or greater is called high-strength concrete. High-strength concrete contains a higher cement content, a low water-to-cement ratio, and stronger aggregates than lower strength concretes.

Water reducing agents, pozzolanas and fly-ash are also common admixtures. The main reason for using high-strength concrete is that it will carry a compression load at less cost. It is recommended for columns and shear walls. For slabs, high-strength concrete will result in reducing the thickness and increasing the amount of steel reinforcement, which will probably offset concrete savings. Other applications include precast and pre-stressed elements where increased concrete strength is a most desirable feature. There is also less creep, which is associated with higher strengths. This may reduce loss due to pre-stressing.

Because of their monolithic characteristics, cast-in-place reinforced concrete structural systems often require more detailed (and to some extent more diverse) structural analysis methods in order to correctly estimate internal forces and to take into account the effect of continuity at the joints. Aside from conventional structural analysis methods using the 'elastic theory', in many cases cast-in-place reinforced concrete structures also need to be analysed using the more elaborate 'limit analysis' method to further evaluate and ascertain specific collapse mechanisms that may be overlooked in a conventional analysis.

foundations
and soil conditions

Foundations are the piling and pile-cap components of the sub-structure of the skyscraper. Piling can in some cases go deeper underground than the skyscraper rises above the ground.

Soil types and soil conditions vary greatly and must be taken into consideration when planning the skyscraper. The soil's weight-bearing capacity will determine the type of foundation system that will be required. In all cases, the skyscraper's total weight must be distributed over a large enough area to permit the soils under its columns and/or walls to support the skyscraper and its loads.

In most cases where poor soil conditions exist, deep piles are required to take the loads down to a better bearing material. The soil must be capable of supporting the super-structure and its loads.

Deep foundations are divided into piles and caissons. A pile is defined as a solid or hollow structural element with a slenderness ratio greater than ten. Whether installed by driving or by filling and excavation with concrete, provisions are made to ensure good contact between the lateral surfaces of the pile and surrounding soil.

Central Plaza,
Kuala Lumpur,
Latitude 3.2°N

bracing

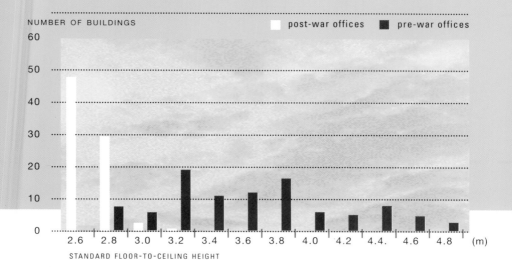

post-war offices ■ pre-war offices

60

50

40

30

20

10

0

2.6 2.8 3.0 3.2 3.4 3.6 3.8 4.0 4.2 4.4. 4.6 4.8 (m)

STANDARD FLOOR-TO-CEILING HEIGHT

Caissons are hollow, having any cross-section and a slenderness ratio of less than ten. A caisson is excavated inside and underneath the edges, and sinks into the ground by its own weight or with the aid of additional deadweight. Other foundations for tall buildings are mat foundations. A mat or raft carries all columns or walls of a building. Either it consists of a single thick slab, with or without base enlargements, or the columns may be joined by beams which receive the ground reaction through the slab.

201

structural implications
of skycourts

Lateral loading due to the action of wind and/or seismic loading governs the structural designs of tall buildings. For the very tall buildings (in excess of 300m in height), lateral loads not only govern the structural design but can dominate the overall architectural form of the building.

The wind-loads for the tall building essentially comprise two components: a steady state component and a dynamic component corresponding to the turbulence along each of the orthogonal axes.

Studies using aeroelastic wind tunnel techniques have shown that the dynamic component can account for up to 70% of the load in the direction of the wind and up to 10% of the load in the orthogonal direction. With the introduction of voids in the building (eg. as skycourts in the bioclimatic skyscraper), reductions in the wind-loads are possible.

structure and super-structure

Throughout the development of the design with the structural engineer, the architect has to be aware that all structural decisions involve:

- area and space planning to ensure that the planning requirements of all parties are met

- keeping tally of the gross floor area (GFA) and net rentable area (NRA) – it should be noted that apart from the loss of rental income, penalty costs may be specified if the building does not achieve the required area of net rentable space

- establishing minimum floor-to-floor requirements, governed by the depth of the structure, requirements of services (present and future), building construction tolerances, and provision for future flexibility (space for access·floors, etc)

- determination of structural column grids (often related to basement car-park planning or the commercial demands of having column-free office space)

- flexibility for future use by tenants in the form of structural provisions for 'compactus' storage areas, provisions for inter-tenancy stairs, etc

The designer should also be aware of a number of constructional approaches which are useful in the erection of the skyscraper, and which may be used depending on the situation (eg. 'top-down construction' where the elevator-core and some of the columns are built before the lower floors are built).

While it is the domain of the engineers, the designer must monitor the 'verticality checks' of the structure of the skyscraper to check for tilts and for constructional off-sets. Equally important are the 'settlement checks' on the sub-structure and the foundations.

'the proportion of sub-structure to super-structure will in the future reverse, and skyscrapers will sit as lightly on the ground as birds' MARTIN PAWLEY

chapter eight

m+e
services
+ intelligent
building systems

'What must be recognised is that skyscrapers are large complex systems.
They are not easily understood
and are difficult to manage.
It is common to find that
such complex buildings are run less
than optimally simply because their
operators do not know how they work
and what state they are in.
The intelligent skyscraper will
eventually look after its inhabitants.
This will become as tricky as robotics,
since after all, the intelligent skyscraper
will be the largest, albeit static,
robot created.'

PROFESSOR BRYAN LAWSON

the building's servicing systems

The initial M&E services design decisions in the tall skyscraper are the adequate provision of *rooms, routes and risers* (the 3 r's) for the building's M&E systems to maintain an efficient floor-plate and an economical floor-to-floor height (3.2 to 4.5 m).

M&E services include the air-conditioning system, ventilation, heating, water supply, electrical power and lighting, telecommunications, sewerage and sanitary systems, computer systems, intelligent building automation systems, security systems, etc.

The bioclimatic skyscraper's air-conditioning, ventilation and heating systems need to be integral with the passive low-energy building systems adopted and with the configuration of the floor-plates (ie. the M&E systems must integrate with the skyscraper's system of internal air-voids, skycourts, etc) as well as with other energy conservation devices used (eg. the cladding system, insulation materials, extent of window area, sunshading devices, etc). The overall intention in the bioclimatic skyscraper is to decrease the dependency of the building's occupants on the M&E systems and to reduce the building's energy consumption through passive means.

Usually at the early stages of the design, the architect must rely on intuition as well as on past experience for critical design choices which include: **ceiling clearances between structure and services, floor-to-floor height, central core configuration, structural floor systems, location and shape of service shafts, and spatial provision for service flexibility to accommodate inevitable future alterations to the building occupancy.**

Local building codes restrict the minimum floor-to-ceiling heights (eg. 2.5 m). However, developers and building owners may often seek to increase (rather than decrease) this for aesthetic reasons and to enable future provision of raised-floors (10 cm clear for routes).

'*Subtract the energy costs of the internal activities from the total energy consumption of the skyscraper and then find a way to create wealth to contribute to the external environment.*' AKIRA SUZUKI

If the ceiling-void depths are increased (eg. beyond 1 m for some local codes), the ceiling void needs to be 'double-sprinkled' (for fire-protection) thereby increasing costs. Fire-voids therefore depend on the structural system adopted, which affects floor beam depths and hence the permissible clear ceiling space for services to run. Another option for the horizontal route zone is to use raised-floors and to dispense with ceilings entirely.

For intelligent building (IB) systems, provision should be made for additional IB risers, machine equipment rooms (MERs) and sub-equipment rooms (SERs) which may further impinge on floor-efficiencies (ie. NRA to GFA ratio).

1851
Air cooling

Air-conditioning came into use in 1851 when Dr John Gorrie used steam-driven compressors to cool air for his patients who had malaria. The term 'air conditioning' was proposed by Stuart Cramer in 1906 to include humidifying, cleaning, heating and ventilating.

SC Building,

Kuala Lumpur.

Latitude 3°

vertical riser routes

The invention of the electric light (1850) and the electric motor (1880) significantly improved interior spaces. Lighting became impossible without the odours, fumes, oxygen reduction and explosion hazards that accompanied gas lighting. The electric fan made it feasible to distribute warm air throughout a building using ducts.

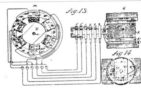

M&E
design objectives

Historically, the utility and feasibility of skyscrapers depended as much upon electric power and light, pumped water, and water-borne sewerage as it did on the elevators and the steel or concrete frame. The possibilities and limitations of these services constrained the diverse forms of the first wave of skyscraper development (c1930s). By that time certain arrangements of the floorplates became common which led to the service-core (ie. the grouping of vertical elements).

The invention of the fluorescent lamp with its lower heat output (compared with the incandescent lamp) combined with air-conditioning made permanent artificial lighting possible and consequently led to much deeper floor plans. However, current trends in the United Kingdom and Germany tend to indicate the return of the shallower floor-plate plan.

The move to air-conditioning even in those regions where the climate did not demand it was stimulated by other pressures. One was the increasingly poor thermal performance of the new tall buildings, a consequence of their reduced mass with the introduction of the 'curtain wall', and, of course, the availability of cheap energy resources.

The acoustic, thermal and luminous environments became highly controlled and integrated at both the gross and system level. At the gross level, the services were organised in the modular false ceiling (in some countries 60 cm x 60 cm).

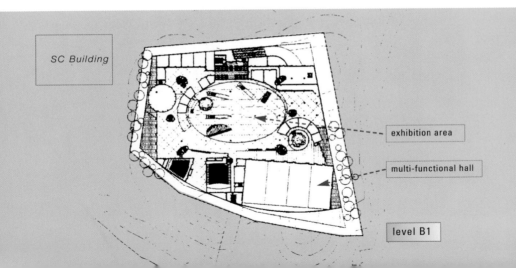

SC Building

exhibition area

multi-functional hall

level B1

Additional experiments with electricity by Westinghouse and General Electric produced commercial fluorescent tubes in 1938. By 1950, fluorescent lighting replaced most incandescent lighting in offices, schools, hospitals, factories and commercial establishments. Fluorescent lighting provided much more light with less electricity and reduced maintenance and replacement costs.

Matching modular room partitioning systems ensured that service points were available in every sub-division. Gradually, as user space standards decreased, the trend led to the use of Systems Furniture (partitionless), to Technology-Desking (desks with built-in partitioning and with interchangeable parts), and to innovative Systems Furniture whose partitions have doors but are not full-height to the ceilings.

Generally, the prime objectives of the sky-scraper's M&E services are to allow the occupants to work or to live at their most effective in a comfortable environment by providing them with the basic framework of facilities, such as power, communication and light. The building's M&E services also provide a secure environment with safety an utmost priority.

207

As with all buildings, but even more so in the skyscraper, M&E system integration and options need to be considered in the preliminary stages of its design as these depend on expected user requirements and marketing requirements. Different systems will have varying mechanical plant-room requirements and distribution systems which will affect building efficiencies and floor-to-floor heights.

The extent of provision of M&E building services as well as its intelligent building (IB) systems in a skyscraper depends entirely upon the owners of the building (ie. on what proportion of costs are to be allocated to the M&E and IB features to be incorporated in the building).

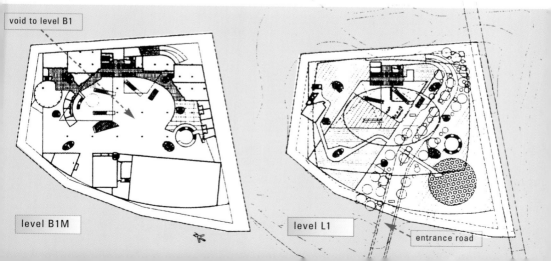

void to level B1

level B1M

level L1

entrance road

The apportionment of energy use in buildings is about 27% in commercial buildings and 29% in domestic buildings. In commercial buildings more than 50% of the energy used is for the occupants' thermal comfort (eg. cooling or heating) and for visual purposes (eg. lighting). These become the target areas for the designer for energy conservation by bioclimatic means.

In a typical high-rise office building, the following consumption of electricity is often found:

AIR-CONDITIONING	40 W/sq m	55%
LIGHTING	18	25
OTHERS (LIFTS, APPLIANCES, ETC)	15	20
	73 W/sq m	100%

Energy-efficient design in the bioclimatic skyscraper can reduce energy consumption, which will not only benefit the building owner/tenant but will assist Utilities in managing their peak demand and a sustainable future through minimising energy use.

IN A FIFTY-YEAR LIFE-CYCLE OF A SKYSCRAPER, ENERGY COSTS CONTRIBUTE 34% OF THE TOTAL COSTS MAKING ENERGY CONSERVATION A JUSTIFIABLE COST SAVING OBJECTIVE.

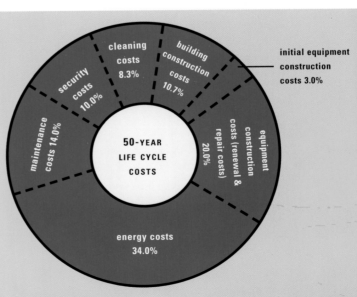

cleaning costs 8.3%
building construction costs 10.7%
initial equipment construction costs 3.0%
security costs 10.0%
maintenance costs 14.0%
50-YEAR LIFE CYCLE COSTS
equipment construction costs (renewal & repair costs) 20.0%
energy costs 34.0%

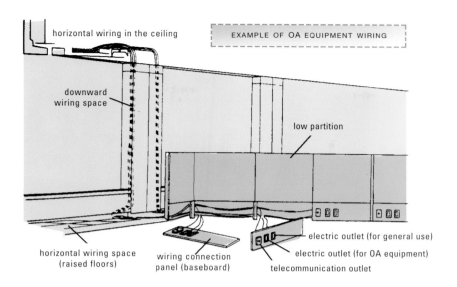

horizontal wiring in the ceiling

downward
wiring space

low partition

horizontal wiring space
(raised floors)

wiring connection
panel (baseboard)

electric outlet (for general use)

electric outlet (for OA equipment)

telecommunication outlet

There are a number of important objectives for the design of the bio-climatic skyscraper's M&E and IB services:

- The systems should be economical to build and operate, be efficient, and minimise energy consumption both during construction and during the life of the building.

- They should maximise human comfort, temperature, acoustics and lighting.

- They should minimise running costs by using ambient energy and heat recovery systems, and reduce heat gain (during summer) and heat loss (during winter).

- They should maximise usable space by reducing equipment areas and maximising structural efficiency.

- They should minimise maintenance costs by using quality materials and equipment, have good maintenance areas, and be simple and reliable.

- They should reduce the environmental impact by installing systems that are quiet, do not discharge pollutants, use materials with no CFCs, and be energy efficient and reduce carbon dioxide production.

- They must provide a flexible framework around which the building can be remodelled, adapted and changed; this being crucial to the life of the building.

209

energy conservation

Building energy consumption accounts for about 15% to 20% of the nationwide electrical power consumption. Typical skyscrapers can consume up to at least 600 Kwhr/m^2 per year prime energy which would contribute to at least 400 kg/m^2 of carbon dioxide emissions per year, equivalent to a total of 20,000 tons per year.

'...the skyscraper of the 21st century requires control centres analogous to the human nervous system...interrelated control and synthesis of all servicing, total environmental integration and balance, structural balance and systems that are monitored, harmonious...' PROFESSOR IVOR RICHARDS

The bioclimatic skyscraper's M&E systems should therefore be designed to consume much less energy than the conventional skyscraper (especially in the reduction of air-conditioning and heating energy requirements).

The bioclimatic skyscraper's design intention is for a low-energy and low-polluting building with minimal negative ecological impact. To achieve this, it incorporates passive solar-architecture with only an absolute 'needs-based rationale' for mechanical heating and cooling, and uses sustainable building materials, equipment and assemblies.

air-conditioning, heating and productivity

The thermal comfort of building users is directly related to their productivity in the workplace. Since personnel costs account for 75-90% of total office expenses, any decline in productivity is of key importance to employers. For many, it follows that the easiest internal environmental solution is to air-condition all commercial buildings in the summer and heat them in the winter (if in the temperate and cold zones).

A free-running design (one with no mechanical air-conditioning or heating) has a greater degree of micro-environmental fluctuation and lack of consistency in the indoor temperatures since it depends on the outdoor climatic conditions which are variable. The design challenge is to maintain an acceptable level of indoor temperatures within comfort zones during the hours in use.

TECHNIQUE	CLIMATIC ZONE			
	HOT & DRY	HOT & HUMID	TEMPERATE	COLD
insulation — THE HEAT-TRANSFER THROUGH THE BUILDING SKIN IS REDUCED: THE HEAT LOSS FROM THE BUILDING IS REDUCED IN WINTER AND HEAT PENETRATION IS PREVENTED IN THE SUMMER	X	X	*	*
mass — MASS STORES HEAT TO STABLISE ROOM AIR TEMPERATURE: FOR HEATING IN WINTER, SOLAR HEAT IS ABSORBED IN DAY TIME AND RELEASED AT NIGHT. FOR COOLING IN SUMMER, MASS IS COOLED AT NIGHT TIME TO KEEP ROOMS COOL IN THE DAY TIME.	X	X	*	*
air lock — AIR LOCK PREVENTS THE HEAT LOSS BY AIR LEAKAGE TO MAKE THE BUILDING AIR-TIGHT.	*	*	*	*
solar glazing — THE SOLAR WINDOW OR SOLAR-COLLECTOR USES SOLAR HEAT POSITIVELY.	X	X	*	*
air-circulation — AIR IS CIRCULATED TO SUPPLY THE HEAT AND HOMOGENIZE THE AIR TEMPERATURE DISTRIBUTION IN THE ROOM.	O	X	X	X
sun space — SUN SPACES ARE ATTACHED TO THE BUILDING IN ORDER TO COLLECT SOLAR HEAT POSITIVELY LIKE GREENHOUSES, CONSERVATORIES, SUN ROOMS, ETC.	O	O	*	
shading — SOLAR INSOLATION IN THE SUMMER IS BLOCKED AND HEAT PENETRATION INTO THE BUILDING IS PREVENTED.	*	*	*	*
cross-ventilation — AIR VENTILATION LETS FRESH AIR IN AND EXHAUSTS HOT ROOM AIR OUT. AIR MOVEMENT PROMOTES HEAT EMISSION FROM THE HUMAN BODY SURFACE AND GIVES A FRESH FEELING.	X	*	X	X
night flushing — MASS OF COOLED AIR IN THE NIGHT TIME IS VENTED THROUGH THE BUILDING TO COOL IT. IT IS EFFECTIVE TO STORE 'COOLNESS'.	O	O	*	*
earth — THE STABLE TEMPERATURE OF THE EARTH CAN BE UTILISED FOR THE PURPOSE OF HEATING AND COOLING. EARTH BERMING ON THE ROOM HAS THE SAME EFFECT.	X	X	*	*
water spray — WATER IS SPRAYED ON THE BUILDING TO PROMOTE EVAPORATION. EVAPORATION COOLING IS EFFECTIVE IN DRY CLIMATES.	X	*	X	X
dehumidification — THIS EXPELS THE DAMPED ROOM AIR AND/OR INTENTIONALLY CONDENSED WATER. THE BUILDING MATERIAL WHICH WORKS AS ASPIRATOR OF HUMIDITY IS ALSO EFFECTIVE.	X	X	O	X
top-lighting — LIGHT IS INTRODUCED INTO THE SPACES AT ALL SEASONS BUT SOLAR CONTROL IS NECESSARY IN SUMMER.	X	X	*	*
side-lighting — HIGH SIDE-LIGHTING IS EFFECTIVE IN DISTRIBUTING THE ILLUMINANCE HOMOGENEOUSLY. SOLAR CONTROL IS NECESSARY DEPENDING ON THE WINDOW ORIENTATION.	X	X	X	X
light guide — SPECIAL DEVICES TRANSFER THE LIGHT TO THE DEEP INTERIOR OF THE BUILDING.	X	X	X	X
light shelf — THE SHELF WHICH IS INSTALLED AT THE GLAZING REFLECTS AND DIFFUSES THE DIRECT BEAM AND THE LIGHT CAN REACH INTO THE DEEP INTERIOR.	*	*	O	O

211

Source: *PLEA (Passive and Low Energy Architecture), Process Architecture*, No 98, Tokyo, Japan, 1991

lighting

For general office tasks, occupants operate most efficiently with illuminance values of 1,000 to 1,500 lux. This leads to electrical loads from lighting in excess of 60w/sqm. For instance, in the equatorial belt, every kilowatt of unnecessary lighting means 2.5 kW of cooling load making a total of 3.5 kW.

The use of task-oriented lighting (say 500 lux at the task) should be used where practical while providing say 200 lux over the whole area as general lighting. In the design of general lighting in the skyscraper with centralised air-conditioning equipment, consideration should be given to integrated lighting and air-conditioning systems which use illuminaries with heat removal capabilities.

Daylighting is an important consideration in minimising energy consumption. Design considerations include:

- for long narrow floor-plates, the envelope zone dominates (6 m to 8 m) and there are opportunities for meeting total lighting requirements in part or in whole from daylighting,
- daylighting of spaces should avoid direct incident radiation and adding glare to workplaces,
- in deeper floor-plates in atrium areas and penthouses, skylighting from the roof or atria can be introduced but any heat gain/loss should not exceed the lighting benefits,
- lighting systems should switch lights off where and when not necessary.

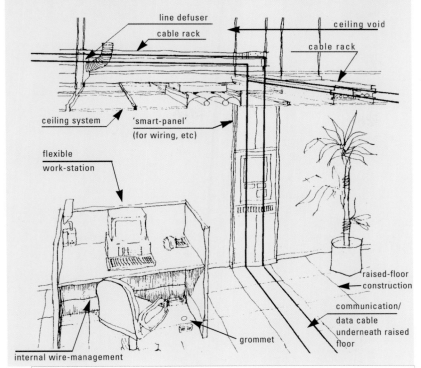

line defuser

cable rack

ceiling void

cable rack

ceiling system

'smart-panel'
(for wiring, etc)

flexible
work-station

raised-floor
construction

communication/
data cable
underneath raised
floor

grommet

internal wire-management

Studies have shown that the use of daylight optimisation techniques can save a significant proportion of lighting energy in commercial buildings. This includes the use of sensors for activating artificial lights on an as-needed basis. The use of energy-efficient lamp-fittings can also make a substantial saving as well as the use of low-level general lighting with additional task lighting as required. The task lighting can be switched off either automatically or manually when not required.

energy moderation

In cold climatic zones, the design strategy is to moderate the energy use:

winter period

The 'peak lopping' of the winter energy demand can be achieved by the following energy strategy:

> minimising heat loss by:
- good insulation
- minimising surface area
- protecting building envelope from the wind

> maximising solar gain by:
- large glazed area to the south
- maximising exposed area to the sun

> Using the thermal mass of the structure as a 24-hour heat store and to dampen sudden temperature changes.

summer period

The 'peak lopping' of the summer energy demand may be achieved by:
> minimising solar heat gain with adequate shading devices
> minimising heat gain cooling load by:
  - good insulation
  - protection from the winds
  - minimising surface areas
> Using the thermal mass of the skyscraper structure as a 24-hour thermal regulation, storing the cool air at night for the following day and dampening climatic changes.

mid-season periods (spring & autumn)

During the mid-seasons, there is no need for either heating or cooling and the skyscraper may be naturally-ventilated.

As the skyscraper comes out of winter, the heating is switched off and the whole building will open up to a warmer climate, although, as the climate warms further, the internal temperature rises and cooling will be required as summer begins. However, higher temperatures are more acceptable if there is good ventilation.

Thus if the switching on of the cooling system for the building is to be delayed, the bioclimatic skyscraper should enhance natural cross-ventilation as much as possible. Wind and solar energy may be used to drive the ventilation of the skyscraper by solar stack effect or wind-suction or wind pressure.

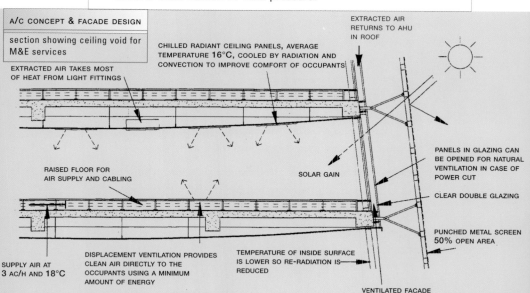

A/C CONCEPT & FACADE DESIGN

section showing ceiling void for M&E services

CHILLED RADIANT CEILING PANELS, AVERAGE TEMPERATURE 16°C, COOLED BY RADIATION AND CONVECTION TO IMPROVE COMFORT OF OCCUPANTS

EXTRACTED AIR RETURNS TO AHU IN ROOF

EXTRACTED AIR TAKES MOST OF HEAT FROM LIGHT FITTINGS

PANELS IN GLAZING CAN BE OPENED FOR NATURAL VENTILATION IN CASE OF POWER CUT

CLEAR DOUBLE GLAZING

RAISED FLOOR FOR AIR SUPPLY AND CABLING

SOLAR GAIN

PUNCHED METAL SCREEN 50% OPEN AREA

SUPPLY AIR AT 3 AC/H AND 18°C

DISPLACEMENT VENTILATION PROVIDES CLEAN AIR DIRECTLY TO THE OCCUPANTS USING A MINIMUM AMOUNT OF ENERGY

TEMPERATURE OF INSIDE SURFACE IS LOWER SO RE-RADIATION IS REDUCED

VENTILATED FACADE

The ventilation of the skyscraper can be driven by both wind and sun during mid-seasons. The temperature rise during the day is minimised by the night-time ventilation. The cool night time is used to pre-cool the structure for the following day.

intelligent building (IB)

The term 'Intelligent Building' (IB) is essentially a misnomer when it is used to describe the responsive automated functions of a building. It might be regarded as a marketing term applied to a building which has certain automatic responsive features to react to certain pre-programmed stimuli. It would appear that the term is in such widespread use that it is here to stay. Accepting the term as commonplace, we should regard its use simply as a simile of human intelligent behaviour.

215

Strictly speaking, the adjective 'intelligent' applies to human beings and (certain) organisms, and not to any inanimate object. Until AI (Artificial Intelligence) is fully realised, no inanimate object (such as a building) can be truly intelligent in the way that a human being is. For instance, a building cannot make independent ethical decisions, although a building can have certain intelligence-like capabilities. The building's intelligent systems can have software programmes that imitate to a limited extent the intelligent behaviour of humans.

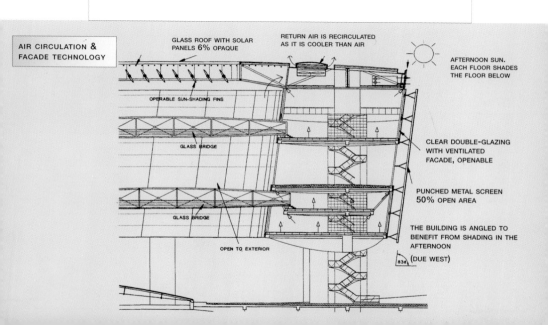

AIR CIRCULATION & FACADE TECHNOLOGY

GLASS ROOF WITH SOLAR PANELS 6% OPAQUE

RETURN AIR IS RECIRCULATED AS IT IS COOLER THAN AIR

AFTERNOON SUN. EACH FLOOR SHADES THE FLOOR BELOW

OPERABLE SUN-SHADING FINS

GLASS BRIDGE

CLEAR DOUBLE-GLAZING WITH VENTILATED FACADE, OPENABLE

GLASS BRIDGE

PUNCHED METAL SCREEN 50% OPEN AREA

THE BUILDING IS ANGLED TO BENEFIT FROM SHADING IN THE AFTERNOON

OPEN TO EXTERIOR

(DUE WEST)

We can use the term intelligent building to refer to a building that has certain intelligence-like capabilities (such as reasoning and responding to pre-programmed stimuli) to optimise its mechanical, electrical and enclosural systems to serve the users and managers of the building. The extent of provision is dependent on the owners of the skyscraper.

There is also the question of the rapidly changing technology. With infra-red, and with cordless phones, the need for cabling within a work-space might be eliminated, which could mean the end of raised floors. With lap-top computers and handphones many staff are not working in the office anymore; they may be working at home, at the customer's office, or in the hotel room and restaurant (see Chapter 3). The argument against this is, of course, that people need to socialise with other people and that the concept of office buildings as common meeting spaces will continue to be valid, but less as conventional workspaces and more as clubs and docking zones for their portables (eg. for information relay and upgrade).

216

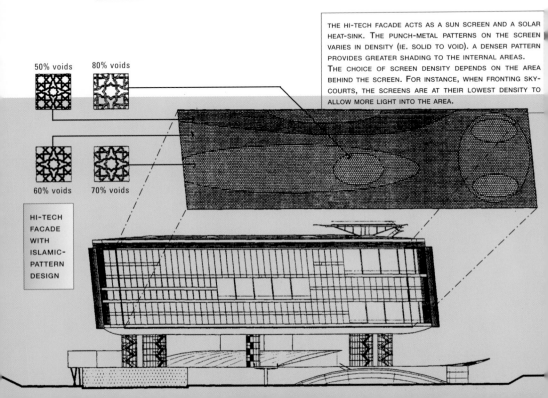

THE HI-TECH FACADE ACTS AS A SUN SCREEN AND A SOLAR HEAT-SINK. THE PUNCH-METAL PATTERNS ON THE SCREEN VARIES IN DENSITY (IE. SOLID TO VOID). A DENSER PATTERN PROVIDES GREATER SHADING TO THE INTERNAL AREAS. THE CHOICE OF SCREEN DENSITY DEPENDS ON THE AREA BEHIND THE SCREEN. FOR INSTANCE, WHEN FRONTING SKY-COURTS, THE SCREENS ARE AT THEIR LOWEST DENSITY TO ALLOW MORE LIGHT INTO THE AREA.

50% voids   80% voids

60% voids   70% voids

HI-TECH FACADE WITH ISLAMIC-PATTERN DESIGN

the IB's sub-systems

The IB has evolved into advanced integrated sub-systems which in varying degrees are part of most buildings today.

IB designs today commonly consist of a:

- BUILDING AUTOMATION SYSTEM (BAS)
- SECURITY SYSTEM
- FIRE AND LIFE SAFETY SYSTEM
- COMMUNICATION SYSTEM
- OFFICE AUTOMATION

Early on in the design process, these components can stand alone or be integrated with one another. In their specification of requirements, owners are instrumental in establishing the IB goals for the building. These components are discussed below (see also Chapter 2).

building automation system (BAS)

The BAS monitors and controls all mechanical, electrical, plumbing, elevator and lighting systems in the building. It can be PC-based, Direct Digital Control (DDC) using distributed microprocessors. Each command centre contains graphic display workstations for monitoring and controlling the various systems. Control stations include inventory tracking and maintenance scheduling. All mechanical and plumbing equipment, including chillers, boilers, cooling towers, pumps and fans, can be monitored and controlled. Each fan-powered office terminal unit might include a microprocessor for temperature, airflow condition, and time-of-day scheduling.

A programmable logic controller (PC) could be designed to co-ordinate between the two incoming lines and the emergency generator system to ensure continuous service to the essential load. It would also control the feeder breaker in terms of priority and events. As part of the electrical management, a micro-logic circuit breaker fitted on main and tie breakers as well as the feeder circuit can provide the capability of maintaining load per phase, record demand power factors, register harmonic distortion, provide control and monitoring capability, and an alarm for the main electrical distribution system. Energy metering can be equipped with digital remote read-out for monitoring tenant usage of electricity.

Lighting control includes: all areas with time-of-day scheduling, unoccupied hours internal off-switching with local override, occupancy recognition system to control lighting based upon room condition, and daylight sensing and lighting control.

The management control system for elevator traffic could be designed around the 'best elevator – best location' parameters, thus ensuring maximum availability of elevators serving a particular floor (see Chapter 2). Artificial Intelligence designed into elevator group supervisory control systems allows continuously adjustable responses to complex and changing traffic patterns in the building.

A control algorithm can be arranged to place elevators in service only as required by building traffic demands. When traffic is very heavy, all elevators will be available for service, while light traffic will be handled by a proportionately smaller number of elevators. A system programme will reduce elevator acceleration and deceleration rates during peak traffic periods, thus reducing energy usage.

All of the above systems can greatly enhance control and monitoring capabilities and substantially reduce maintenance and operation costs.

fire and life
safety system

The fire detection, alarm and communication system can be a non-coded, zoned, electrically supervised, fully-addressable multiplex system.

A two-channel, two-way telephone communication system could provide a link between the central control station and the entry to the enclosed exit stairway on every level, in the exit stairway at every fifth level, in elevator lobbies and vestibules, in each elevator cab, and at the fire pump controller location for use by the fire-fighting department.

The oldest built-in fire safety device is the automatic sprinkler, dating from 1850 in the form of perforated water pipes activated when needed. In 1882, Frederick Grinnell patented the first automatic sprinkler device in America, based on techniques still used today.

A voice alarm and public address system may be provided from the central control station (usually located in the skyscraper base) for rooms, corridors, elevator lobbies and vestibules, at exit stairways and other critical locations for fire department and other authority announcements.

security system

The access control and alarm monitoring system can be a fully supervised, digital multiplex system and interfaced to the closed-circuit television (CCTV) system. This system makes provision for alarm call up and initiation of real-time video recording for overhead security cameras associated with alarms. Alarm monitoring will occur at all perimeter doors by use of magnetic contacts, and intrusion detection will be provided for all ground level glass by means of glass-break detectors.

Access-card readers can be located at staff entrances, entrances to the skyscraper for after hours access, and between the loading dock and back of house areas of the building. The access card can be a magnetic-stripe card.

The CCTV system can be solid-state electronics and, if possible, use colour cameras and monitors installed at all entrances to the skyscraper, elevator lobbies, main building lobbies and areas of refuge. The switch can be microprocessor-based to permit flexibility in selection of cameras being viewed, sequencing of cameras and monitors, and alarm call up functions. Television monitors for routine viewing should have larger (say 23 cm diagonal) screens. The CCTV inputs to the VCR's can be digitally encoded for ease of review and playback.

communication system

In addition to Direct Tenant Services (DTS) from the local telecommunication company, Shared Tenant Services (STS) can be offered for both voice and data. An advantage is that telephone service to a new tenant becomes available in a timely manner and without negotiation with the local telecommunications company. This can be a strong marketing advantage, particularly for the international tenant's home office needing immediate telephone accessibility. This may also allow for direct billing to tenants for services provided and master operator/directory assistance. In addition, access to Community Antenna Television (CATV), Master Antenna Television (MATV), satellite and microwave antennas can be on a dedicated base on each floor. Video and teleconferencing can be made available in the skyscraper's conference areas.

A data network conversion facility could offer any combination required by the tenant. Typically, users might have one standard and need to convert to another. This facility will also provide media conversion capability (eg. from UTP to STP or even to Fibre, AUI/DIX to UTP or Fibre or any combination thereof). Bridging and routing capabilities in the skyscraper should also filter or offer 'like' segmented environments with different network address schemes. For tenants and other hot-desking users who may not want to make address changes, this system allows the user to filter or automatically convert addressing and routing.

The skyscraper could have a well-placed business centre to accommodate multi-purpose rooms and to provide the tenants and visitors with common fax, copy and telecommunication centres. PC terminals could be available with a wide range of popular business and graphic software with high-speed access to the internet and other international services. There should also be document manufacturing facilities with equipment for high-speed printing. This, as well as the other services, should be accessible to the tenants through the cable highway discussed on the next page.

system integration

Each of the skyscraper's IB systems should perform these functions continuously during the operation of the building and perform the majority of these alone without communication with the other systems. However, integration of the systems will provide further increased building intelligence. For instance, the fire alarm system must activate the smoke exhaust system by communication with the BAS. The former is still required in some cities, but today most local authority jurisdictions accept actuation of smoke control through the BAS.

There are three basic methods by which these two systems can communicate with each other and other systems. One method is to allow a single vendor to bid, supply and install all the systems, thereby assuring communication connectivity. One drawback of this method is that it does not allow the best vendor of each system type to be used. An alternate method is to use a company to interconnect the systems. This company may be one of the sub-system vendors or a third party vendor. Finally, the third method is where digital inputs/outputs are used to pass the specific information to the other system through an interface board. In general, a complete assessment of the magnitude of information that needs to be passed between systems is necessary to select the best method of a project.

cable highway

The intelligent skyscraper has a cable highway. This addresses the product-specific applications that meet tenant and building management needs, tenant business characteristics, and space designation. The cabling system might include a structured-cabling system of both copper and fibre facilities (with separate compartments for data/video, power and telephone) or might be entirely in a raised floor system.

SC Building

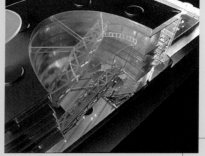

Atrium
cut-away

The cable highway infrastructure will prevent the need to run additional cabling for tenant turnover, expansion or acquisition of new technology. There are two types of cable highway systems within the building: the horizontal and riser sub-systems. Both of these systems make up the basic cable highway for the riser backbone and the horizontal work position connectivity. This cable highway infrastructure will support both STS as well as DTS needs.

The skyscraper's 'intelligence' can be nested in several components that use a vertical and horizontal cable highway emerging from an 'intelligent building cabinet' located on each floor.

This cable highway can consist of both single-mode and multi-mode fibre optic cable and unshielded twisted pair cable. The highway is optimised to accommodate extensive types of tenants, building services and future technological interconnectivity for data, voice and video, including ATM and Fibre Digital Data Interface (FDDI). Tenants may be offered both DTS and STS for voice through the cable highway, and a building Private Branch Exchange (PBX). STS for data can be offered as well as the cable plant for inter-tenant Local Area Networks (LAN).

As mentioned earlier, the skyscraper's amenities might include a central common business centre with fax and copy centres, high-speed print centres with user PCs and high density data recording, document manufacturing, training, audio-visual and teleconference centres, and private convention facilities.

If the skyscraper is a top-class hotel, it could incorporate intelligent guest-room controllers for lighting, HVAC, drapery control, automated mini-bar billing, and a host of in-house audio and video guest amenities.

The skyscraper's cable highway can serve all parts of the building (eg. office, retail and hotel zones) allowing amenities to be shared and the systems of each function to be intergrated, thereby enhancing ease of operation and maintenance.

222

The cable highway for the skyscraper will have to be optimised to accommodate various types of tenants, building service, and future technological interconnectivity for data, voice, video and building services functions. Within the next five years it is anticipated that ATM and FDDI will become more prevalent and video tele-conferencing, voice and data networks may become part of a single cabling infrastructure.

command centres

It is likely that the basic system architecture will have a number of main 'command centres' (eg. for the retail area, the hotel and the office if these are in the same skyscraper). The office command centre can also serve as the master building command centre. The command centre and all areas of the skyscraper would be served by a cabling system (eg. copper and fibre optic structured cabling system).

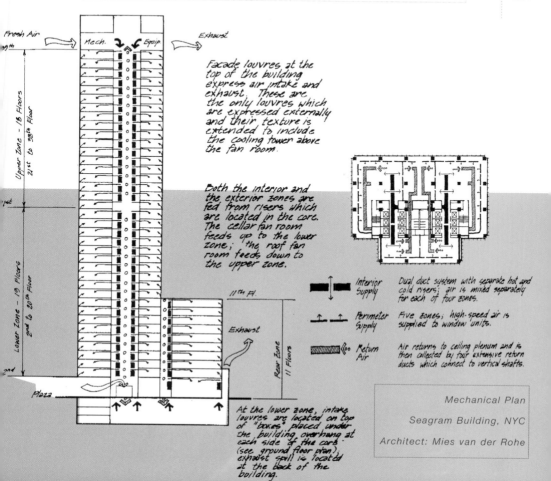

Facade louvres at the top of the building express air intake and exhaust. These are the only louvres which are expressed externally and their texture is extended to include the cooling tower above the fan room.

Both the interior and the exterior zones are fed from risers which are located in the core. The cellar fan room feeds up to the lower zone; the roof fan room feeds down to the upper zone.

Interior Supply — Dual duct system with separate hot and cold risers; air is mixed separately for each of four zones.

Perimeter Supply — Five zones; high-speed air is supplied to window units.

Return Air — Air returns to ceiling plenum and is then collected by four extensive return ducts which connect to vertical shafts.

At the lower zone, intake louvres are located on top of "boxes" placed under the building overhang at each side of the core (see ground floor plan); exhaust spill is located at the back of the building.

Mechanical Plan

Seagram Building, NYC

Architect: Mies van der Rohe

use of thermal mass

Thermal mass integrated with the M&E systems functioning in the bioclimatic skyscraper can be used not only to delay the time of peak indoor temperature compared to outdoor temperature, but also to reduce it significantly. Design considerations include:

- where mass is used for warmth, it should be exposed to incident solar radiation,

- where mass is required for cooling, it may be better placed in a shaded zone,

- buildings may be pre-heated using electric or hot-water tubing embedded in the mass (usually floors),

- buildings may be pre-cooled by night-flushing using cool night air from outside, although this requires significant amounts of exposed mass, and may be necessary only at certain times of the year. Where little mass is used, night-purge cooling removes warm indoor air and replaces it with cool air from outside.

In buildings with extended hours of use, thermal mass heated during the day can also be a cause of discomfort during the night when the heat is released.

SC Building

external wall
cross-section

224

EXPERT CHECKLIST

1 ENVELOPE SYSTEM
Exterior wall
Window glazing
Roof
Subgrade
Notable overall performance
System integration

2 STRUCTURAL SYSTEM
General system
Notable overall performance
System integration

3 INTERIOR SYSTEM
Ceiling
Floor
Fixed interior wall
Furnishings

4 MECHANICAL SYSTEM
Heating, ventilating, and air-conditioning
Service generators, conduits and terminals
Energy management control systems (EMCS)
Central and Local management systems
Lighting
Service generator, conduits and terminals
Lighting/dynamic control systems
Plumbing
Service generator, conduits and terminals
Fire safety
Service generator, conduits and terminals
Vertical transportation
Notable overall performance
System integration

5 POWER & TELECOMMUNICATION
Service generator (External Signal)
Power
Data/video
Telephone
Service conduits (Internal Signal)
Power
Wire management systems
Telephone
Service terminals
Power
Telephone
Computers & peripherals
Dynamic controls
MIS/ Telecommunications planning module
Notable overall performance
System integration

6 PHYSICAL SECURITY SYSTEMS
Security system
Notable overall performance
System integration

7 OVERALL BUILDING PERFORMANCE

chapter nine

the geography
of the
skyscraper

- multi-storey urban design
- relationship with pedestrians & street
- relationship with the city block
- relationship with the city

'skyscrapers rake the night sky as they mark the core of our city, and they create incredible landscapes when temperature inversions clothe their bases in cloud and leave their heads in the sun. We discover again that we are on a spherical planet.'

PROFESSOR LEON VAN SCHAIK

focal super-tall
skyscraper

geography

When designing the skyscraper, the designer must also look at the greater environmental impact and contextual implications of the building in relation to the site, the city block and the city itself. These considerations constitute the geography of the skyscraper, its spatial and urban relationship with its surroundings.

Skyscrapers are evidently massive structures and, simply by virtue of their overwhelming physical presence and inorganic intensity, they have come to represent the contemporary city of the developed world. Skyscrapers can be said to make up the city. This building type has, within the incredibly short period of its urban history (since its introduction in the 1890s), become the key influence on the city, its workings and its society.

In many instances, skyscrapers constitute the city itself: in most cities, they already form the city's core, CBD and financial hubs. This is true for just about every city with a population of over 100,000 in the world today.

The geography of the skyscraper consists of the locational constraints and opportunities that affect its design. Geographically, the pressures of increased land-values, urban accessibility, expanding urban populations, globalization of national economies, and locational preferences of businesses make the skyscraper in the developing world an inevitability. Rather than an endless debate on its viability and acceptability, what should be of greater concern (in view of rampantly developing Asia) is how these skyscrapers are designed and whether there are effective planning controls for their location, design, building height, form and beneficial characteristics.

Economically, the skyscraper's existence is derived from high land values which are related to urban accessibility, which in turn is a product of road and rail services. Thus, skyscrapers result from their geographical optimisation of land costs and building economics, the locational preferences of their occupants, their owner's desire for flagship status (induced by the assertive image associated with the high-rise), and their ingenious feats and inventions of architectural and engineering design.

Financially, the skyscraper is a 'wealth-creating' mechanism that operates in an urban economy. Commercially and aesthetically, skyscrapers have become for many the objects of personal wealth and power. They have evolved as the logical extension of the development of real estate. They are the obvious solution to how to make more money out of a small piece of scarce urban land resource. The commercial objective is simply to build more and more equivalents of the basic plot, stacking them up as high as possible to better utilise and multiply a limited resource. For the commercial developer, the higher the stacking, the higher the returns. This can extend upwards until limited by local authorities, constraints and building economics where the construction costs vis-à-vis height makes the financial returns on investment unviable.

The growth of the skyscraper began during the latter decades of the nineteenth century when the business corporation emerged as the dominant new commercial institution. By the twentieth century a pronounced split had occurred between the production and the administrative facilities in many of the businesses thereby affecting city-planning geographically.

Factories then became relegated to the suburbs, on cheap land, with plenty of room for expansion. Meanwhile, skyscrapers containing thousands of clerical and service-based workers with new business machines and equipment were clustered near the centres of finance in the CBD's of the city. The process began to transform the profile of cities and the geography of the urban development, notably in North America.

The office building as a skyscraper became the flagship of major corporations or speculative accommodation for multiple small-business tenants. The proliferation of the North American stereotypical office building led to its degradation from its fine, specific and rational late nineteenth-century origins to the built 'stock-in-trade' of anyone anywhere who wished to develop, design and build for the rising property market whether in Chicago, Tokyo, Hong Kong or Kuala Lumpur.

227

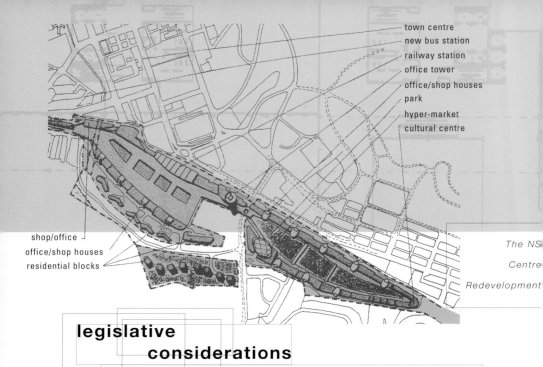

town centre
new bus station
railway station
office tower
office/shop houses
park
hyper-market
cultural centre

shop/office
office/shop houses
residential blocks

The NS
Centre
Redevelopment

legislative considerations

        The local government town planning legislation for the city determines the extent to which the skyscraper can be built (eg. its footprint, its height limitations, set-back lines, basement lines, ingress and egress positions, car-parking provisions and any other communal requirements that are mandatory for that location, eg. public rooms, rail interchanges, etc).

        The local planning authorities usually control the extent of permissible built-up space for the plot as a permitted plot ratio (or FAR, the Floor-Area-Ratio) and site-coverage (eg. permissible building footprint of plinth-ratio). From this, the designer initially analyses the extent of the permitted gross built-up area (GFA) for the plot area. This is simply the site area multiplied by the permitted plot ratio for the site (eg. the ratio may be 1:12) (see Chapter 1).

        Costings are usually calculated at this stage. For instance, assumptions on the building efficiencies (ie. as a net-to-gross (NFA) ratio percentage) are made to derive the net rentable/saleable area and total GFA areas for the plot.

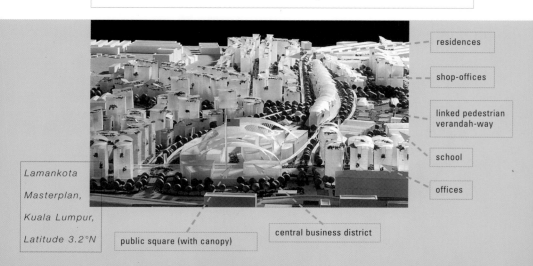

residences

shop-offices

linked pedestrian verandah-way

school

offices

Lamankota Masterplan, Kuala Lumpur, Latitude 3.2°N

public square (with canopy)

central business district

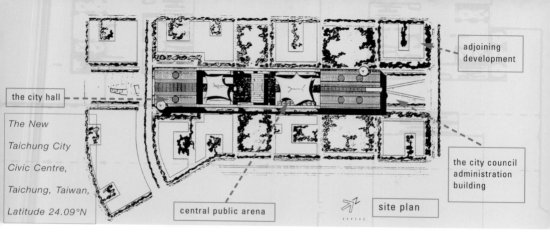

the city hall

The New

Taichung City

Civic Centre,

Taichung, Taiwan,

Latitude 24.09°N

adjoining
development

the city council
administration
building

central public arena

site plan

Others factors include delineating the permissible building envelopes (which may include height restrictions) and permissible building footprints (as a percentage of the site area), and the extent of car-parking provisions and their location (ie. whether above ground, below ground or elsewhere).

From these figures, the financial analyses or ROI (Returns-On-Investment) are made to establish the building's viability taking into account other costs such as legislative charges, saleable/rentable rates and financing costs.

Real estate marketing considerations related to the locality and its surroundings are also taken into consideration.

However, as most skyscrapers are on compact urban sites, crucial design considerations include the extent of road-widening, building set-back line from boundary lines, extent of building volume in relation to provision of fire-engine access (eg. fire-fighting access to skyscraper facades), vehicular ingress and egress points, and other town planning requirements.

229

Lamankota

Masterplan

(Residential Segment)

The New
Taichung City
Civic Centre

building orientation
and shadows

Skyscrapers are exposed more directly than other buildings to the full impact of external temperature and direct sunlight, so their overall orientation has an important bearing on energy-conservation within the building and the shadow it may cast on surrounding sites.

The greatest source of heat gain can be the solar radiation entering through the window. The direct radiation transmitted varies markedly with the time of the day and the angle of incidence.

Site planning and building orientation decisions that are made by the designer early in the design process can have a significant impact. Issues to consider include:

- solar orientation with respect to the sunpath to create opportunities for appropriate form development and solar access,

- stringent sun-control for the building throughout the year, using knowledge of summer-winter sunpaths,

- overshadowing effects of other buildings and vegetation on the building and other parts of the site.

230

avenues

boulevard

2,000 m long
verandah-way

Lamankota
Masterplan
(Low-cost Residential Sector)

LRT to reduce energy-cost
of motor-vehicular travel

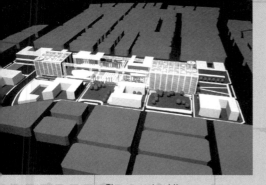
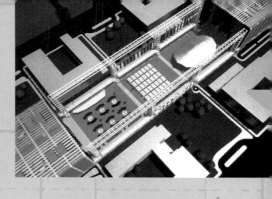

The central public arena
as variable seasonal
community activity zone

contextual relationship

The tall building has three levels of physical and climatic relationship with its urban context: firstly, at the level of the city as a whole, including its image and infrastructural physical-social-economic systems; secondly, at the level of the city-block; and lastly, at the level of the pedestrian (and existing patterns of life around, inside and through the building's lower floors).

CBD
town centre

up-market residential clusters

avenues

hotel

public plaza

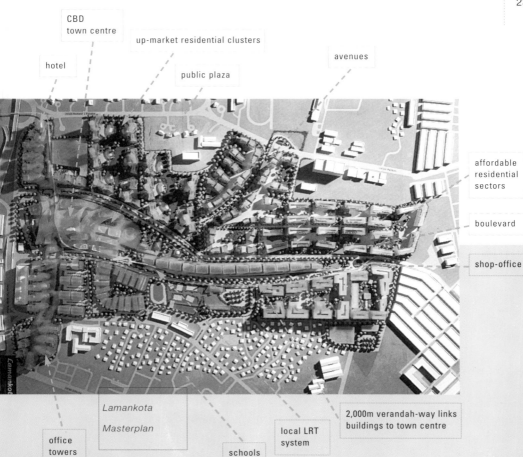

affordable
residential
sectors

boulevard

shop-office

office
towers

Lamankota
Masterplan

schools

local LRT
system

2,000m verandah-way links
buildings to town centre

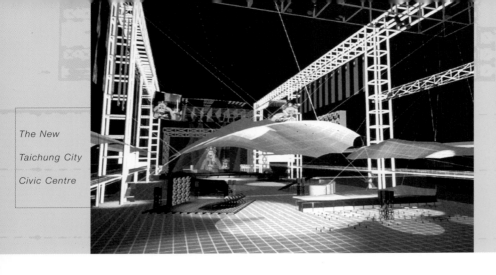

Normally, the erection of a new building on a vacant site increases the site's overall density of inorganic mass. The environmental impact of this at the city level is compounded by that of its servicing systems, power, lighting, air-conditioning, and waste output which not only consume energy in their operations but may also make polluting discharges. All these need to be addressed by passive climatic-control systems which reduce and control energy consumption and polluting systems.

The overall energy exchange of the city, if seen holistically as an ecosystem, is increased with the introduction of any new skyscraper. Depending upon the shading and micro-climate wind-flow of the locality, the new building may lead to enhanced 'heat-island' effects and other micro-climatic problems. These need to be counteracted by the introduction of vertical landscaping, the use of heat-sink claddings, and the reduction of air-conditioning use which increases the heat-discharges from their condensers.

At the city-block level, a new skyscraper affects the wind-flow around adjoining buildings at both the upper levels and the lower levels, and wind-tunnel tests should be carried out early on to ascertain the impact on the site and on the surroundings.

The heat emitted by the skyscraper's systems also affects the micro-climate of the locality. The introduction of vertical landscaping into the skyscraper, however, increases the biotic components in the local ecosystem.

It is clear that in terms of urban planning skyscraper built forms and massing can affect several city-blocks with local environmental factors that can influence the comfort and well-being of other city inhabitants. The skyscraper's designer should therefore carefully consider the pattern of sun and shade; the degree of protection from radiation, rain and wind; and the ventilation conditions arising from the new building. These in turn, will be influenced by the dimensions and particularly the heights of the locality's existent

skyscrapers, the spacing of the skyscrapers, the variation in heights in any one section of a town, the orientation of the street network, and the distribution and extent of open spaces and gardens. For the designer, the site planning of the new skyscraper should be directed towards optimization of natural ventilation conditions and providing the maximum protection from solar radiation and other undesirable climatic factors (eg. the North wind in temperate and cold climates).

street relationships

The street relationship of the skyscraper is particularly important in its design by virtue of its magnitude and height. Pedestrians perceive and visually react to the skyscraper generally up to its 4th or 5th floors only (eg. as seen from the opposite side of the street). Beyond this they have to strain their necks to see the upper parts of the building.

What should the pedestrian's relationship to the skyscraper be? Ideally, the pedestrian should be able to enter the skyscraper as high up as possible from the ground plane – through ramps, escalators and earth berms – so that the distanced relationship with the upper-parts of the skyscraper is reduced.

The relationship of the skyscraper's ground plane to the street outside is also important. In many parts of the world, the advent of the sealed indoor air-conditioned atrium has marked the demise of street-life. The ground plane of the skyscraper deserves special consideration. Preferably, it should be entirely open to the outside as a naturally-ventilating space. It should not be enclosed or air-conditioned. In this way, it serves effectively as a 'transitional space' between the outside and the enclosed interior of the building.

Pan Global
Tower,
Johore
Baru,
Latitude 1.4°N

entrance canopy

Hartamas Town Centre
Studies, Kuala Lumpur
Latitude 2°N

the U-shaped configuration with
low-rise and high-rise
built-forms combined

low-rise in
U-shape
layouts

skyscrapers located
at street-edge

Where climatically possible, as pedestrians approach the skyscraper they should come not to an abrupt glass-facade but to an 'open-to-the sky' space before entering the elevators into the upper-parts of the building. However, care should be taken to keep out wind-swept rain and wind-turbulence at the skyscraper's base. In temperate and cold climates, the gradual transition from outside to inside can be achieved by an air-curtain (heated in winter).

Urban design should discourage free-standing skyscrapers which can increase alienation from the street. They reduce the pedestrian communication and movement into and around buildings from the street. This results in the classic 'island site' situation (see Lamankota verandah city layout which rectifies this through linked verandah-ways, pages 228-231).

relationship
with the block

At the level of the city block, the sky-scraper's design becomes an important component of the block's urban design. The skyscraper has to be designed in relation to the massing of the entire block, while the block itself must relate to the other adjoining blocks and streets.

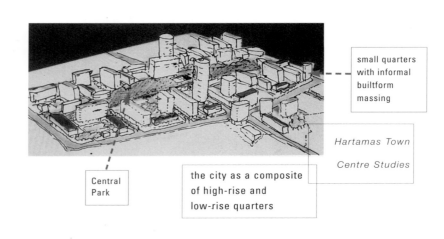

small quarters
with informal
builtform
massing

Hartamas Town
Centre Studies

Central
Park

the city as a composite
of high-rise and
low-rise quarters

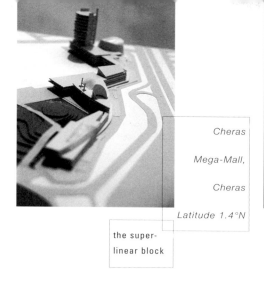

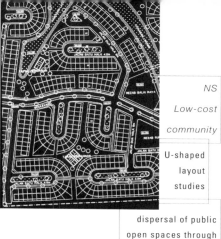

Cheras

Mega-Mall,

Cheras

Latitude 1.4°N

the super-
linear block

NS

Low-cost

community

U-shaped
layout
studies

dispersal of public
open spaces through
U-shaped layouts.

The linkages of the skyscraper have to be considered (eg. vehicular, pedestrian, public transport, service vehicles, etc). The skyscraper's design has to be seen with regard to 'place-making' within the city (eg. as part of the city's squares, boulevards, promenades, broad-walks, etc).

Clusters of skyscrapers make sense from the standpoint of business togetherness, but not always from the standpoint of urban design. Many famous buildings, for instance, cannot be seen because taller buildings have grown all around them.

235

Prior to the twentieth century, the growth of the common 'solids of the city' (ie. its urban 'fabric') was primarily horizontal. In the twentieth century, it is vertical, the solids standing up and altering the continuous profile along the horizon. The impact of this development on the city block is most visible in its contrast to the medieval tissue of old world cities or the early colonial period shop-house city in East Asia. Over the grid patterns in the new world cities, the skyscraper block can be designed to be an improvement, adding a vertical dimension to the regularity of the gridiron plan.

In the old world cities and in the cities in the East where the gridiron street plan did not exist, the new sky-scrapers can also generate undesirable problems, destroying existent streetscapes, creating a line of island sites along previously arcadian boulevards, and introducing new problems of tall builtform relationships with the city block and with the city's skyline.

'When the cities of Asia come to resemble their
European counterparts, as clusters of skyscrapers,
the concept of geography will inevitably
disappear from the earth.' AKIRA SUZUKI

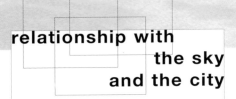

relationship with the sky and the city

The other level of relationship the skyscraper has with its surrounding is with the city as a whole. Superficially, this includes the skyscraper's impact on the city's skyline. Unlike other building types, the top of the skyscraper is an important design consideration.

While the skyscraper makes significant demands on the city's services and infrastructure (eg. public transport, garbage collection, maintenance, electrical lighting, telephones, sewerage, water supply, etc), it can also be seen as beneficial: contributing increased property taxes back to the city.

236

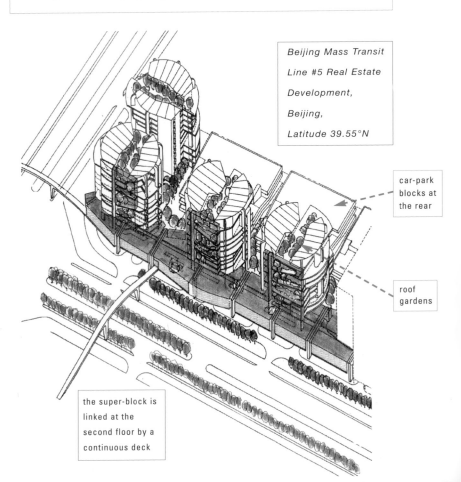

Beijing Mass Transit Line #5 Real Estate Development, Beijing, Latitude 39.55°N

car-park blocks at the rear

roof gardens

the super-block is linked at the second floor by a continuous deck

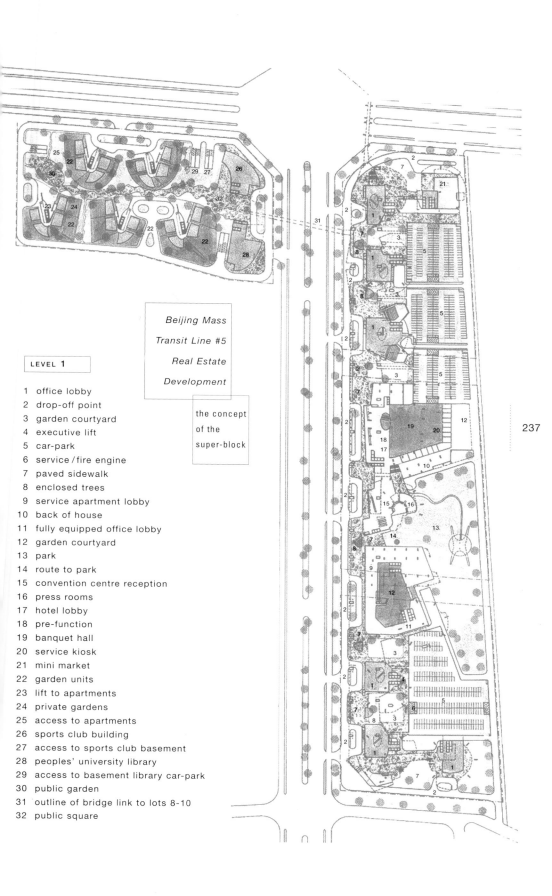

Beijing Mass
Transit Line #5
Real Estate
Development

the concept
of the
super-block

LEVEL 1

1 office lobby
2 drop-off point
3 garden courtyard
4 executive lift
5 car-park
6 service / fire engine
7 paved sidewalk
8 enclosed trees
9 service apartment lobby
10 back of house
11 fully equipped office lobby
12 garden courtyard
13 park
14 route to park
15 convention centre reception
16 press rooms
17 hotel lobby
18 pre-function
19 banquet hall
20 service kiosk
21 mini market
22 garden units
23 lift to apartments
24 private gardens
25 access to apartments
26 sports club building
27 access to sports club basement
28 peoples' university library
29 access to basement library car-park
30 public garden
31 outline of bridge link to lots 8-10
32 public square

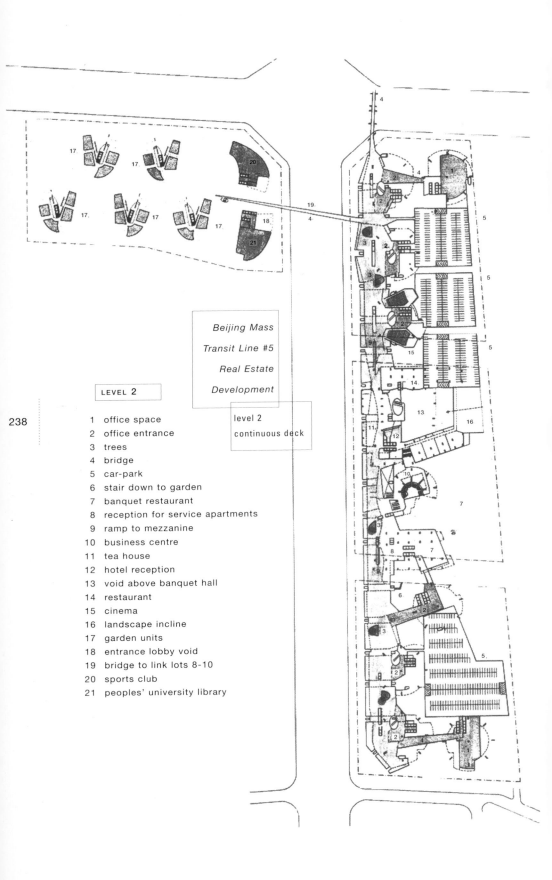

238

*Beijing Mass
Transit Line #5
Real Estate
Development*

LEVEL **2**

level 2
continuous deck

1 office space
2 office entrance
3 trees
4 bridge
5 car-park
6 stair down to garden
7 banquet restaurant
8 reception for service apartments
9 ramp to mezzanine
10 business centre
11 tea house
12 hotel reception
13 void above banquet hall
14 restaurant
15 cinema
16 landscape incline
17 garden units
18 entrance lobby void
19 bridge to link lots 8-10
20 sports club
21 peoples' university library

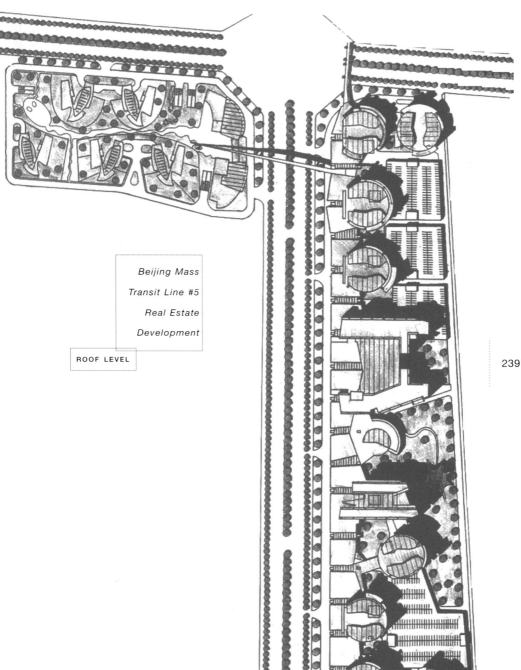

*Beijing Mass
Transit Line #5
Real Estate
Development*

ROOF LEVEL

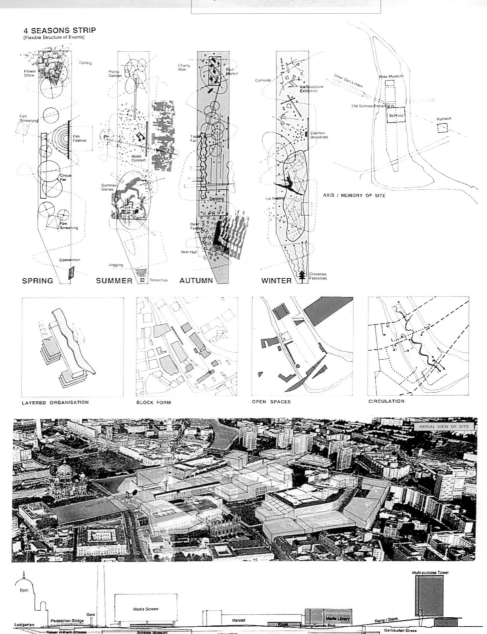

4 SEASONS STRIP
[Flexible Structure of Events]

SPRING SUMMER AUTUMN WINTER

AXIS / MEMORY OF SITE

LAYERED ORGANISATION   BLOCK FORM   OPEN SPACES   CIRCULATION

240

AERIAL VIEW OF SITE

LONGITUDINAL SECTION 1 : 2000

The public realm is designed as
a community stage that responds to
local cultural activities that change
with the seasons of the year.

conclusion + future R & D

'We would all like to have the
penthouse please. Failing
that, let our skyscrapers
enfold us with soft breezes,
falling petals and the sound
of laughter from on high.'

PROFESSOR LEON VAN SCHAIK

what is the future of the skyscraper?

Will the skyscraper become obsolete? Considering the rapid pace of technological change in urban development worldwide (especially in the developing world), this is the most pressing question affecting all building designers.

The importance of office work for a nation's economy will be more and more recognised. At the same time, office, hotel and residential skyscrapers already are and will continue to be the single largest item in any nation's asset base.

Some might argue that with the changing workplace, the office building as an edifice is a thing of the past. However, with the current rate of urbanisation and urban migration, especially in the Far East, this is unlikely to be so. It is contended that skyscrapers are synonymous with the twentieth century and are likely to be synonymous with the twenty-first century as well.

As mentioned earlier, lap-tops and hand-phones mean that many people no longer work in the office. The role of the office will continue to change to one of a communal meeting space. The offices will become less a conventional workspace and more a 'club' and a docking zone for employees' portables (eg. for information relay and upgrade).

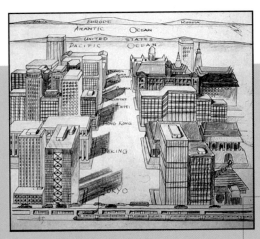

Towers rising in the East

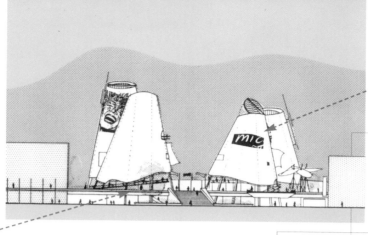

bioclimatic
community
interactive
towers

Saitama

Hiroba,

Saitama, Japan

Latitude 36°N

public plaza

The office-less future may
focus on the public plaza as
communal meeting &
recreational zone.

office design
as hospitality design

The innate desire for human company and
society is hardier than we realise and is likely to survive even in the
presence of a 500-channel interactive-cable system. People will still
want to meet other people.

The complex geographical genesis of the
tall building is found in demographics, location and land values, resulting from society's need for growth. This growth persists and has been
increasing exponentially since the beginning of urbanisation. There is
no reason to expect this trend to change.

243

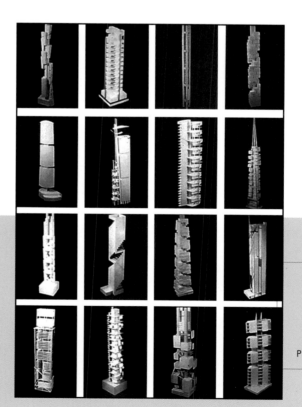

Skyscraper
Morphology
Studies
(at Hong Kong
University with
Professor Eric Lye)

Saitama Hiroba

bioclimatic fabric-clad towers

The skyscraper offices of the future will become more like hotels (eg. the office environment having the hospitality services, work-stations, room services, conference and other retail and business facilities of a hotel).

Offices will have:

- CHOICE IN RELATIONSHIP WITH OUTSIDE ENVIRONMENT
- TRANSITIONAL SPACES BETWEEN THE INSIDE AND THE OUTSIDE
- COMMUNITY ZONES AS OPPORTUNITY AREAS FOR MEETING (EG. SKYCOURTS, LIFT-LOBBIES, ETC)
- FOOD AND EATING PROVISIONS, PANTRY AREAS
- NATURAL SUNLIGHT ACCESS
- NATURAL VENTILATION (FRESH-AIR) ACCESS
- COMMUNITY AND PRIVACY CONSIDERATIONS
- RE-CREATION OF GROUND CONDITIONS IN THE AIR
- INCREASED WASH ROOM PROVISIONS, SHOWERS, AND GREATER ACCESSIBILITY
- LIGHTING CONDITIONS AS SIMILAR TO THE OUTSIDE AS POSSIBLE
- USE OF CLEAR GLASS IN GLAZING

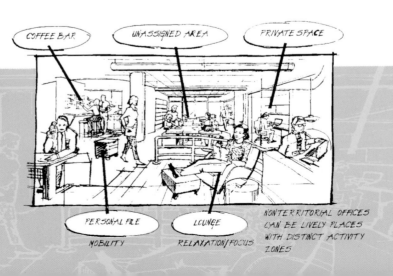

COFFEE BAR

UNASSIGNED AREA

PRIVATE SPACE

PERSONAL FILE

MOBILITY

LOUNGE

RELAXATION/FOCUS

NONTERRITORIAL OFFICES CAN BE LIVELY PLACES WITH DISTINCT ACTIVITY ZONES

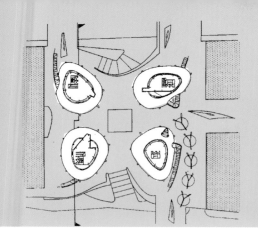

The future residential skyscraper may well become more and more like an upmarket hotel. It will have better designed public areas, more comfortable private areas, butler services, service elevators, and washroom and communal recreational facilities. Its building management might even become more similar to hotel management and be complete with 'back-of-house' facilities providing ordered meals and other amenities to offices like a hotel's range of room services.

Conversely, the future hotel skyscraper will be more like a 'state-of-the-art office' with linked intelligent systems. Rooms will have interactive work-stations as in an office and will be networked to the entire building's facilities and those elsewhere in the world.

Luxury up-market apartment dwellers will have their cars parked in 'garages-in-the-sky' right next to their high-rise apartment.

Source: M Shirow,
Ghost in the Shell, Dark Horse Comics,
Milwaukee, USA, 1995.

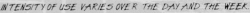

INTENSITY OF USE VARIES OVER THE DAY AND THE WEEK.

View of interior of the
future wall-climber

skyscraper design
as urban design

While studies into the relationship between skyscraper development and the city planning concept continue, it is evident that as the skyscraper increases in intensity of development and in height, the need for a 'vertical urban design theory' becomes even more pressing.

All the usual urban design concepts commonly planned horizontally in the ground plane for good city and civic design must now be re-interpreted vertically for the skyscraper. (These include place-making, vista creation, boulevards, promenades, urban squares, figure-ground and massing linkages).

TUESDAY AFTERNOON

View as the elevator
door opens to the
arrival floor

Source: M Shirow,
Ghost in the Shell,
Dark Horse Comics,
Milwaukee, USA, 1995.

from the bioclimatic
skyscraper to the
ecological skyscraper

Is the bioclimatic skyscraper a conundrum? Should ecological design be intensive? These are as much questions of economics as they are of ecology and urban planning.

The proposition of re-planning and re-building all of today's cities on a clean slate, based on ecological principles, may mean whole-scale waste of the existing building stock and infrastructure. It is clear that skyscrapers will continue to be built regardless of current piecemeal achievements of ecological proponents.

Kuala Lumpur Garden City, year 2020

247

Source: F Becker,
F Steele,
Work Place By Design,
Jossey-Bass Perkl,
San Francisco, 1994.

Where building intensity continues, the
designer should seek to design buildings based on ecological principles. The bioclimatic approach to skyscraper design is in effect only a
subset of the ecological approach, and it is hoped that the development of the bioclimatic approach will lead to a comprehensive, 'green'
skyscraper design. Not only could energy be conserved, but the entire
cycle of energy and material use should be considered throughout the
lifecycle of the skyscraper for a sustainable future.

Guthrie
Pavilion,
Petaling,
Latitude 3°N

'the future office
will be a
club-house'

pneumatic pillow-canopy

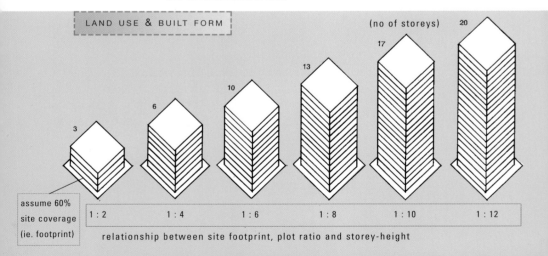

LAND USE & BUILT FORM   (no of storeys)   20

                                                          17

                                              13

                                  10

                      6

          3

assume 60%   1 : 2   1 : 4   1 : 6   1 : 8   1 : 10   1 : 12
site coverage
(ie. footprint)

relationship between site footprint, plot ratio and storey-height

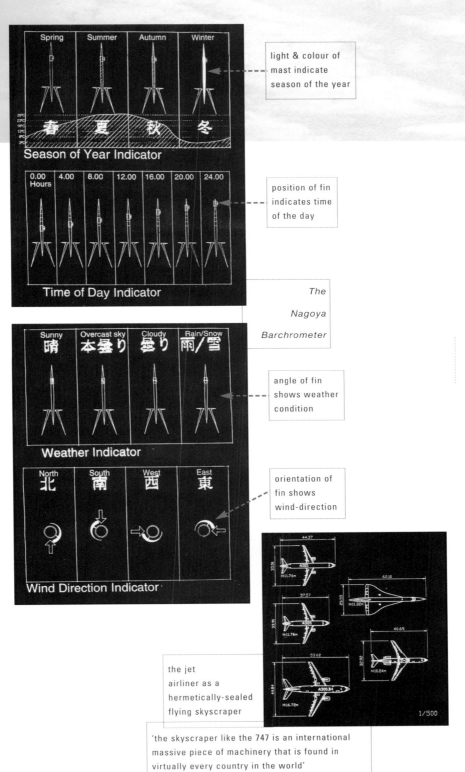

Season of Year Indicator

Spring	Summer	Autumn	Winter

春 夏 秋 冬

light & colour of mast indicate season of the year

Time of Day Indicator

0.00 Hours	4.00	8.00	12.00	16.00	20.00	24.00

position of fin indicates time of the day

The

Nagoya

Barchrometer

Weather Indicator

Sunny	Overcast sky	Cloudy	Rain/Snow
晴	本曇り	曇り	雨/雪

angle of fin shows weather condition

Wind Direction Indicator

North	South	West	East
北	南	西	東

orientation of fin shows wind-direction

the jet airliner as a hermetically-sealed flying skyscraper

'the skyscraper like the 747 is an international massive piece of machinery that is found in virtually every country in the world'

THE ONE HUNDRED TALLEST BUILDINGS IN THE WORLD

(SOURCE: COUNCIL ON TALL BUILDINGS AND URBAN HABITAT, 1994)

Note: * Height is measured from sidewalk level of main entrance to structural top of building. (Television, radio antennas, and poles are not included.)

	BUILDING	CITY	YEAR	STORE*
1	Petronas Tower 1	Kuala Lumpur	UC97	88
2	Petronas Tower 2	Kuala Lumpur	UC97	88
3	Sears Tower	Chicago	1974	110
4	Jin Mao Building	Shanghai	UC98	88
5	1 World Trade Center	New York	1972	110
6	2 World Trade Center	New York	1973	110
7	Empire State Building	New York	1931	102
8	Central Plaza	Hong Kong	1992	78
9	Bank of China Building	Hong Kong	1990	70
10	Sky Central Plaza	Guangzhou	UC96	80
11	T & C Tower	Kaoshiung	UC97	85
12	Amoco	Chicago	1973	80
13	John Hancock Center	Chicago	1968	100
14	Chrysler Building	New York	1930	77
15	Nations Bank Plaza	Atlanta	1993	55
16	First Interstate World Center	Los Angeles	1989	75
17	Texas Commerce Tower	Houston	1982	75
18	2 Prudential Plaza	Chicago	1990	64
19	Ryugyong Hotel	Pyongyang	1992	105
20	First Interstate Bank Plaza	Houston	1983	71
21	Landmark Tower	Yokohama	1993	70
22	311 South Wacker Drive	Chicago	1990	65
23	Columbia Center	Seattle	1984	76
24	American International Building	New York	1992	67
25	1 Liberty Place	Philadelphia	1987	60
26	First Bank Tower	Toronto	1975	72
27	40 Wall Tower	New York	1966	71
28	National Bank Plaza	Dallas	1985	71
29	Republic Plaza	Singapore	UC96	-
30	Overseas Union Bank	Singapore	1986	66

* UC - under construction

HEIGHT *			
m	ft	MATERIAL	USE
450	1476	Mixed	Multiple
450	1476	Mixed	Multiple
443	1454	Steel	Office
418	1371	Mixed	Multiple
417	1368	Steel	Office
415	1362	Steel	Office
381	1250	Steel	Office
374	1227	Concrete	Office
368	1209	Mixed	Office
364	1193	Concrete	Office
347	1140	Steel	Office
346	1136	Steel	Office
344	1127	Steel	Multiple
319	1046	Steel	Office
312	1023	Mixed	Office
310	1018	Mixed	Office
305	1000	Mixed	Office
303	995	Concrete	Office
300	984	Concrete	Hotel
296	972	Steel	Office
296	971	Steel	Multiple
296	970	Concrete	Office
291	954	Mixed	Office
290	950	Steel	Office
287	945	Steel	Office
285	935	Steel	Office
283	927	Steel	Office
281	921	Mixed	Office
280	919	-	Office
280	919	Steel	Office

	BUILDING	CITY	YEAR	STOREY
31	United Overseas Bank	Singapore	1992	66
32	Citicorp Center	New York	1977	59
33	Scotia Plaza	Toronto	1988	68
34	Transco Tower	Houston	1983	64
35	Society Center	Cleveland	1991	57
36	AT & T Corporate Center	New York	1988	60
37	Nations Bank Corporate Center	Charlotte	1992	60
38	900 North Michigan	Chicago	1989	66
39	Canada Trust Tower	Toronto	1990	51
40	Water Tower Place	Chicago	1976	74
41	First Interstate Tower	Los Angeles	1974	62
42	1 Peachtree Center	Altanta	1992	60
43	Parque Central Torres de Oficina	Caracas	1978	62
44	Transamerica Pyramid	San Francisco	1972	48
45	First National Bank	Chicago	1969	60
46	GE Rockefeller Center	New York	1933	70
47	Messeturm	Frankfurt	1990	70
48	USX Tower	Pittsburgh	1970	64
49	Gate Tower	Osaka	UC96	-
50	Osaka World Trade Center	Osaka	UC96	55
51	Altantic Center (IBM)	Atlanta	1988	50
52	Governor Philip Tower	Sydney	1993	61
53	City Spire	New York	1987	72
54	1 Chase Manhattan Plaza	New York	1961	60
55	Metropolitan Life	New York	1963	59
56	Malayan Banking Berhad	Kuala Lumpur	1990	54
57	City Hall Complex	Tokyo	1991	48
58	Rialto Tower	Melbourne	1985	60
59	Mellon Bank	Philadelphia	1990	56
60	Woolworth Building	New York	1913	57
61	John Hancock Tower	Boston	1976	60
62	Palace of Culture and Science	Warsaw	1955	42
63	Moscow State University	Moscow	1953	
64	Momentum Place	Dallas	1987	60
65	Commerce Court West	Toronto	1973	57
66	Nations Bank Center	Houston	1983	56
67	1 Worldwide Plaza	New York	1989	47
68	Bank of America	San Francisco	1969	52
69	Office Tower	Caracas	1985	60
70	1 Canada Square	London	1991	49

HEIGHT *		MATERIAL	USE
m	ft		
280	918	-	Office
278	915	Steel	Multiple
275	901	Mixed	Office
275	901	Steel	Office
271	888	Mixed	Office
267	885	Mixed	Office
253	875	Concrete	Office
267	871	Mixed	Multiple
265	869	-	Office
262	859	Concrete	Multiple
262	858	Steel	Office
260	853	Concrete	Office
260	853	Concrete	Multiple
260	853	Steel	Office
259	850	Steel	Office
259	850	Steel	Office
259	850	Concrete	Office
256	841	Steel	Office
254	833	-	Office
252	827	Mixed	Office
250	820	Mixed	Office
250	820	-	Office
248	814	Concrete	Multiple
248	813	Steel	Office
246	808	Steel	Office
244	799	Concrete	Office
243	796	Mixed	Office
242	794	Concrete	Office
241	792	Steel	Office
241	792	Steel	Office
241	790	Steel	Office
241	790	Mixed	Office
240	787	-	-
240	787	Mixed	Office
239	784	Mixed	Office
238	780	Steel	Office
237	778	Steel	Office
237	778	Steel	Office
237	778	Mixed	Office
236	775	Steel	Office

	BUILDING	CITY	YEAR	STOREYS
71	3 First National Plaza	Chicago	1981	58
72	First Bank Place	Minneapolis	1992	55
73	Norwest Center	Minneapolis	1988	57
74	Singapore Treasury Building	Singapore	1986	52
75	IDS Center	Minneapolis	1972	57
76	Korea Insurance Co	Seoul	1986	63
77	Heritage Plaza	Houston	1987	53
78	Tun Abdul Razak Building	Penang	1985	65
79	Carnegie Hall Tower	New York	1991	60
80	Equitable Tower	New York	1986	54
81	Maine Montparnasse	Paris	1973	60
82	1 Penn Plaza	New York	1972	57
83	1251 Avenue of the Americas	New York	1971	54
84	Prudential Center	Boston	1964	52
85	MLC Centre	Sydney	1978	65
86	First International Plaza	Houston	1981	55
87	Korea Trade Tower	Seoul	1988	54
88	JP Morgan Headquarters	New York	1989	50
89	Republic Plaza	Denver	1983	56
90	2 Union Square	Seattle	1989	56
91	Security Pacific Plaza	Los Angeles	1974	55
92	1 Liberty Plaza (US Steel)	New York	1973	54
93	Ikebukuro Tower (Sunshine 60)	Tokyo	1978	60
94	Chicago Title and Trust	Chicago	1992	51
95	20 Exchange Place (Citibank)	New York	1931	55
96	The Westin Stamford	Singapore	1986	70
97	Wells Fargo Tower	Los Angeles	1983	54
98	191 Peachtree	Atlanta	1992	50
99	The Westin	Detroit	1977	73
100	World Financial Center	New York	1984	51

HEIGHT *		MATERIAL	USE
m	ft		
236	775	Mixed	Office
236	775	Steel	Office
235	770	Steel	Office
235	770	Mixed	Office
235	770	Mixed	Office
233	764	Steel	Office
232	762	Steel	Office
232	761	Concrete	Office
231	757	Concrete	Office
230	752	Steel	Office
210	751	Mixed	Office
229	750	Steel	Office
229	750	Steel	Office
229	750	Steel	Office
228	749	Concrete	Office
228	748	Mixed	Office
228	748	Steel	Office
227	745	Steel	Office
227	745	Mixed	Office
226	743	Mixed	Multiple
227	743	Steel	Office
226	742	Steel	Office
226	742	Steel	Office
226	742	Mixed	Office
226	741	Steel	Office
226	741	Concrete	Hotel
225	740	Steel	Multiple
225	740	-	Office
225	739	Concrete	Hotel
225	739	Mixed	Office

Abu Dhabi Tower
Project Architect • Goon Li Ching
Design Architect • Goon Li Ching
Project Team • David Fu

Beijing Mass Transit Line #5
Project Architect • Seow Ji Nee
Design Architects • Mark Gurney,
Paul Mathews
Project Team • Ng Wai Tuck, Mariani
Abdullah, Margaret Ng, Loh Mun Chee,
Azman Che Mat

BP Building
Project Architect • James Chua Ching Ern
Design Architect • Huat Lim
Project Team • James Chua Ching Ern,
Huat Lim

Central Plaza
Project Architect • Lim Piek Boon,
Yew Ai Choo
Design Architects • Azahari Muhammad,
Rachel Atthis, Heng Jee Seng
Project Team • Ooi Poh Lye, Margaret Ng,
Loh Mun Chee, Yap Yow Kong, Russell Harnett,
Hannah Cherry

Cheras Mega-Mall
Project Architect • Indrani Vanniasingham
Design Architect • Eleena Jamil
Project Team • Claudia Monazenska

China Haikou Tower #2
Project Architect • Ang Chee Cheong
Design Architect • Indrani Vanniasingham
Project Team • Ng Wai Tuck, Margaret Ng,
Don Allan Ismail, Laurent Lim, Ng En-Loong,
Sacha Noordin, Derick Ng, Guy Westbrook,
Indrani Vanniasingham, Wang Qiyou

China Haikou Tower #3
Project Architect • Ang Chee Cheong
Design Architect • Ang Chee Cheong
Project Team • Ng Wai Tuck, Margaret Ng,
Don Allan Ismail, Laurent Lim, Ng En-Loong,
Sacha Noordin, Derick Ng, Guy Westbrook,
Indrani Vanniasingham, Wang Qiyou

Chongqing Tower
Project Architect • Shamsul Baharin
Design Architect • Shamsul Baharin
Project Team • Norindar-Hamzah Yeang
Architectural Engineering Design Co Ltd

Guthrie Pavilion
Project Architect • Seow Ji Nee
Design Architects • Ian Morris,
Paul Mathews, Tim Mellor
Project Team • Loh Mun Chee,
Warren Williams, Margaret Ng, Yap Yow Kong

Hartamas Town Centre
Project Architect • Jay Low
Design Architects • Mariani Abdullah,
Philip Tan
Project Team • Derick Ng, Ho Eng Ling,
Sow Sun Fung, Paul Brady, Simon Doody

Hitechniaga Tower
Project Architect • Don Allan Ismail
Design Architect • Sacha Noordin
Project Team • Guy Westbrook, Margaret Ng,
Tomas Quijano

IBM Plaza
Project Architect • Chee Soo Teng
Design Architect • Woon Chung Nam
Project Team • Mak Meng Fook, David Fu

256

JA Tower
Project Architect • Mark Gurney
Design Architect • Mark Gurney
Project Team • Margaret Ng, Loh Mun Chee,
Aoife Hooulihan, Shamsul Baharin,
Azman Che Mat, Eleena Jamil, Tomas Quijano

Lamankota Masterplan
Project Architect • Eddie Chan Kin Leong
Design Architect • Yvonne Ho Wooi Lee
Project Team • Aidan Hoggard,
Chew Tick Wah, Stephanie Lee, Leow Ai Boon

MBf Tower Penang
Project Architect • Laurent Lim, Yap Lip Pien
Design Architects • Haslina Ali,
Normala Arifin
Project Team • Don Allan Ismail, Hazlinda
Hashim, Rahimah Lasim, Ooi Poh Lye,
Sneha Mathews, Shamsul Baharin

Menara Boustead
Project Architect • Yeoh Soon Teck
Design Architect • Chee Soo Teng
Project Team • Mak Meng Fook,
Mun Khai Yip, Joe Khoo

Menara Budaya
Project Architect • Seow Ji Nee,
Chong Voon Wee, Ahmad Kamil
Design Architects • Normala Arifin,
Ken Wong, Seow Ji Nee
Project Team • Paul Mathews, David Fu,
Margaret Ng, Loh Mun Chee, Ooi Poh Lye

Menara Mesiniaga
Project Architect • Too Kah Hoe
Design Architects • Heng Jee Seng,
Seow Ji Nee
Project Team • Don Allan Ismail,
Sacha Noordin, Lyn Yap,
Yusof Zainal Abidin, Philip Tan Hui Lee,
Ooi Poh Lye, Rahimah Lasim, Tomas Quijano,
Mohamad Pital Maarof

Menara UMNO Penang
Project Architect • Shamsul Baharin
Design Architects • Ang Chee Cheong,
Tim Mellor
Project Team • Warren William,
Anthony Ogden, Ooi Poh Lye, Margaret Ng,
Yap Yow Kong, Hazlinda Hashim, Azizan,
Mah Lek, Loh Mun Chee, Deborah Rogger,
Tomas Quijano

Nagoya Barchrometer
Project Architect • Aoife Hooulihan
Design Architect • Aoife Hooulihan
Project Team • Azman Che Mat

New Taichung City Civic Centre
Project Architect • Houston Morris
Design Architects • Houston Morris,
Roshan Gurung
Project Team • Rajiv Ratnarajah,
Alvise Simondetti, Margaret Ng, Loh Mun Chee,
Yap Yow Kong, Yvonne Ho Wooi Lee

NS Centre Redevelopment
Project Architect • Indrani Vanniasingham
Design Architect • Indrani Vanniasingham
Project Team • Shamsul Baharin, Ho Eng Ling,
Paul Brady

Pan Global Tower
Project Architect • Siti Aminah Abd Shukor
Design Architect • Paul Mathews
Project Team • Tim Mellor, Indrani
Vanniasingham, Margaret Ng

Plaza Atrium
Project Architect • Yeoh Soon Teck
Design Architects • Mak Meng Fook,
Rahim Din
Project Team • Mak Meng Fook, David Fu

PNBIT Tower
Project Architect • Sneha Mathews
Design Architect • Philip Tan Hui Lee
Project Team • Eleena Jamil

Roof Roof House
Project Architect • Rahim Din
Design Architects • Rahim Din,
Mak Meng Fook
Project Team • Mak Meng Fook, David Fu
Rahimah Lasim, Kon Liam

Saitama Hiroba
Project Architect • Ang Chee Cheong
Design Architect • Paul Brady

SC Building
Project Architect • Houston Morris
Design Architects • Joshua Levine,
Ang Chee Cheong, Houston Morris
Project Team • Margaret Ng, Loh Mun Chee,
Yap Yow Kong, Derick Ng, Carlo Matta

Schindler Advanced Elevator Designs
Project Architect • Sneha Mathews
Design Architect • Yee Kwai Hoong
Project Team • Han Kooi Peng, Adam
Osbourne, Nik Hasliza Suriati

Shanghai Armoury Tower
Project Architects • Eddie Chan Kin Leong,
Song Guofu
Design Architects • Ridzwa Fathan,
Dang Wei Dong
Project Team • Roshan Gurung,
Yvonne Ho Wooi Lee, Margaret Ng,
Loh Mun Chee

SJCC Block
Project Architect • Andy Chong
Design Architect • Mohamad Pital Maarof
Project Team • Margaret Ng, Loh Mun Chee,

Tomas Quijano, Derick Ng, Mariani Abdullah,
Voon Quek Wah, Ooi Poh Lye

Spreeinsel Berlin
Project Architect • Ng En Loong
Design Architects • Ang Chee Cheong,
Ng En Loong
Project Team • Derick Ng, Ng Wai Tuck

SUEP (Taipan Crest)
Project Architect • Lim Piek Boon
Design Architect • Azahari Muhammad
Project Team • Margaret Ng,
Voon Quek Wah

Tokyo-Nara Tower
Project Architect • Puvan Selvanathan
Design Architects • Puvan Selvanathan,
Vincent Le Feuvre
Project Team • Emmy Lim

Wisma Kencana
Project Architect • Rahim Din
Design Architect • Rahim Din
Project Team • Mak Meng Fook

Wisma SMI
Project Architect • Lim Pay Chye
Design Architect • Mak Meng Fook
Project Team • Mak Meng Fook, David Fu

TR Hamzah & Yeang Sdn Bhd
8 Jalan Satu
Taman Sri Ukay
68000 Ampang
Selangor, Malaysia
Tel ~ 6 03 4571966
Fax ~ 6 03 4561005
E-mail ~ kynnet@pc.jaring.my

The Skyscraper and Tall Buildings

Adler, Jerry, *High Rise*, Harper Collins, NYC, USA, 1993.

Ali, Mir, M, et al (Eds), *Architecture of Tall Buildings,* Council on Tall Buildings and Urban Habitat, McGraw-Hill Inc, NYC, USA, 1995.

Aregger, H, & Glaus, O, *High-Rise Building and Urban Design,* private publication, Zurich, Switzerland, 1967.

Balfour, A, *Rockefeller Center, Architecture as Theatre,* McGraw-Hill, NYC, USA, 1978.

Ballard, JG, *High-Rise,* Flamingo, imprint of Harper & Row, London, England, 1993.

Beedle, L (Ed), *High-Rise Building: Recent Progress,* Council on Tall Buildings and Urban Habitat, LeHigh University Publ, Bethlehem, USA, 1986.

Beedle, L (Ed), *Tall Buildings – 2000 and Beyond,* Council on Tall Buildings and Urban Habitat, LeHigh University Publ, Bethlehem, USA, 1990.

Beedle, L (Ed), 'Habitat and the High-Rise, Tradition and Innovation', Proceedings of the 5th World Congress, 14-19 May, 1995, Council on Tall Buildings and Urban Habitat, LeHigh University Publ, Bethlehem, USA, 1995.

Bennett, David, *Skyscrapers, Form and Function,* Simon & Schuster, NYC, USA, 1995.

Garber, Joseph, R, *Vertical Run,* Simon & Schuster, England, 1996.

Goldberger, Paul, *The Skyscraper,* Alfred A Knoph, NY, USA, 1989.

Huxtable, AL, *The Tall Building, Artistically Reconsidered: The Search for a Skyscraper Style,* University of California Press, Berkeley and LA, USA, 1992.

Hyde, K, & Warwicker, J, *Mmm...Skyscraper, I Love You,* Booth-Clibborn Editions, London, UK, 1994.

Irace, F, *Emerging Skylines, The New American Skyscrapers*, Whitney Library of Design, NYC, USA, 1988.

Jencks, C, *Skyscrapers-Skycities,* Rizzoli, NYC, USA, 1980.

Kerr, Philip, *Gridiron,* Chatto and Windus, London, England, 1995.

Kilham, WH Jr, *Raymond Hood, Architect: Form Through Function in the American Skyscraper,* Architectural Book Publishing Co, NYC, USA, 1973.

Klotz, H, with Sabau, L, *New York Architecture, 1970-1990*, Prestel-Verlag, Munich, Germany, 1989.

Koolhaas, Rem, *Delirious New York, A Retroactive Manifesto for Manhattan,* 010 Publishers, Rotterdam, The Netherlands, 1994.

Mujica, F, Mandell, J, *Trump Tower,* Lyle Stuart Inc, NJ, USA, 1984.

Reina, P, 'No End to Asia's High-Rise Binge', in *ENR,* 29 May 1995, pp10-11.

Sabbagh, Karl, *Skyscraper*, Viking (Penguin Group), NYC, USA, 1990.

Mierop, Caroline, *Skyscrapers, Higher and Higher,* Norma Editions, Paris, France, 1995.

Saliga, PA (Ed), *The Sky's the Limit, A Century of Chicago Skyscrapers,* Rizzoli, NYC, USA, 1990.

Scuri, Piera, *Late-Twentieth-Century Skyscrapers,* Van Nostrand Reinhold, NYC, USA, 1990.

Tauranac, J, *The Empire State Building, The Making of a Landmark,* Scribner, NYC, USA, 1995.

Toy, Maggie, *Reaching For the Skies,* Architectural Design Profile No 116, *Architectural Design,* Academy Group, London, England, 1995.

Van Leeuven, TAP, *The Skyward Trend of Thought,* The MIT Press, Cambridge, USA, 1988.

Note: For further reference, refer to monographs and books published by the Council on Tall Buildings and Urban Habitat, by McGraw-Hill, NYC, and by LeHigh University, Bethlehem, USA.

Structure

Billington, DP, and Goldsmith, M (Eds), 'Technique and Aesthetics in the Design of Tall Buildings', in *Proceedings Annual Fall Meeting, American Society of Structural and Civil Engineers, Houston, 19 October, 1993.*

Hawkes, N, *Structures, Man-Made Wonders of the World,* Readers Digest Press, Australia, 1990.

Microys, H, et al (Eds), *Cast-in-Place Concrete in Tall Buildings Design and Construction,* Council on Tall Buildings and Urban Habitat, McGraw-Hill, NYC, USA, 1991.

Stephens, John, H, *The Guinness Book of Structures (Bridges, Towers, Tunnels, Dams),* Guiness Superlatives Ltd, UK, 1976.

Hainle, E, Leonhardt, F, *Towers, A Historical Survey,* Rizzoli, NYC, USA, 1989.

Workplaces

Applebly, S, 'What is wrong with the office?', in *Blueprint,* May 1993, pp30-31, 1993.

Damacion, MC (Ed), *Office,* Access, The Understanding Business Publication, SF, USA, 1992.

Becker, F, and Steele, F, *Workplace by Design, Mapping the High-Performance Workscape,* Jossey-Bass Publishers, SF, USA, 1995.

Duffy, F, 'Offices: Escape from the banal', in *Architectural Review,* November 1983, Volume CLXXIV No 1041, pp31-35, 1983.

Duffy, F, Laing, A, and Crisp, V, *The Responsible Workplace, The Redesign of Work and Offices,* Butterworth Architecture in assoc with Estates Gazette, Oxford, England, 1993.

Freiman, Z, 'Hype vs Reality: The changing workplace', in *Progressive Architecture,* March 1994, pp48-55.

Salmon, G, *The Working Office,* Design Council Publications, distrib by Heinemann Educational Books Ltd UK, 1979

Elevators

Lampugnani, V, et al, *Elevators, Escalators, Paternosters: A Cultural History of Vertical Transportation,* Ernst and Sohn, Berlin, Germany, 1994.
Note: For further reference, please refer to Catalogues and Brochures of Otis, Schindler, Boral, Mitsubishi, etc.

Environmental Design

Alvarez, S, et al (Eds), *'Architecture and Urban Space', Proceedings of the 9th International PLEA Conference, Seville, Spain, 24-27 September, 1991,* Klower Academic Publishers, Dordrecht, The Netherlands, 1991.

Brown, GZ, *Sun, Wind, and Light; Architectural Design Strategies,* John Wiley & Sons, NYC, USA, 1985.

Davis, AJ & Schubert, RP, *Alternative Natural Energy Sources in Building Design,* Van Nostrand Reinhold Company, NYC, USA, 1974.

Fry, M, Drew, J, *Tropical Architecture,* Batsford, London, England, 1964.

Gabel, M, et al, *Energy, Earth and Everyone,* Straight Arrow Books, San Francisco, USA, 1975.

Giovoni, B, *Man, Climate and Architecture,* Elsevier Publishers, NYC, USA, 1969.

Kodama, Yuichiro, et al (Eds), *PLEA: Passive and Low Energy Architecture,* Process Architecture, No 98, Tokyo, Japan, 1991.

Koenigsberger, OH, Ingersoll, T, Mayhew, A, and Szokolay, S, *Manual of Tropical Housing and Building, Part One: Climatic Design,* Longman Group, London, England, 1973.

Lam, JC & Chan ALS Chan, 'Building energy audits and site surveys', in *Building Research and Information,* E & FN Spon, Chapman & Hall, UK, 1995.

Lim, B B-P, *Environmental Design Criteria of Tall Buildings,* Council on Tall Buildings and Urban Habitat, LeHigh University Publ, Bethlehem, USA, 1994.

Olgay, Victor, *Design With Climate,* Princeton University Press, Princeton NJ, USA, 1963.

Paks, M, & Hira, A, Multi-disciplinary Design Approach to the Design of Tall Buildings – The Trend Beyond 2001, *Proceedings of the 3rd International Kerensky Conference on Structural Engineering,* Singapore, 20-22 July 1994.

Roaf, S, & Hancock, M, (Eds), *Energy Efficient Building, A Design Guide,* John Wiley & Sons, NYC, USA, 1992.

Saini, Balwant Singh, *Architecture in Tropical Australia,* Architectural Association Paper No 6, Lund Humphries for the Architectural Association, London, England, 1970.

Yannas, Simos, *Solar Energy and Housing Design, Volumes 1 & 2,* Architectural Association Publ, London, England, 1994.

Wind and Ventilation

Irwin, Peter, *Applications of Wind Engineering to Large Building Projects,*
Private Paper of Rowan Williams Davies and Irwin, Ontario, Canada, 1991.

Daniels, Klaus, et al, *The Skyscraper Naturally Ventilated?,* Technical Paper #2,
Top E, European Consulting Engineering Network, Munich,
Germany, 1994.

Chandra, S, et al, *A Handbook for Designing Ventilated Buildings,* Private
Publication of Florida Solar Energy Center, USA, 1983.

Ismail, M, *Wind-flow Study of High-rise Office Buildings in the Hot-Humid
Tropics of Malaysia: Design Considerations,* private paper, Department
of Architecture, University of Cardiff, Wales, UK, 1994.

External Wall & Cladding

Lao, Desmond, *Curtain Wall Testing Methods,* Mechanical Technology
Centre, private paper, Singapore Institute of Standards and
Industrial Research.

Heintges, Robert A, 'Semantics of the Curtain (or) Wall: Surface or
Substance?', in *SIAJ (Singapore Institute of Architects Journal),*
March/April 1994, pp52-54.

Sakhnosky, AA, 'Why test Curtain Walls?', in *SIAJ (Singapore Institute of
Architects Journal),* March/April 1994, pp45-46.

Sturdevant, JR, 'What makes a good Curtain Wall?', in *Progressive
Architecture,* February 1994, pp70-77.

Wang, ML (Ed), et al, *Cladding,* Council on Tall Buildings and Urban
Habitat, McGraw-Hill Inc, NYC, USA.

Wilson, Forrest, 'The Changing Nature of Building Skins', in *Architecture,*
March 1989, pp66-70.

Geography of the Skyscraper

Ford, LR, *Cities and Buildings: Skyscrapers, Skid Rows and Suburbs,*
John Hopkins University Press, Baltimore, USA, 1994.

Hall, Peter, *Cities of Tomorrow,* Blackwell, Oxford, England, 1988.

Money, DC, *Climate and Environmental Systems,* Collins Educational,
London, England, 1988.

Morris, AEJ, *History of Urban Form: Before the Industrial Revolution,*
Longman Scientific and Technical, Harlow, England, 1994.

Pye, M, *Maximum City, The Biography of New York,* Sinclair-Stevenson,
England, 1991.

Sudjic Deyan, *Hundred Mile City,* Andre Deutsch, London, England, 1992.

Zunz, O, *Making America Corporate 1870-1920,* Universiity of Chicago
Press, Chicago, USA, 1992.

262

263

265